JOURNAL

OF

A RESIDENCE AND TOUR

IN

THE UNITED STATES

OF

NORTH AMERICA,

FROM APRIL, 1833, TO OCTOBER, 1834.

BY E. S. ABDY,

FELLOW OF JESUS COLLEGE, CAMBRIDGE.

" As far as experience may shew errors in our establishments, we are bound to correct them; and, if any practices exist contrary to the principles of justice and humanity, within the reach of our laws or our influence, we are inexcusable if we do not exert ourselves to restrain and abolish them."—D. WEBSTER, *Discourse at Plymouth on the second centenary of the settlement of New England.*

" The distinction of color is unknown in Europe."—*Speech of Chancellor* KENT *in the New York State Convention.*

IN THREE VOLUMES.

VOL. III.

NEGRO UNIVERSITIES PRESS
NEW YORK

E 165
. A 13
1 9 6 9
Vol. 3

GL

Originally published in 1835
by John Murray, London

Reprinted 1969 by
Negro Universities Press
A DIVISION OF GREENWOOD PUBLISHING CORP.
NEW YORK

SBN 8371-1917-0

PRINTED IN UNITED STATES OF AMERICA

CONTENTS

OF VOL. III.

CHAPTER XXIV.

CHAPTER XXV.

CHAPTER XXVI.

CHAPTER XXVII.

CHAPTER XXVIII.

CHAPTER XXIX.

CHAPTER XXXIII.

JOURNAL

OF A

RESIDENCE AND TOUR,

ETC.

CHAPTER XXIV.

Official Report from Liberia.—Proofs of Africo-American Industry.—Ignominious Mode of Interment.—Inadmissibility of Free Blacks' Evidence in Ohio.—White Slave and her Children.—Blacks have " Notice to quit ".—Sketch of Louisiana.—Courage of a Mulatto.—Blacklegs at Cincinnati.

THE Colonization Society, while its agent was painting the prosperous condition of Liberia, had documents in its possession that would at once have exposed the falsity of the statement. The auxiliary society of Georgetown, in Brown County, (Ohio,) who had sent out a Baptist missionary, of the name of Jones, (a colored man,) to inquire into the state of the colony, had, a few months before, received his report, together with another from a convention of the settlers, called by the agent of Liberia for the same purpose. A copy of these documents was sent by one of the Lane students, Mr. Wattles, to the Cincinnati Journal. He had procured them from the society's secretary, (Dr. Buckner,) in addition to some letters transmitted to the committee of the Board of Managers of the Presbyterian missions by their agent, Mr. Temple, whom they had sent out to Africa. The journal refused them a place in its columns. All these documents gave a very unfavorable account of the colony. The convention, whose names are appended to the report, state, among other things, that the settlers, " on their arrival, are placed in public receptacles ; and, in almost every instance, their lands are withheld from them till they are over the fever. Consequently, many who do not take the fever for several weeks, and are anxious to do something, but not having their lands assigned them, turn their attention to traffic ; and those who are disposed to do nothing, let themselves down, depending upon what they get from the public stores. The fever now takes them, and is of such a nature that it generally brings on a train of diseases, and is also calculated to produce indolence in almost every case. About the time they are half through with the fever, the six months are expired, and they are turned out of doors, sick, weak, and debilitated ; and, from the loss of friends and relatives, many are broken-hearted, and are thus brought to an untimely grave. Others are so discouraged, as to have no inclination to help themselves, and consequently so many afflicted widows and orphans become burthensome upon society." Mr. Jones says, in his report, that "there are hundreds there who would rather come back and be slaves, than stay in Liberia." " Of all misery, and all poverty, and all repining, that my imagination had ever conceived,"—such are his words,—" it never had reached what my eyes now saw, and my ears heard. Hundreds of poor creatures, squalid, ragged, hungry, without employment,—some actually starving to death, and all praying most fervently that they might get home to America once more. Even the emancipated slave craved the boon of returning again to bondage, that he might once more have the pains of hunger satisfied. They would sit down and "tell us" (he was accompanied by another missionary) "their tale of suffering and of sorrow, with such a dejected and woe-begone aspect, that it would almost break one's heart. They would weep as they talked of their sorrows here, and their joys in America; and we mingled our tears freely with theirs. This part of the population included, as near as we could judge, two-thirds of the inhabitants of Monrovia." " I was particularly requested", he adds, " by some of the most respectable citizens, to disabuse the American public on the present condition of the colony, and fearlessly to state the facts as they exist. For the agents who have been here, said they, have done as much harm by giving more flat-

tering accounts than the truth would warrant; and
by this means have induced many to come, who ever
have been, and ever will be, a burthen to themselves
and the colony. Others again, who were in good
circumstances in America, and might live in the first
style in the colony, have been so deceived by these
agents, that they have returned home perfectly sick-
ened with disappointment."

Speaking of the natives, he says, they are treated
like slaves. " All the colonists, who can afford it,
have a native or two to do their work. The natives
never go into the house, but always eat and sleep in
the kitchen. When they go to the door to speak to
the master, they always take their hats off, and appear as though they desired to be very submissive."
Yet these unfortunate colonists are made to say, in a
circular addressed by them to their brethren at home,
and published by the Colonization Society, that they
were " grateful to God and their American patrons,
for the happy change which had taken place in their
situation." Eels, we have been told, do not suffer
when they are flayed alive, because they are used to
it. The cook has never asserted that they thanked
her.

The document I have before quoted was brought
from Liberia by a person whom I afterwards saw.
Part of it I transcribed from a copy lent me by one
of the Lane students. It came from " a convention
of the citizens of Liberia, called by order of the

agent of the American Colonization Society, for the purpose of inquiring " into the actual state of the colony.

" In answer," they say, " to the inquiry made of the total neglect of agriculture, we would briefly remark that much depends upon the location of the newly arrived emigrants. The early settlers of the colony were located on Cape Mesurado ;—a thirsty barren rock, unproductive, and on which nothing can be raised to any extent, and on which expedition after expedition was continued to be located for several years—which was very essential, as the colony was then surrounded by thousands of heathen enemies. So far agriculture was neglected through necessity. During this time, the settlers of course turned their attention to trading. The population being small, the supplies from the natives were sufficient to serve them : therefore, the necessity of farming was not felt. This caused a total neglect, till the settlement of Caldwell was established. By this time the settlers, who were successful in trade, were so bound by their interests in mercantile pursuits, that farming to them could not be an object ; and those who were unsuccessful, had neither courage nor means to attempt to farm. Caldwell being now settled, where the land is fertile, better things might have been expected ; but the misfortune is, the people located there were generally poor, and in indigent circumstances—whose expectations were raised to so great a height by flattering reports be-

fore they left the United States, that they were induced to believe that they were going to a country
in which they would enjoy a liberty attended with
little or no difficulty in acquiring the common comforts of life. Now, on their arrival, they are placed
in public receptacles; and in almost every instance
their lands are withheld from them, &c.", till they
become " burthensome upon society."

The report recommends that land should be ap-
portioned to the emigrants as they arrive. " The
emigrants would not then be forced into the swamps,
as they now are, to get lumber to sell, in order
to support a starving family. This unprofitable and
health-destroying employment had destroyed many
and would destroy more." In another passage they
say:—" Monrovia, our first and capital settlement,
can only appear a town of considerable size, when
delineated on the map. There its fine churches, its
Lancasterian schools, and its market, and its forts,
are shewn to great advantage; but, upon inspecting,
the originals appear as dark shades. The cause,
which we would assign, is, the want of a colonial
coin." Signed by the convention. The last paragraph, as well as the whole style of this report, shews
clearly that it was written with great caution, and
under an apprehension of giving offence to the authorities at home. It affords, however, sufficient
evidence, that the grossest fraud and mismanage-
ment prevail, both in the colony and in the board of
managers.

There is no State in the Union that has carried
its enmity to these people so far as Ohio. In the
public burying-ground, or "Potter's Field," as it is
called, at Cincinnati, the difference of position, in
which the bodies below are laid, points out the difference of complexion by which they were distinguished while living. The pride of the white man
pursues its victim even beyond the grave. The one
lies from East to West: the other, from North to
South. I visited the spot with a benevolent Quaker,
Mr. Davis, to whom I am indebted for many civilities. I saw the unchristian distinction amid all that
is calculated to humble the pride of man: and I
wished that the shame of Cincinnati might be known
in every village of Europe. None but the poor and
destitute are buried in this humiliating manner; as
those who can scrape together a few dollars, would
rather purchase a few feet of earth in some cemetery than
submit to the supposed degradation of interment in the
Potter's Field. It is thus that the corporation of the
city unites with the legislature of the State, in pan-
dering to the popular superstition; and the ingenuity of malice is racked to make life and death
equally ignominious to its object: as if "the wicked"
would not "cease from troubling," nor the weary
be permitted to "be at rest" even in "the narrow
house."

The ignominious mode of interment, to which the
poor among this neglected race are subject, is deeply
felt by them. A young man, speaking to me upon

the subject, said, with tears in his eyes, " I was much shocked to find, on my return to the city after a short absence, that one of my female relatives had been buried in this way. I visited the spot, and saw the grave : it cut me to the heart, we could and would have raised enough among ourselves to bury her decently, but it was too late." Another observed to me, that he had often been insultingly told by the whites that there would be a separate place in heaven for him and his people.—" But," added the man, " I always tell them we shall have a good boss in the next world—not a white boss."

It was in the year 1807 that the act, disqualifying colored persons from giving evidence, where whites are concerned, was passed, to the eternal dishonor of the State. It is therein expressly provided, that " no black or mulatto person shall hereafter be permitted to be sworn or give evidence in any court of record or elsewhere in this State, in any cause depending, or matter of controversy, where either party to the same is a white person ; or in any prosecution which shall be instituted in behalf of this State against any white person."

Mr. Davis related to me an instance of human depravity, almost unequalled in the annals of crime. He was personally acquainted with the parties. It occurred in Virginia thirty or forty years ago : and the legal proceedings to which it gave rise, are now upon record. An orphan girl was indentured as an apprentice, to a man of the name of Jones, who died insolvent before the term, for which she was bound, had expired; and a Scotchman, (Hook,) a creditor of the deceased, got possession of her. She was a white woman. Hook, however, treated her as a slave, and compelled her to marry, or rather to co-habit with, a negro, by whom she had several children. The whole affair was subsequently brought into a court of justice; and, after a long and tedious litigation, the mother and the offspring were declared free. Whether the action was of a civil or a criminal nature,—whether any damages were awarded, or any punishment inflicted,—I was unable to learn. It is not very likely, however, that either the judge or the jury would be very severe against an act, which I have erroneously termed unequalled, as they were, probably, in the habit of committing it, directly or indirectly, themselves;—with this difference only, that compulsion, in their case, has the sanction of law, and is not exercised upon *white* women. After all, the children would have obtained but the mother's freedom. The father's disabilities would remain with them for life, and, perhaps, still longer.

This woman, whose name is Pagee, often comes to Cincinnati, in the neighborhood of which she lives. She had borne a white child, before her forced connexion with the slave; and her master, whose name he now bears, is thought to have been the father. According to a MS. narrative Mr. Davis shewed me:
" It is supposed the degraded condition of his mother

and her children, induced him to leave them, when their situation was known, to remove to the Western country; where his qualifications for usefulness have procured him an office of honor and profit. His mother, having passed the prime of her life in slavery, and being destitute of the means of subsistence, and probably looking to this son for support in her declining years, followed him to the West; but it is believed, they never have recognized each other in the relation in which they stand to each other. Her daughter Charlotte had been taken into the family of General Jessup; and, when he passed through Cincinnati some years ago, she, with great care and difficulty, sought out her mother, and with much delicacy and filial tenderness, obtained a private interview with her, and kindly offered to administer to her wants."

Before I left Cincinnati, I obtained a copy of the advertisement, which was published in the newspapers relative to the security required of the free blacks. It is as follows :

" TO THE PUBLIC.

" The undersigned, trustees and overseers of the poor of the township of Cincinnati, hereby give notice, that the duties required of them by the act of the General Assembly of Ohio, entitled an act to regulate black and mulatto persons, and the act emendatory thereto, will hereafter be rigidly enforced; and all black and mulatto persons, now residents of the said Cincinnati township, and who have emigrated to and settled within the township of Cincinnati, without complying with the requisitions of the first section of the amended act aforesaid, are informed, that unless they enter into bond, as the said act directs, within thirty days from this date, they may expect, at the expiration of that time, the law to be rigidly enforced. And the undersigned further insert herein, for the information of the Cincinnati township, the third section of the emendatory act aforesaid, as follows :—that, if any person, being a resident of the State, shall employ, harbor, or conceal any such negro, or mulatto person aforesaid, contrary to the provisions of the first section of this act, any person so offending, shall forfeit and pay, for every such offence, any sum not exceeding 100 dollars, the one half to the informer, and the other half for the use of the poor of the township in which such person may reside, to be recovered by action of debt, before any court having competent jurisdiction; and, moreover, be liable for the maintenance and support of such negro or mulatto ; provided he or they shall become unable to support themselves.

" The co-operation of the public is expected in carrying these laws into full effect.

" WILLIAM MILLS,   } Trustees
  BENJAMIN HOPKINS, of the
  GEORGE LEE,   } Township.

" June 29th, 1829."

The public took the hint; and the outrage detailed in the preceding volume, was perpetrated.

The person, for whom I brought a letter from his
brother in Washington, was a man, who would have
been looked up to in any other country for his good
sense and pleasing manners. He had just received
a printed circular, addressed to the people of his
race, by the editor of the Genius of Universal Emancipation, an active and able advocate of the black
man, when he had few friends. The letter was written in Mexico; and the writer (Lundy) stated that
he had had a personal communication with the government of that country, and that he had reason to
believe a grant of land in the Texas would be made,
for the reception of colored people from Tennessee.
What a reverse and retaliation of fortune! The
descendants of the bigoted Spaniards are more tole-
rant than the descendants of the liberal English!
While the latter are driving away their own subjects,
the former offer them an asylum! The policy, however, that impoverished Spain and enriched England,
was dictated by the spirit of the age and the religion
of the country: that which is now strengthening
Mexico, at the expense of the United States, is
opposed to both.

The following sketch of what may be seen in
Louisiana I had from an eye-witness, whom I met
with at Cincinnati, and whose veracity I have no
reason to doubt. Slaves for sale at New Orleans are

publicly exposed at the mart, or auction-room; the men ranged on one side, and the women on the other. Purchasers are in the habit of examining the mouth and the limbs, in the same way that a horse is subjected to the scrutinising touch of the buyer. The joints are tried, and turned, to see if they are strong and supple. Should the back, or shoulders, or any other part of the body, exhibit marks of frequent or severe flogging, the " animal" is set aside, as rebellious and refractory. Twice a week, an exhibition takes place, during the season; and the human cattle are paraded through the streets, decently dressed, and in regular file, to attract customers. While at work in the streets, or on the banks of the river, they are frequently chained together by the ancle—women as well as men. Sometimes they wheel barrows on the road with a chain and a heavy ball at the end of it, affixed to one of their legs. The ball they place, when they can, in the barrow, as a temporary relief from the burthen. They work during the heat of the day, and few of them are decently clothed or sufficiently fed. They are usually allowed an hour for dinner, which consists of rice and bullock's head. Something is given them to eat before they start, at an early hour, and when the toils of the day are over. On the Red River, a peck of corn a-week is the allowance for each. They must grind it and cook it themselves.

On the cotton plantations, they are half-naked,

and avoid, with feelings of shame and confusion, the
gaze of the traveller. No exemption from toil is
granted to the females, many of whom, while suck-
ling their infants, are prohibited from seeing them
till their return at night. Individuals, of both sexes
and of all ages, may often be seen with iron collars,
from which spikes of six inches' length protrude,
round the neck, as a punishment for stealing*.
That they do steal and will steal, they make no
scruple to acknowledge and avow:—they must steal
or starve. The number of Virginians imported by
the "soul-drivers" is so great, that it is supposed
there must be, annually, nearly 10,000 sent to the
Southern market by the "Old Dominion." Such is
the substance of what was related to me; and there
is no lack of testimony from other quarters to corro-
borate the statement. The iron collars alluded to
are of such a nature that the wearer cannot lie down.
He sleeps sitting up. Such was the statement made
to Mr. Elizar Wright by a slave from Georgia—the

* "If any person or persons, &c., shall cut or break any iron
chain or collar, which any master of slaves should have used in
order to prevent the running away or escape of any such slave
or slaves, such person, &c., so offending shall, on conviction, &c.,
be fined not less than 200 dollars nor exceeding 1000 dollars;
and suffer imprisonment for a term, not exceeding two years,
nor less than six months."—Act of Louisiana Assembly, 1819.
Severity of punishment measures extent of crime. What then
must be the amount of suffering which prompted the offence,
and that of cruelty which suggested the repression?

property of a minister of the gospel, who had himself directed the overseer to put it on a man for running away. The evidence was corroborated, as far as it could be, by Mr. Joshua Coffin of Philadelphia.

It has been asserted by those who have an interest in concealing the truth, or are too indolent to seek it, that the slave has neither the inclination nor the ability to provide for himself, and that to give him freedom would be to misapply kindness by injuring its object. I had abundant opportunity of submitting these assertions to the only test, by which their accuracy can be ascertained; and I can honestly declare, that an impartial induction from indisputable facts has led me to an opposite conclusion. I conversed freely and frequently with many of those who had passed immediately from bondage to freedom, and were pursuing the same course of industry, which had purchased them the blessing of the transition. I found them as intelligent, civil, and attentive to the duties required of them in their several employments and relations of life, as any of those who are neither disfranchised of their natural rights, nor exposed to the scorn and bad passions of their neighbors. While visiting at their houses, I remarked as much concern for each other's welfare as I have ever found in any other rank or order of society, and a much greater attention to the civilities and courtesies of society than I ever saw among their white fellow countrymen. Though they are under the necessity, in consequence of their civil disqualifications, of securing themselves against fraud by the presence of a white person, whenever they make a bargain with a member of the favored caste, there is no proof that honesty or punctuality is wanting on their side. That they suffer from the want of both in the other party is too often the case, and is naturally to be expected while men are disposed to take advantage of the law's injustice.

On entering one of their houses, with almost the only white companion I could have found—one of the students,—my attention was particularly directed to the respectable appearance of the mistress, an elderly woman,—and the unaffected ease with which she received us. She had the manners and good-breeding of a gentlewoman. Her husband, who had been emancipated by his owner, had bought her freedom, and that of her children, for the sum of 1375 dollars. It was after much solicitation, and a considerable lapse of time, that he succeeded in his object, as her master retained her in bondage with the view of enhancing her price, till she had had seven children. The husband was obliged to borrow part of the money; and he who is not, in a free State, believed on his oath, had his bond for 250 dollars accepted in a slave State. The wife and the children were, all this time, maintained by him, and he received no deduction or remuneration whatever on that account.

While we were at tea, I was much distressed by the mistress of the house declining to take any thing. As I suspected the reason, I prevailed upon her, at last, to partake of " her own labors," and share in the good things she had provided for us. I told her it was most painful to me to be distinguished in a manner that to an European mind conveyed the feelings of self-reproach and humiliation. I was so ashamed and embarrassed by her deference to the folly of my own race, that it was some time before I could make up my mind to ask an explanation involving such odious associations, and intreat that I might be exempted from the observance of an usage that I utterly loathe and abominate.

She assured me, while speaking of Liberia, that she had never known nor heard of a slave, who would not prefer remaining in his native land, if he could be free, to a settlement in any other country. This I had often heard from others; and nothing but a complete disregard for truth, or unthinking credulity, can assert or believe the contrary. My companion and I were ridiculing the bugbear of " amalgamation," when he told me that a justice of the peace had mentioned, in his presence, the circumstance of his having married four white men to colored women in the course of one winter. There is a practising physician in Cincinnati, who has taken unto himself a wife from this degraded caste; not agreeing with the general opinion, that a connexion of this sort is made culpable by the matrimonial tie, and excusable without it.

Among the persons we visited during the evening, was a man between fifty and sixty years of age. He had given 1,200 dollars—the fruits of hard work and strict economy, for himself, his wife, and his children. To compass this object of his fondest wish required no less than sixteen years: during which time he had to support the whole family himself, and pay his master annually 120 dollars—the sum stipulated for his hire as a bricklayer and plasterer. He contrived to give his children a good education. Part of the money he paid his master, was advanced to him by some of his white friends, who were induced, at his earnest solicitation, to purchase his wife, when she was put up to auction with her children, to pay her master's debts. This part of the story he related in the presence of his wife, with great feeling and simplicity of manner. He discharged all his debts with interest. A certificate of character, which he put into my hands, from several of the principal inhabitants of Lewisburgh in Virginia, was signed by about sixty persons, among whom were the mayor and recorder of the city. Higher testimony to good conduct, than this document presented, few men can obtain, whether black or white—whether in America or in Europe. Yet this certificate would be a piece of blank paper in any court of Ohio justice. Evidence, that would be taken, without it, in Louisiana, would be rejected, with it, here, though backed by fifty others from every State in the Union.

So far is it from being true that self-respect is a feeling almost unknown to all of African descent, that I have never seen more indications of its influence on any men of any class or of any country, than among these very people : and I believe this favorable opinion is entertained by all who have seen as much of them. My companion, who was one of those that had undertaken the care of the " colored schools," lived almost exclusively among this part of the population, as it was pretty plainly intimated to him, that his visits would not be acceptable elsewhere. In making our calls, he took me, at my request, to see a man, who had been indebted to his Herculean strength and extraordinary courage, for his escape from an attempt made by some ruffians to take him by force out of his house. He was a freed slave from Kentucky, and was serving as a cook at one of the hotels. His whole history, with the details of the brutal outrage, I had from his own mouth. The facts are well known to the inhabitants of Cincinnati.

I may preface the narrative by stating that he was a short sturdy man about thirty years of age, with a frame of adamant and a heart of invincible bravery.

A form more adapted for feats of agility and athletic exercise, I never beheld. Mendoza, though taller, never, with all his boasting, could produce such an arm. He was a model of manly strength and perfect proportions. His master, who knew his value, and dreaded the effects of his resolution, had often promised to set him free; and, at last, as an inducement to remain with him, had entered upon record a grant to him of fifty acres of land, rented at two dollars an acre—to be made over to him when he should obtain his freedom. He had, though a mere lad, accumulated, by working extra hours, a considerable sum of money; and his master, wanting cash to complete a purchase he had made, was induced to sell him his freedom for 650 dollars. Having surmounted all the obstacles that were thrown in his way, he, at last, procured the legal proofs of his freedom, and set off, with his papers, for Ohio. On the road thither, he was attacked by three men, who seized him by the shoulders, and attempted to detain him. He threw them from him on the ground; and, running to the river, near which the assault had been made, he leaped into a boat, and crossed over to the other side.

Having resided some years in Cincinnati, he was, one night in the winter of 1833, aroused, while in bed with his wife, by a noise at the door. Thinking, however, that it was occasioned by some drunken men, he paid little attention to it. "Had I known what was coming," said he, " I could have killed every one of them." Efforts had often been made to induce him to return to Kentucky; but he was not prepared for the sort of persuasion that was now to be used with him. His bed-room door was burst open, and fourteen men rushed in, headed by a person of the name of Samuel Goodin—lately appointed by the Judges, and rejected by the proper authorities, as Clerk to the County Court. They called out that they would have him dead or alive. He had but just time to leap from his bed, when, seizing a chair, he knocked two of them down; and, though severely wounded by their dirks in both arms, in the ribs, and in the intestines, made his escape down stairs, pursued by the gang into the yard. Here he discovered that his bowels were protruding from one of the wounds; when he supported them, as well as he could, with one hand, and, stooping down, laid hold with the other of a log of wood. With this weapon he laid about him so effectually, that he felled no less than seven of them to the ground.

In the mean time, (the whole combat lasted from one till two o'clock,) the wife, and a female cousin, who was in the house at the time, had borne their share in the fight, and had collected the neighbors by their screams for succor. No one ventured to rescue them; as the number of the assailants, the execrations they uttered, and the brandishing of

their dirks and knives, kept every one aloof. At
length, in attempting to escape, they broke down
the fence; and the victim of their fury, while pursuing them, stumbled upon a stake, and, dragging
his intestines after him, fainted away. One man
only was secured on the spot, and another was subsequently taken. They were admitted to bail, and
are not likely to make their appearance, should they
be "wanted." Goodin is also under bail for the
assault.

As soon as the field of battle was cleared, and the
enemy had fled, every assistance was rendered to the
wounded man. He was confined for two or three
months; and the expenses he incurred, for medical
attendance and proper nourishment, amounted to
140 dollars, not one cent of which has ever been
repaid him. The object, in trying to get possession
of his person, was to make away with him by violent
means, or by sending him to the South. The estate,
which his master made over to him, is still legally
his; and though he has never received any rents,
he is entitled both to the land and the arrears. Since
this occurrence, he has been shot at; and the parties
interested have openly expressed their determination
to effect his removal, whatever it may cost, or whatever be the mode. I asked him why he did not go
to Canada. He smiled, and said he was not afraid
of any man; and, though his strength was much
reduced, he was fully prepared to repel force by

force. The poor fellow was covered with deep scars, and suffered much from atmospheric changes. But he seemed to care little about the attack, and still less to dread its renewal. He was altogether a very extraordinary man. Neither boast nor threat escaped his lips. He knew the white man was his enemy; and he despised him too much to fear him.

A great many slaves,—no less, probably, than 300 every year, pass through Cincinnati on their way to Canada. Their propensity to run away from Kentucky is so well known, that few planters in Mississippi and Missouri will buy them, if they come from that State. This will account for the persecution against the freed men at Cincinnati, who give them an asylum, and speed them on their road to the British provinces; while it affords the owners an additional motive for granting them the privilege of buying what they might take without asking. The process of self-emancipation is, in fact, going on very largely; and the same policy which suggested it, will give it extension, as new converts are made in the North to the doctrines of abolition. It will be found the safest and the easiest way to "back out" of a system, that is fast becoming as odious in one section of the Union as it is destructive in the other.

The vicinity of Ohio has brought into closer contact and contrast the results of slave and of free labor; and Kentucky has seen, in the rapid progress of her neighbor, the causes that retard her own.

The hardships to which the disqualifying statute exposes its objects, in such a mixed population as that of Cincinnati, may be readily conceived. When the unhealthy season drives away the idle and the wealthy from New Orleans, those who live by gambling and swindling either follow their prey, or seek some other quarry. Many come up the river to exercise their trade in the western metropolis. Here the law supplies them with a "scape goat" in case of "accidents." It is easy to throw suspicion on those whom it has already condemned; self-defence is not allowed: and the penitentiary buries within its walls the crimes of the one party and the wrongs of the other. One of the latter class, whose master spoke of him to me as a very honest boy, ("boy" is an expression of kindness, "fellow" of its opposite,) told me one day that he considered himself very fortunate in never having been accused of a theft, as many others had been, by the rogues and rascals who frequented the house.

CHAPTER XXV.

A Son's Feelings.—Ripley.—Georgetown.—Colony of Emancipated Slaves.—Mr. Samuel Gist's Will.—Mormonites.—Liberia, by an Eye-witness.—Certificate of Emancipation.—Gist's
benevolent Intentions defeated.—Return to Cincinnati.—Book
of Mormon.

On the 12th I left Cincinnati. When I arrived at
thé boat which was to convey me to Ripley, about
sixty miles up the river, the porter, who carried my
luggage, was accosted by a white man on board, and
I went in search of the captain. On my return, I
saw that the "boy" had received some afflicting
intelligence; for his lips quivered, and his countenance was painfully dejected. He had just been
informed that his mother, whom he had left a slave
in Kentucky, had been brutally flogged by her
master's brother-in-law, who had got her into his
possession, during the other's bankruptcy.

The story of the porter's misfortunes is similar to
that of hundreds in Cincinnati. I had it, when he
was gone, from the white man, who was going to

Paris, in Kentucky, where he had known him before he obtained his freedom. " Sir," said he, " that boy is one of the best-hearted and most honest men to be found anywhere. He worked night and day to buy himself; and, when he had paid the purchase-money, (600 dollars,) the sheriff took him in execution for his master's debts; and he would have been sold, if he had not made his escape. He is now saving what he can scrape together to buy his mother,—a most respectable old woman, and one of the most faithful servants I ever knew. I would buy her myself on his account, and he would repay me, but I cannot afford the money. Both parent and son have the good-will of all who know them. She is now at Postlethwaite's hotel for sale. They ask 200 dollars for her;—too much for a woman who is almost past her work. Her master always treated her well; but his brother-in-law is a bad-tempered hard-hearted man." I found, by this conversation, that she was at Lexington, at the very house I had put up at. She is safe, I thought, under Postlethwaite's roof; but what is to become of the poor creature if she is sold, and sent off to a distance?

It was about one o'clock when the boat quitted Cincinnati, and past midnight when it reached Ripley. There were, fortunately, two men waiting on the bank, with some luggage to be carried up the river; and one of them assisted me to carry my port-

manteau to the inn, where we found all fast and in
bed. Upon our knocking at the door, the owner
came down in " an undress" and let me in. What
sort of a place it was I had no means of ascertaining:
all I could make out, when I had groped my way in
the dark to my berth, was, that there were at least
three generations under the same roof with me; for
I heard an infant squalling, an old woman coughing
incessantly, and two men snoring a duet with great
vigor and perseverance.

The next morning I called upon Mr. Rankin, a
Presbyterian minister, highly esteemed by the abolitionists for some valuable letters he published, when
in Kentucky, against slavery. My object in the visit
I made, was to obtain from him some information
relative to a colony of free blacks, who formerly belonged to an Englishman of the name of Samuel
Gist, and who had been, in pursuance of his munifi-
cent bequest, emancipated, and transferred from his
plantations in Virginia to the lands they now occupy
in the neighborhood.

Mr. Rankin was unable to state more than I had
already heard at Cincinnati. He very kindly, however, directed me to the proper quarter. He was
superintending the erection of a chapel : among the
workmen were one or two blacks and a Cherokee.
He had, he said, seen a great deal of the former
race, as the settlers generally made his house their
home when they quitted or returned to " the camps",

as the two colonies they have formed are called.
Sometimes there would be as many as ten or twelve
at a time in his house; yet, though his property was
left exposed, nothing was ever taken by them. He
could find, he said, no kind of difference, moral or
intellectual, between the sable and the pale races.
They were possessed of the same feelings, and directed by the same motives. He ridiculed, very
happily, the dread of " amalgamation"; conceiving
that perfect freedom of choice should be left to regulate this like every other matter in which society can
never have such an interest as the parties directly
concerned. His sentiments, upon these and other
subjects, were characterised by great good sense, and
implied an originality of mind and an independence
of thinking very far in advance of the spirit of his
country. I have seldom met with a man more decided in his principles of benevolence, or more mild
in expressing them.

There is a passage in his " Letters on Slavery" so
painfully descriptive of its abominations, that I was
anxious to know, from his own lips, whether it was
not too highly colored. He assured me the facts it
alluded to were too true. I have heard the same
from equally good authority; and I would ask the
Southerners, whether they really allow their male
slaves to go alone into the sleeping-rooms of the
white women, for the purpose of lighting the fires
when they are in bed.

" It often happens", says Mr. Rankin, in his ninth
letter, " that the master's children practise the same
vices which prevail among his slaves; and even the
master himself is liable to be overwhelmed by the
floods of temptation: and, in some instances, the
father and his sons are involved in one common
ruin: nor do the daughters always escape this im-
petuous fountain of pollution. Were it necessary, I
could refer you to several instances of slaves actually
seducing the daughters of their masters! Such se-
ductions sometimes happen even in the most respectable slave-holding families."

The next day I started for the Camps, having left
my portmanteau with the landlord at Ripley. When
the stage reached Georgetown, twelve miles from the
latter place, I was informed that some of the settlers,
of whom I was in search, were at work in the town.
From them I learnt that the colony was two or three
miles off. I told them I should ride over to see
them. They begged I would wait till six o'clock,
and they would shew me the way. It was then four
o'clock; and it was near eight before we set off, as
they had to settle an account with a store-keeper,
who kept them waiting for some money he owed
them, and, after all, left the matter for future arrangement. The claim of one was for ten dollars.
He told me they were often cheated and vexed, unless they could get a white witness; neither their

word nor their oath being of any value on these occasions.

After we had walked upwards of two miles on a
very bad road, which a heavy shower had rendered
wet and dirty, I desired my companions to go on, and
I would follow, after I had rested myself and recovered from a violent seizure of spasms in the stomach,
to which I am occasionally subject. One of them
had a bundle which I had entrusted to his care,
and was unwilling to proceed with it till I had assured him that I felt no distrust about it. Having
recovered in the course of an hour or two, I resumed
my journey, avoiding the ruts and holes in the road
when the moon, as it shone through the trees, enabled me. I began at last to despair of finding my
way, by the guidance of instructions that were neither clearly given nor easily remembered, and I
bawled out till I was hoarse. A light, however, appeared at a little distance, and a voice from the
house where it was responded to my call,—" Who
are you?—what do you want?" The owner of the
voice was one of the settlers; and the precaution it
bespoke arose from the frequent insults and annoyances he had met with. I soon explained to him the
object of my visit, and gained his confidence. He then
took me with him to the house of his father-in-law,
about a quarter of a mile through the fields. On
knocking at the door, the same questions were asked,

and the same reluctance to open it exhibited, till as-
surance was given that we were friends. It was nearly
eleven o'clock, and the family in bed. A blazing
fire, however, cast its light upon every object in the
log-hut, and threw a cheerful aspect upon the welcome with which I was greeted. The women soon
made their appearance; and, after taking a cup of
coffee, and talking over the affairs of the colony, I
betook myself to a clean and comfortable bed about
one o'clock in the morning.

The substance of what I heard, on the condition
and prospect of the settlers, was as follows:—They
had been "located" in the lands they occupied
about fifteen years; and their owner, Mr. Samuel
Gist, had died some time before they left his plantation in Virginia. It seems they had been defrauded
of their rights, and would probably have remained in
ignorance of the bountiful provision made for them,
had not an elderly man, who had been present when
their master breathed his last, arrived from England
to see how they were going on. From him they learnt
that they were free, and that the land on which they
were at work belonged to them. Their owner had
always been kind to them, and would never allow any
flogging upon the plantation. They were much attached to him; and the relation between them was that
which exists between servants devoted to their master, and a master who has confidence in his servants.
As soon as this joyful intelligence was communicated

to them, they refused to work any longer without wages. They were compelled, however, by stripes and the most barbarous usage, to continue in bondage; their protector, who had gone to another part of the State, and promised to return, having died—it was supposed of poison. They struggled on in this way for some time, with no alleviation of their sufferings, and no hope of redress, when the indignation of some of the neighboring whites was excited by their piteous situation,—beaten, half-starved, and badly clothed as they were; and they were advised to apply for their freedom at Richmond, from which they were distant upwards of twenty miles. Here they were treated with great cruelty, and were imprisoned till they were reduced to the most loathsome state by filth and vermin. At length, after they had endured the greatest hardships,—their numbers being reduced by violence, and many having been hunted down and shot like wild beasts,—they were put in possession of their liberty, and were sent off under a military escort.

It would be painful and tedious to detail all that they underwent from the scoffs, the brutality, and the villainy they encountered, on their passage to the State of Ohio; where they were carted out, as it were, on uncleared land, without provisions, and without the necessary implements for husbandry. The soil was the worst in the State; and at times so wet that nothing could be raised upon great part of it. My host, whose name (as far as I could make it out) was Peter Vicy, had but three hoes given him, while his family consisted of sixteen members. His wife had borne him twenty children. Each member of the community had eight acres as an allotment—of little or no value now to some of the possessors, who are married and have large families. They have none of them any legal title to their lands; and if they had, it would be difficult to establish their claims under the disabilities which affect them. It is not very creditable to the agent employed by the court, which had finally given judgement in the matter, that he should have selected the most ineligible situation in the most unfavorable State of the Union for their residence, as they can neither live upon the produce of their allotments, nor obtain work without being liable to be defrauded by men who shelter their iniquity under the cloak of the law. They were strongly impressed with a belief that Mr. Gist had left a large sum of money for their support, and to provide three years' education for their children. Had it not been for some benevolent Quakers, who came to see them, soon after their arrival, they must have perished of hunger in the woods. Such was the melancholy prospect before them, that one of that society was so affected by what he saw and heard of their destitute condition, that he sat down in the midst of them and wept like a child. Two boats, loaded with clothing, and provisions, and tools, were sent to them by the Friends, and the Shakers were not behind them in charity. They brought them a vast quantity of things they stood in need of, having no less than six wagons filled with them. According to Peter's account, there were 360 in all when they left Virginia ; though it would seem, by a letter written by Dr. John Adams, from Richmond Hill, in 1815, to the Pennsylvania Society for promoting the abolition of slavery, that there were not so many.

He stated in that communication, that " a certain Samuel Guest*, deceased, had, by his will, directed that his slaves, amounting to about 300, should be emancipated, and his lands sold for their benefit; which being prohibited by law, unless they should be removed out of the boundaries of the commonwealth of Virginia, he requests the aid of the society, and recommends their transportation to Guinea." The committee, to whom this letter was referred, reported that it did not appear that the convention could, at present, propose any specific plan for accomplishing the benevolent intention of Samuel Guest. I have extracted the above from a note to a work entitled, " A Portraiture of Domestic Slavery in the United States, &c.", by Jesse Torrey, Jun., Physician, published at Philadelphia in 1817. This account seems to confirm Peter's statement;

* This appears to be the same person :—the name is properly Gist.

and it may fairly be concluded, that if the personal friend of the testator had not visited the spot, and excited a spirit of inquiry among the slaves themselves, nothing ever would have been done for these unfortunate creatures. The author adds a circumstance that almost confirms this conjecture. The legislature of Indiana had just taken into consideration a petition from a person of the name of Sumner, resident in Williamson county, Tennessee, and had decided that his request was inconsistent with the constitution of the State. " I have about forty slaves," says the writer, " and my intention is, if permitted by the laws of Indiana, to bring and free them, to purchase land for them and settle them on it, to give them provisions for the first year, and furnish them with tools for agriculture and domestic manufactory, and next spring with domestic animals. You must be aware, that this must be attended with no small expenditure of money and trouble. I think that, after a man has had the use of slaves, and their ancestors, twenty or thirty years, it is unjust and inhuman to set them free unprovided with a home, &c. All that I have were raised by my father and myself, and the oldest is about my age (forty-six). I am also very desirous to leave the slave States, and spend my few remaining days in that State, where involuntary slavery is not admissible ; and will, with the blessing of God, prepare to do so as soon as I can settle my affairs." Not being allowed to enrich Indiana, " at the expense of her neighbor " Tennessee, this generous-hearted man consulted the abolition society of Pennsylvania, and received a similar reply to that which had been sent to Dr. Adams.

Since the emigrants have been settled here, their number has nearly doubled itself. The other colony is more fully peopled. They still retain the name of Camps,—an appellation that marks the length of time that elapsed before they could get any thing better than a tent to rest their weary heads in ;—an appellation that will carry down to the remotest posterity the dishonor of their oppressors and persecutors. They are still liable to the intrusion of slave-traders and marauders, who break open their doors, and subject them to outrage or insult, at all hours of the night, in violation of the law of the land as it affects the white, but in accordance with its spirit as it bears on the black man. Three weeks before my visit, one of them was cruelly beaten, his dog shot, and his gun broken, by a gang of these wretches. He was confined several days to his bed by the injuries he received, and the lawyer to whom he applied, could obtain no redress for him, as neither his evidence, nor that of his neighbors, was admissible. Often has Peter to entertain travellers who are sent to his cabin by the whites, and never has he had any remuneration for his ready hospitality, except from an English lady, who came one night with her carriage and servants. She would not allow him to persist in the refusal he made to accept any money from her. The agent, William Wickham, of Richmond, in Virginia, had, he told me, promised to come and see them. He had not only never been near them, but had not answered the letters they had procured to be sent to him. Under all these difficulties, and discouragements, some of them had contrived to build themselves comfortable log-huts, and to bring up their children, as decently as the want of education, and the few opportunities they have for religious instruction, from the occasional visits of white preachers, will admit of.

Peter has about eighty acres of land under cultivation:—the two last years the produce was not sufficient for his family, and they were compelled to draw upon their hard savings for a supply. Still they seemed cheerful and contented. One of their sons was employed at Cincinnati. I had some conversation with him, while there, about the settlement. Peter had two milch cows—a yoke of young oxen, and three calves—four horses and a wagon—fifteen head of sheep—a good stock of poultry—and forty or fifty hogs. All these were acquired by the industry of this man and his family, under an accumulation of difficulties that few would have had the courage to encounter, or the perseverance to overcome. They would often go many miles in search of work; and, when they got any, would be fed with offals hardly fit for dogs or pigs. Sometimes, after toiling a week, they could obtain no more than a quarter or half dollar to return home with. They were ignorant and unsuspicious; and their employers were unscrupulous in using every advantage that want of legal protection gave them. Death, or even slavery, seemed preferable to their lot in the wilderness. Some of the whites in the country (their most bitter enemies are generally in the towns) would, now and then, give them a little assistance; but no one, when they had lost a valuable horse, which had often been borrowed by the neighbors, would stir a foot to detect the thief, who had been seen lurking about. Peter pays the taxes and does road-work the same as the whites, though he is excluded from their privileges, and has no protection from the State. By a statute passed in 1831, blacks and mulattoes in Ohio are exempted from the school-tax.

All the whites with whom I conversed upon the subject, admitted that they had been defrauded—but then their color! What right had they to remain where they were—they were marked as a distinct people—they could never associate with the chosen race—they must go to Liberia—there were plenty of persons in Georgetown ready to make up a purse to pay their passage—it would be easy to turn them out of their lands, as they had no title—the trustees could enforce the law—as they could not procure securities, they might be driven out of the township. Such were the sentiments of the tavern-keeper at Georgetown—an Englishman of the name of Wilson. A more brutal reviler of these harmless hard-working people I could hardly have found in the whole State of Ohio. I listened for some time to his abuse of the abolitionists, and his nonsense about a scheme that would ruin the country of his adoption, by transporting its best hands, and throwing away a large portion of its capital. At last I asked him where he would find a place to receive them, ships to carry them away, and funds to defray the expense: whether they had ever committed any crime to be compared with that of their oppressors—whether there was any thing in reason or religion to justify what he recommended—and whether he thought the laws of nature were to be reversed in a young country, among a race remarkable for its tenacity of life and its tendency to increase. " At all events," he replied, " we can get rid of these settlers,—they are an eye-sore and a nuisance,—and they have no business among us." I felt strongly inclined to say—" What business have you here ? If the blacks have no business in America, what business have the whites in Africa ?" But I was silent : convinced that the day of reckoning is coming upon a nation so disgraced by cruelty and wickedness.

While I was at Peter's, two or three of his white

neighbors came in, and treated him with respect.
One of them, an old man, appeared to be speech-
less with astonishment at the sight of a white man
sitting at the same table with a black. It was some
time before he recovered himself; when he made
up for lost time, by his loquacity and inquisitive-
ness. He was very anxious to know who and
what the stranger was; though he did not venture to put any direct questions. As soon as I had
ascertained that he was "raised" in Kentucky, I
turned the tables upon him, and began to cross-
examine him as to the state of that country. He
had left it in consequence of the cruelties he had
witnessed. He could bear it no longer. To see
human beings tortured till the blood flowed from
them in streams, or dying with hunger;—to witness
the sale of children by their own parents, and the
separation of infants and mothers from each other,
had turned the current of his feelings, and driven
him into voluntary exile. " A judgement," he exclaimed, " will come upon the land, and the whites
will be driven out."

I found, in the course of conversation, that the
Kentuckian was well acquainted with the Mormons,
or Mormonites, some of whom had been settled in
the neighborhood before they went further to the
west. Their present number, he thought, amounted
to five or six thousand. The founder of the sect
(Smith) had published what he called his seal.

There were six remaining to be revealed, as the world became prepared to receive them. It is partly historical and partly prophetic and didactic. The members of the society live in common ; and their intercourse with one another is characterised by equality and harmony. They have some excellent preachers among them, and are the most moral well-behaved people my informant ever knew. They maintain that the Indian tribes will finally recover their lands, and the blacks gain the ascendancy over the whites. Their practice corresponds with their principles; and no invidious distinctions are allowed to humiliate one portion of the community and elevate the other. In such opinions and habits it is easy to perceive the causes of that hatred and hostility by which they have been assailed.

Having settled in Jackson county, in the State of Missouri, and invited the free people of color to join them, they were attacked by an armed band of forty or fifty men, and driven into the woods, with their women and children. The next day, another settlement, about ten miles off from the former, suffered a similar fate:—the shops were plundered, and the houses broken into. Some days after, a regular engagement took place, (the injured party having taken up arms in self-defence,) and several were killed on both sides. A man was seized in the act of ransacking a store, and carried before a magistrate, who refused to take cognizance of the affair. The accused then turned upon the accusers, and they were committed to gaol, by a warrant for false imprisonment, the mob declaring that they should never come out alive.   These and other facts were communicated to a Missouri paper by a Mormonite (Orsan Hyde).   The other party, in reply, accused the settlers of having opened an asylum for rogues and vagabonds, and free blacks.   As I evinced a considerable degree of interest about these singular people, and expressed a wish to visit them, the talkative old man fancied I wanted to join them, and become a preacher.   " What could he want," said he, " with the colored people?   Did he come all the way from England to see them?   I'm sure he's a real gentleman from his dress and manner.   His skin was quite white.   Why, Nelly," (turning to a young woman who was present,) " his complexion was much fairer than yours.   I'd give any thing to know his name."

Such was the description given by Peter's daughter, who was an excellent mimic, and who had been present at the man's recital of what he had seen. This young woman was a great support to the family, by her good sense and industry.   She had a loom in an adjoining hut, and added considerably to the common stock by the proceeds of her weaving. She had acquired the art, as it were, by piece-meal; the whites having thrown every obstacle in the way of its acquirement.   None of her own race could teach her; and very few of the other were willing to give her any instruction, even in the most simple kinds of work. She had succeeded, however, in making herself mistress of the employment, and was not idle in the use of her skill.

While I was conversing with Peter and his wife, they said the whole colony, if they were once righted, would willingly pay any expenses that an agent, to or from England, might incur in prosecuting their claims. They had no one to befriend them; and they were becoming every day more impoverished and more despised. To add to their distress, the whites had succeeded in sowing dissension among them, and Peter himself, as well as his family, was looked upon with jealousy and envy by all the rest. This I discovered on inquiring why the men, who had been my guides, had never been to the log-hut, where I was, though they had told me that the people, old and young, would be rejoiced to see me. They took great care, however, of the bundle, which I recovered without any difficulty.

There are several other settlements of the same kind in the State; but in none of them has the common enemy been so successful in creating divisions and distinctions. If something be not done for the lower Camp, to defend the settlers and instruct their children, it will not be long before it is abandoned in great part, if not entirely.

As Jones, who had been sent out to Liberia by

the Brown County Colonization Society, was living within eight or ten miles, Peter sent his son over for him the next day, and he arrived, with his wife, in the evening, too late for me to get back to Ripley that night. I remained, therefore, another night in the cabin, being anxious to obtain information about the African colony. It was some time before Jones would dismiss his suspicions, and speak out, fairly and fully, his opinions. He had been so much abused and persecuted by the colonizationists, who were displeased with him for divulging the truth, that he was fearful of committing himself before a stranger, who might, for aught he knew, have been sent as a spy to entrap him. He was, in fact, placed in a situation that required great caution and circumspection. He was still a slave. Part of his purchase-money he had paid to his master in Kentucky; and the remainder the Brown County Society had promised to advance, as one of the conditions of his mission to Liberia. This agreement had never been fulfilled; his unfavourable report having furnished a motive and a reason for the refusal. He was but three weeks in the colony; and, not being a man of quick conception or comprehensive views, his account was necessarily defective; no just grounds, however, exist for doubting its accuracy; particularly as it is confirmed by the testimony of others, who had a stronger interest in favor of the truth, and more time for observation.

One third of the settlers, he informed me, died the first year after their arrival. Of 300 emigrants from Norfolk, in Virginia, 106 had perished by the end of the year. This statement he had from Governor Mechlin.

The largest farm in cultivation there, does not exceed three or four acres; and sufficient produce is not raised for one twentieth part of the population. The chief dependence for support is on the natives, whom they pay for the commodities they want, in rum, gunpowder, and tobacco. The latter may be considered the currency of the country. A commission, appointed by the governor to make inquiries into the state of the colony, had reported that two-thirds of the settlers had not more than one meal in their houses; and that the funds appropriated to the erection of a saw-mill and the completion of a road, had been embezzled or misapplied. There were other parts of the report highly unfavorable to the governor, who brought home with him, on his return to America, one copy; while Jones, who got back in the preceding February, was the bearer of another. The Colonization Society, it is generally believed, has not yet laid the contents of these despatches before the public. One of the charges referred to the substitution, by the store-keeper, of bad provisions for those brought out in a good condition by the Lafayette. The copy I saw at Cincinnati of this document, contained no accusation of the kind. That part and others of a similar nature might have been omitted in the transcript. It was lent to me by one of the Lane students, (Mr. Wattles,) who obtained it from Dr. Buckner, of Georgetown, as I have before stated.

Some of the early settlers, who were maintained by the Society for the first twelve months, are doing well. They are merchants—not agriculturists; and may be considered as the medium of communication between the natives and the importers of goods, whose profits from the trade thus carried on are enormous. The natives are ignorant, and submissive to the colonists, who employ them to do all the laborious part of their work,—the heat of the climate, they assert, being beyond their strength. They are too proud or too lazy even to carry a parcel; and as wages are extremely low, they do little or nothing that requires manual exertion. There is small hope, therefore, that the settlers will turn their attention to the cultivation of the soil, or make any attempt to civilize the aborigines; as the Americans, whether of European or of African descent, feel it their interest to keep them in a state of debasement and subjection. There are other causes too in operation, for diverting industry from agriculture to trade. The elective franchise depends on the possession of land; and, where opposition to the governing party is apprehended, allotments are delayed till the

pending elections are over,—to the great detriment
and discouragement of the claimants.   There are
many tribes in the neighborhood : some of them have
already shewn unequivocal symptoms of hostility.
Though subdued for the present, they would become
formidable if they acted in concert, or had some experienced leader to organize them, and teach them
the use of fire-arms,—an article they have recently
manifested an inclination to receive in payment for
the ivory, palm-oil, and other things with which they
supply the traders.

Of the schools and churches, Jones spoke favorably.   Most, if not all, of the white missionaries,
who had been sent out from America, had found the
climate too hot and unhealthy for their constitutions.
There are now about 3000 settlers remaining in the
colony.   Jones declared that, after all he had seen
and heard of Liberia, nothing should induce him to
live there ; and that it would be madness for any one,
unless he had some capital, to settle at that place.

The next day I returned to Ripley on one of Peter's horses, and his son accompanied me on another.
These good people seemed much affected by my
visit.   They begged I would not interfere in their
behalf, if they were likely to be placed, by such a
step, in a worse situation.   They were reconciled to
their fate, and would continue to trust in a higher
Power for relief from their sufferings, or support under them.   They were desirous that their children

should be instructed, and all discord cease in the Camp; that they might live peaceably and amicably with one another, and shew, by their good conduct, that they did not deserve the cruel treatment they were receiving from the whites. I called on three or four of the other settlers; but the men were out; and one or two of the women, whom I saw, were either not inclined, or (more likely) not enabled, to give me any satisfactory information. I endeavored to impress upon one of them the policy, as well as the duty, of being united; as they had a common enemy to deal with, who would be better pleased to set them all at variance with one another, than promote the interests of any. She said I had told her more than she had ever heard before, and that there was much truth in it.

If schools were established, and a white preacher —to protect them—appointed, they might, perhaps, emerge from the state of despondency in which I left them. Mr. Rankin informed me that the Presbytery of Chillicothe (Ohio) had resolved upon sending a schoolmaster to instruct their children. The first and most important thing to be done by their friends, is to obtain from the legislature the repeal of that iniquitous statute which has given them up as a prey to the designing and the unprincipled, and put the seal of legal authority on the prejudice that debases them, and the roguery that defrauds them.

The young females are often brought back by their

employers in a condition which reflects more dishonor on the villainy that has betrayed them, than on
their own imprudence. In the case of a white woman, an oath is sufficient to filiate. Here the mother
can obtain neither reparation for herself, nor maintenance for her child. Her evidence is worthless.
No explanation can be given by the injured party,
and no punishment inflicted on the guilty. She is
left in the middle of the Camps, to find her home, if
she have one, and assistance where she can.

The people of the hotel where I lodged, at Ripley,
were much pleased when I acquainted them with the
object of my visit to the Camps. They had heard a
great deal of the oppression and fraud from which
their inhabitants had suffered. Their wrongs ought
to be known, they said, to the family, if any remained, of their benevolent owner, that ample redress
might be obtained from them. I was particularly
warned to be on my guard with a person who was a
sort of sub-agent for these poor people, and who was
living at Hillsborough; to which place it was my
intention to proceed, for the purpose of making further inquiries. Some years ago, a man had been
appointed to reside at Georgetown, and administer
to the wants of the settlers from Virginia. He was
in very indigent circumstances when he arrived; but
having set up a store, in which he appeared to be
making money, he suddenly decamped, and is now
living, in the State of Illinois, on some land he is

supposed to have purchased with the fruits of his successful speculation in the Camps.

Samuel Gist left two daughters, both of whom were always remarkably kind to the slaves. One of them was married, and is said to have had a son; the other was also married, and her husband quitted England. This was all the information I could obtain about the family; and my informants could neither write nor read.

I was shewn several papers of freedom while at Peter's house. The following is a copy of one of them :—

" Virginia to wit.

" By virtue of the act of the General Assembly, intituled ' An Act giving effect to the last will and testament of Samuel Gist, deceased, late of the city of London', passed the 26th day of February, 1816, Anthony　　　　, one of the slaves belonging to the estate of the said Samuel Gist, deceased, aged about six years, was, by a decree of the Superior Court of Chancery for the Richmond district, pronounced the third day of July *, declared to be emancipated and free to all intents and purposes.

" WM. W. HERRING, C.S.G., C.R.D."

---

* I am not certain about the date here. As I transcribed it, it appears to be 1813; but that must be a mistake. As the decree was made in pursuance of an act of the legislature, to give effect to the will, the codicil, (as it appears in the Ap-

There were two documents of this kind,—the sur-
name not inserted in either, though room was left
for it. The persons thus enfranchised were children
of Peter Vicy or Visy.

I subjoin a transcript from a copy of a letter to a
Quaker of the name of Woodrow, at Hillsborough in
Highland County, Ohio. The copy was taken by
W. Patterson, (a colored man,) who taught a school
in the settlement one quarter. He boarded with Peter,
who was never remunerated by those who had sent
the man. On the back of the paper was written :
" This letter is only a copy of Mr. Wickham's letter;
and there may be some words not legally taken
down, in consequence of its being very hard to read." .

" Hanover Court House, 10 July, 1828.
" Dear Sir,

" I have just received your letter of the 1st instant.
The estate of Mr. Gist in Virginia now amounts,
according to my estimate, from 8000 to 10,000 dollars. The whole subject is placed by an act of
Assembly under the control of the chancellor for
the Richmond district; and no step is ever taken,
except by his own (here some word was wanting).
The property, by our general laws, by a special provision in this case, is subject to the claims of cre-

pendix,) appended to the latter, follows the condition on which
it was made, and is null. The slaves have obtained their freedom; but what has become of the estate?

ditors; and the estate has already been very much diminished by a decree rendered by C. J. Marshall in favour of W. Anderson, representative, for 50,000 dollars. This decree has been satisfied. There are now two suits brought by the aty. [I presume attorney] of Jos. Smith and of John Smith against the estate. Appeals, death, have caused delay in bringing their cause to a hearing: about two months ago they were reversed [I am not sure whether the word be not 'revised']. The Court meets in Oct., and I shall exert myself to have them tried as soon as possible. It is impossible to say at what time they can be brought on: but I shall be much disappointed, if the term passes without a decision. The opinion of the chancellor was against the claim; and I am very sanguine it will be affirmed. Should it, however, be revised, it cannot now be known what effect it will have on the estate. If we succeed in their cause, there will be no obstacle, of which I am at present advised, that can delay the claims of the concerns of the estate. In that event, the Chancellor, according to the will of Mr. Gist, will have the funds noted [vested?] in some productive stock, and the extents applied to the benefit of the aged and infirm. There are still in Virginia from eighteen to twenty negroes, whom I hope to remove, if the decision of the Court of Appeals be, as I anticipate, in the next spring, &c. &c.

" WM. B. WICKHAM."

I left Ripley the next day for Cincinnati, with the
view of seeing whether something might not be done
for the poor people at the Camps, and with the intention of proceeding from that city to Hillsborough.
In the boat was a young man, with whom I had
travelled from Ripley, and who had left the stage, in
consequence of illness, before it reached Georgetown.
We immediately recognized each other, and recipro-
cated civilities.   He enquired the result of my expedition, and told me he had lived within a mile of
the Camps, and was well acquainted with all the
circumstances connected with the colony.   The conduct of the whites towards them had been most
brutal and vexatious.   They had, in the first instance,
endeavored to drive them away, declaring that they
had no business there ; had ever since insulted and
threatened them ; and were only waiting till they
were themselves sufficiently numerous, to expel them
by force.   He had no doubt, he said, that gross injustice had been practised upon these helpless
people ; and that if it were not for the employment
some of them got on the river and at Cincinnati,
they would long since have been exterminated, or
driven away, by starvation.   The inhabitants of
Georgetown cared little what became of them, if
they could but get rid of them.   He had little to say
in praise of Mr. Wilson ; and I was not inclined to
defend his character, as the loss of a pair of razors I
left under his care had not tended to remove my

dislike of his violent and insolent abuse of the
" niggers."

Though I had no opportunity of visiting any
Mormon settlement, I am enabled to give some account of the people to be found there,—a society
that appears to be adding very rapidly to its numbers, if credit is to be given to one of the preachers,
who signs his name " Gladden Bishop " to a letter
recently published in one of the newspapers of the
country. He there states, that there are already
20,000 converts to the doctrines he professes ; that
they have 800 ministers, though there were but six
in 1830, when the sect first became known : that
two printing-offices, as many stores, and a large
meeting-house, built of stone, belong to them.

Joseph Smith, the founder of the new faith, who
is reported to have recently been shot in a conflict
with its enemies, published, a few years ago, " an
account, written by the hand of Mormon upon plates
taken from the plates of Nephi." As the "account"
was, when found, in " an unknown tongue ", the
world would have been but little the better or the
wiser for it, if the discoverer of this precious document had not been inspired to interpret its contents.
Whether through delusion or collusion, there were
found eleven persons willing to testify, by their sig-
natures, to the truth of this apocalypse. Eight names
of living and respectable witnesses were affixed to
one certificate, and three to another. The former

had this declaration: "We have seen and hefted and know of a surety, that the said Smith has got the plates of which we have spoken: and we also saw the engravings thereon, all of which have the appearance of ancient work and of curious workmanship." The other was to the same effect. "That an angel of God", such are the words used, "came down from heaven, and he brought and laid before our eyes, that we beheld and saw the plates and the engravings thereon."

Absurd as this "account" is, or perhaps because it is absurd, it has imposed upon many; while the prophet, under whose standard they are gathering, has contrived, by his cunning, to reconcile attachment to received truths with the natural love of the new and the marvellous. In acknowledging the authenticity of the Bible, he brings forward a supplement to its supposed omissions, and interweaves its doctrines and sanctions with the narrative of his own mission.

The chief peculiarities of the sect are the gift of preaching in unknown tongues, plainness of apparel, and gratuitous services in all who are chosen to minister to the secular and spiritual wants of the community. One passage in this curious Koran clearly points to the place of its concoction, and the prepossessions of its author; who would doubtless ground a claim for the prophetic spirit on this very objection from the unbeliever. It alludes, most un-

equivocally, to the free-masons; Ontario county, in
the State of New York, being the place where
Morgan's murder excited such a spirit of hostility to
" the craft."   " Satan ", says the plate, " did stir up
the hearts of the more part of the Nephites, inso-
much that they did unite with those bands of robbers,
and did enter into their covenants and their oaths,
that they would protect and preserve one another, in
whatever difficult circumstances they should be
placed; that they should not suffer for their murders,
and their plunderings, and their stealings.   And it
came to pass, that they did have their signs, yea, their
secret signs, and their secret words: and this that they
might distinguish a brother, who had entered into
the covenant, that, whatever wickedness his brother
should do, he should not be injured by his brother,
nor by those who did belong to his band, who had
taken this covenant: and whosoever of their band
should reveal unto the world their wickedness and
their abominations, should be tried, not according
to the laws of their country, but according to the
laws of their wickedness which had been given by
Gadianton and Kishkumen."

The prophetic and didactic portions of Smith's
work are such as might be expected from one, who
would make a belief in the Christian revelation sub-
servient to his purposes.   The historical part chiefly
narrates the deeds and misdeeds of the Lamanites
and Nephites—descended from Laman and Nephi;

two out of four brothers, who, with their parents, Lehi and Sarai, fled, in the first year of King Zedekiah, from the ill-fated city of Jerusalem into the wilderness. The plates had been previously obtained by their father, who sent his sons back to their former place of abode for these genealogical records of his family. Lehi is described as a lineal descendant of Joseph, the son of Jacob. The Lamanites represent the rebellious, and the Nephites the obedient, portion of the family; and, through them, of the whole human race. Nephi, the youngest son, built, in obedience to the commands of the Holy Spirit, a vessel, in which the whole family sailed to a distant and an unknown land. Our Saviour, after his resurrection, is described as appearing, in the character of teacher, to the Nephites—the chosen people of the New World, who were ultimately subdued by their less worthy kindred. The "plates" were, we are told, "hid up unto the Lord in the earth, to be brought forth in due time by the hand of the Gentile." Such is the outline, which the fortunes and characters of the two great branches, that sprang from the adventurous Patriarch, who first planted himself in the western wilds, present. Their disputes and reconciliations; their wars and their alliances, are detailed with tedious minuteness; and the mounds of earth, which, as they now exist in that part of the country, have given rise to so much interest and speculation, are referred to, by the preachers of the Mormon faith, as proofs of the existence of these theocratic tribes.

As the promulgators of this extraordinary legend maintain the natural equality of mankind, without excepting the native Indians or the African race, there is little reason to be surprised at the cruel persecution by which they have suffered, and still less at the continued accession of converts among those who sympathize with the wrongs of others or seek an asylum for their own.

The preachers and believers of the following doctrines were not likely to remain, unmolested, in the State of Missouri.

" The Lord God hath commanded that men should not murder; that they should not lie; that they should not steal, &c. He inviteth them all to come unto him and partake of his goodness : and he denieth none that come unto him ; black and white— bond and free, male and female ; and he remembereth the heathen ; and all are alike unto God, both Jew and Gentile." Again : " Behold ! the Lamanites, your brethren, whom ye hate, because of their filthiness and the cursings which hath come upon their skins, are more righteous than you ; for they have not forgotten the commandment of the Lord, which was given unto our fathers, &c. Wherefore the Lord God will not destroy them ; but will be merciful to them ; and one day they shall become a blessed people." " O my brethren, I fear, that, unless ye shall repent of your sins, that their skins shall be whiter than yours, when ye shall be brought with them before the throne of God*. Wherefore a commandment I give unto you, which is the word of God, that ye revile no more against them because of the darkness of their skins," &c. " The king saith unto him, yea! if the Lord saith unto us, go! we will go down unto our brethren, and we will be their slaves, until we repair unto them the many murders and sins, which we have committed against them. But Ammon saith unto him, it is against the law of our brethren, which was established by my father, that there should be any slaves among them. Therefore let us go down and rely upon the mercies of our brethren."

---

* This ridiculous notion is to be found, where few would think of looking for it, in Dr. Lettsom's letters. Speaking of one among the patrimonial slaves whom he had emancipated, the benevolent Quaker says, quite unconscious that he was sanctioning a distinction equally foolish and wicked,—" Poor Teresa! Thou little thinkest how much thy master values thy present. He will probably never see thee in this world! In the next thou mayest appear white as an European, and happy as he who has said ' be free !'"

CHAPTER XXVI.

ON my second visit to Cincinnati, I went to a private house in preference to an hotel, having found the one I lodged at very crowded and noisy, without a counter-balance to be found in an agreeable or polished society. It was some time before I could find what I wanted. Wherever I applied, I met with great civility, and a readiness to assist me in searching for a house that would accommodate me. Very erroneous opinions are often formed of a place from the company at the taverns. The reception I found at the establishment, to which I was admitted, was such that I must have been "hard to please" if I had found fault with it; and my fellow-lodgers were obliging and courteous. While conversing

with one of the students, of whom I have before
spoken, he shewed me a letter he had received from
Lewis Tappan, of New York. I took the following
extract from it, as it shews the state of the public
press in America. After relating what had passed
during the examination, at a public meeting, of a
person who had been some time at Liberia, of
which place he gave a most lamentable account,
the writer adds : "The newspapers have endeavoured
to mislead the public on this subject, and have done
it to a considerable extent. We cannot get any explanation into any influential paper, except the
Evangelist, unless by chance. Charles King—editor of the American—told me the abolitionists are
right. ' Why don't you say so in your paper ?' he
laughed and replied : 'The time has not come yet,'
and in a few days he admitted a piece against us.
One of the editors of the Daily Advertiser, of the
name of Townsend, told me, our cause was a just
one. ' Why then do you not publish articles on
our side ?' He looked angry, and said, ' The paper
is my property : I'm not going to injure it.' So he
says nothing on either side."

Among my colored friends at this place was one
from North Carolina, who was well acquainted with
Damon Jones, having lived in the same part of the
country with him for some time. He spoke of him
as an industrious honest man, temperate in his habits,
and respected by those who knew him. He had heard

of the ill treatment he had met with. The last time he saw him was on the public road, in company with a white man. They appeared to be going towards the South. This corresponds exactly with what Damon told me—that he was decoyed into Alabama. Of Mr. Gaston my informant expressed himself in very different terms. He described him as a hard master, and an advocate in the legislature of the State, for severe measures against the slaves. Free blacks have the elective franchise in North Carolina; and in some districts it has happened that they have been almost the only voters at an election. Some of them are wealthy; and all who conduct themselves with propriety are much less insulted and molested than their brethren in the northern states. This disgraceful pre-eminence in injustice is an indisputable fact; and I never met with a free black from the South who could not testify to its truth from the experience of his own feelings. There are but few States where these people enjoy the elective franchise: and they are, I believe, in the free,—Maine, New Hampshire, Vermont, Massachusetts, New York, and Pennsylvania; but they seldom or never make any use of it in Philadelphia: North Carolina and Tennessee alone of the Slave States, allow them the privilege of voting. Their political and social disabilities are almost as various as the States to which they belong; and while both are subject to modifications by their removal from one to another, they still remain in the lowest rank of society, with an impassable barrier between themselves and others who occupy the scale above.

They appear to be further removed from the common sympathies of our nature in Eastern Virginia than in any other part of the Union; and to be, in some respects, in a less enviable situation than those slaves who have fallen into the hands of humane masters. I could always distinguish a free man from a slave at Richmond, by the former taking off his hat to me as he passed—a piece of conciliatory civility which the other feels to be a work of supererogation, as his master will protect *him*. The better the coat, the more submissive was the bow of the wearer. A remarkably fine-looking man of very respectable appearance touched his hat to me one day as I was going by. As there was no other person where he stood, I stopped and entered into conversation with him, and asked him whether he was not free. " No, Sir!" was his reply—" most people think as you do but I am not so." It was civility that induced him to bow: in most others it is fear.

There are few places in the States where capital can be more advantageously employed than at Cincinnati. Money is frequently let at fifteen, twenty, and even twenty-five per cent. per annum. A land agent in the city told me he had just obtained a mortgage at ten per cent. on the best land security. At New

York, a mortgage, except for small sums and short periods, can seldom be had for more than six per cent. The legal interest is seven. In Ohio, the legislative Procrustes has not put the honest and industrious borrower into the same bed with the rogue and the spendthrift. The necessaries of life are cheap here. Board and lodging may be had for two dollars and a half a week. Mechanics pay generally about half that sum, though they can earn from one to three dollars a-day, according to their skill and the kind of employment. They are, in fact, considering the changes and chances to which men in business are subject, in a more eligible situation than many of the store-keepers and small capitalists, as their remuneration is secure from almost every risk but that which arises from their own want of prudence. The value of land in the vicinity of the city has risen with its extension. Lots, that twelve years ago were hardly worth four or five dollars an acre, now fetch as many hundreds. Land, at the distance of ten to fifty miles, is worth from 50 to 100 dollars an acre, with intermediate prices, corresponding to the degrees of proximity. As the great emporium of trade to the Western States, Cincinnati cannot fail to become, in the course of a few years, a populous and wealthy city.

Twenty years ago, a journey from New Orleans to this place would have taken ninety days; it can now be performed in twelve. The cost of freight has diminished in a greater proportion. Seventy cents the cwt. from Philadelphia are, at present, about the average for goods, which, at that time, were charged twelve dollars. The city contains between thirty and forty thousand souls; and, from the advantages it enjoys as a manufacturing and shipping town, may be expected to continue at its present rate of increase. It supplies the Southern market with machinery of various kinds, implements of husbandry, and articles of furniture. Hence, in a great measure, the bitter hostility it has manifested against every thing that may lead to the abolition or amelioration of a system on which it thinks, as Liverpool once thought of the slave-trade, its interests depend. There was but a small addition made to the city the year in which I visited it; the number of new buildings, which had averaged 500 annually, having dwindled down to little more than fifty, owing to the war carried on by " the hero of New Orleans" against the currency of the country.

On the 20th I left Cincinnati, at nine A.M., and arrived, about the same time P.M., at Hillsborough. The distance is fifty-six miles. The road was hilly and bad; great part of it being what is vulgarly called " corduroy", or " bang-up", or " rail-road". The term alludes to the planks or rails, which are placed transversely; so that the road presents the appearance of that sort of stuff which, in honor of some monarch, announces to the world that his ma-

jesty once deigned to have his inexpressibles made
of it—(corde-du-roi).

The greater part of the country we passed through
was uncleared; the soil being of an inferior nature,
swampy, and covered with beech-trees, interspersed
with " bottoms", or alluvial land of excellent quality.
The towns and villages presented a lively picture of
industry and cheerfulness. Where the land has been
recently cleared, the log-hut and its inhabitants give
striking evidence of hard toil, and severe privation.
The women, in particular, seem to be worn out, and
the children are frequently ragged and squalid. The
wilderness is no paradise to the first settlers. Nothing but the love of independence, or the hope of
bettering their condition, could support them under
the discouragements that await them in a new country. The drudgery to which the females are necessarily exposed, is, indeed, most painful and harassing. Few can afford to hire " help"; and the better
it is when obtained, the less is the chance of retain-
ing it. Of the female servants, the blacks are preferable, both for industry and skill, to the whites.
They are equally prone to change. A fixed establishment is out of the question. Even the children
go forth " to seek their fortune", as soon as years or
opportunity admit. This early want of stability fixes
an indelible stamp upon individual character; and
forms, as it unfolds and extends its influence through
the innumerable ramifications of society, no small

item in those deductions which an impartial estimate
will make, from the supposed advantages of the new
over the old world.

It is not only in the woods that the wives and
daughters of settlers have such a laborious and irksome life to lead. It is very difficult for women in
the villages, however wealthy their condition and re-
fined their feelings, to meet with that sort of "help"
on which they can depend for a regular supply of
their domestic wants. They must make their own
soap and candles, and bake their own bread; while
they are often obliged to perform themselves all the
minutiæ and drudgery of the culinary department.
Those who are poor, and prepared to work hard,
may do well in the back woods; but where habits
have sprung from the enjoyment of comfort and leisure, the immediate sacrifices to be made by an emigrant to the "far west", would scarcely be indemni-
fied by the prospective benefits of an ample provision
for the future.

When wages are spoken of here, it is to be observed that the amount is, in some measure, nomi-
nal; a large proportion being generally paid in goods,
on the barter or truck system. The clergy often
" take their tithes in kind". Hence some tact is
required on the part of the workman, not only in
fixing upon what he shall receive in lieu of money,
but in making such arrangements with the store-
keeper, with whom he must bargain to give him ar-

ticles in return, that may not subject him to loss when he disposes of them to others, or appropriates them to his own use. It will readily be seen that the tradesman has, in like manner, to traffic with the merchant at a distance, to insure his own profits: and thus it is that the want of a currency, and the imperfect distribution of employment, have the effect of sharpening the faculties of all, and producing in each individual a greater degree of acuteness and caution in some things, than prevails among a people whose commercial machinery is more simple, because more perfect. The general fund of knowledge is less, as the exigencies of society are more limited; while the share of each is greater, as his necessities are less easily supplied.

The profits of capital must be very high in Ohio, as the borrower pays a high interest for it. There is a man at Hillsborough, who gets, upon an average, twenty-five per cent. for the small sums he lets out. The law allows six per cent. per annum upon debts, but lays no restriction on loans—the act of 1804, for the prevention of usury, having been repealed in 1824.

No State has added to its numbers so rapidly as Ohio. Its population, which was 581,434 in 1820, amounted, in 1830, to 937,679. It is now the third in the Union; and will probably outstrip them all in the number of its citizens, before many years have passed. One cause of its increase may be

found in its liberal policy towards foreigners, whose
capital is attracted to it, as well by the security as
by the profits of investment which it offers.   In the
State of New York, an alien cannot legally hold a
mortgage upon land.   In Ohio he may hold all kinds
of real estate " as fully and completely as any citizen of the United States."   Great caution, however,
is necessary here in lending money or making bar-
gains, as, to use the words of a writer in the American Jurist, (Jan. 1834,) " the balance turns too
much in favour of the debtor ; for, unless he be particularly honest and conscientious, the creditor
stands but little chance in making his claim."   " We
speak," he adds, " from dismal experience.   We
have known suits commenced against merchants,
who had at the time in their stores goods amounting to fifty or sixty thousand dollars.   We have
heard them declare, that those creditors, who were
so ungentlemanly as to sue, should never receive one
cent. We have besought a court of chancery to interfere by injunction, or compel an assignment for the
benefit of all the creditors; alleging, among other
facts, that these merchants were then forcing off
their goods at auction, at forty per cent. less than the
first cost; but chancery has told us it could not interfere.   We have pursued the case to judgment,
and our execution has been returned " no property."
All has been disposed of, we know not how.   Nay,
more, we have heard such men, when examined, on

application for the benefit of the insolvent act, admit, that, for the purpose of arranging their affairs, they have been paying one quarter per cent. a day for money, and that at the same time, they were selling off their goods at forty and fifty per cent. loss; and yet, after making these disclosures, we have known them to be permitted to take the benefit of the act, on the ground that such was the custom here.   It is high time that this enormous system of fraud was broken up, either by enacting a genuine bankrupt law, which should take from a debtor all control of his property after the first act of bankruptcy; or by giving a creditor the power of attaching his property in the first instance, instead of arresting his body.   Unless some remedy like this be interposed, our law of debtor and creditor should be entitled, ' a law for the encouragement of fraud.' "
It should be observed, that, by the existing law on the subject, a debtor's property cannot be touched, till after judgment, as long as an arrest can be made; and the latter is a mere farce, since the prisoner can have the privilege of " the limits," which embrace the whole county.

The day after my arrival at Hillsborough, I called at Joshua Woodrow's store, and found him busy behind the counter.   As soon as I announced to him the object of my errand, he crossed over, and commenced his replies to my inquiries, with a tone of voice and change of countenance that bespoke no

slight degree of discretion, and recalled to my mind
the hints I had received at Ripley.   He informed
me that he was one of three local agents, all Quakers, who had been nominated by the manumission
society at Philadelphia to look after the interests of
Mr. Gist's emancipated slaves.   The other two were
Levi Warner, of Chillicothe, and Enoch Lewis, who
resided near one of the settlements.   He had, at
first, declined accepting the commission, as he was
too much occupied and too old to pay proper attention to its duties.   He was induced, however, from
motives of humanity alone, to undertake the office.
There were, he said, altogether, three colonies ;—
two called the Camps, upper and lower, founded at
the same time, at the distance of ten miles from
each other, and containing about 300 souls. The other
had been " located " but two or three years. From
the agent, (Wickham,) at Richmond, he had heard
that, after all claims upon the estate were satisfied,
and legal expenses paid, there would remain somewhat more than 5000 dollars, the interest of which
was to be employed for the relief of the aged and
the infirm.   It was to carry these objects into effect
that he had been appointed.   Speaking of the lower
Camps, my visit to which I had concealed from him
till his questions elicited the fact from me, he endeavored to impress my mind with an unfavorable
opinion of the settlers.   " To tell you the truth,"
said he, with a mysterious look and in a low voice,

" I do not wish this to be known publicly—I have
heard that they are rather too fond of a glass of
whiskey." This delicacy towards a despised race
rather surprised me; and the more so, as I felt assured, from what I had seen, that the imputation
could not be justly laid upon my friend Peter, as he
would naturally have offered me a glass of spirits,
had there been any in the log-hut, when I entered
it fatigued and unwell. But if the charge had any
foundation, it was the duty of the agent to report it
to his employers, rather than to whisper it to a
stranger. When I informed him of my intention to
visit the new colony of which he had spoken, he
strongly urged me to call on Enoch Lewis, who
lived near the place, and take him with me. He
seemed particularly anxious that I should have the
benefit of his company, as a guide and an interpreter. On my return to the inn, he sent me a mes-
sage to say, that there was a man at his house who
was going that way, and would ride with me. I
found in the uncertain state of the weather an excuse for declining the offer; and, a few hours after,
when the day had cleared up, I set off on horseback
by myself, having received the necessary instructions
from the prudent Joshua.

    After riding five or six miles, and surmounting the
difficulties of choice which the concurrence of cross-
roads presented, I rode up to a house that stood at
the distance of a quarter of a mile, and inquired the

way of a young woman who was standing at the
door. She referred me to her father. He came up
very civilly to the place where I stood, and supplied
me with the information I wanted. The usual in-
terrogatory a stranger meets with in the woods was
put; and as soon as I had answered that I was from
England, and wished to see how the blacks were
going on, the farmer offered to conduct me himself,
as he knew the people well,—had occasionally given
them employment, and felt great interest in their
welfare, both from their good conduct while working
for him, and the reports that were current of the ill-
usage they had met with. I was rather puzzled what
to do. He was a near neighbor of Enoch; and I
thought it not unlikely that Joshua had sent him a
hint, through my intended companion, of what was
going on, that he might either send over to Enoch,
or prevent, by his presence, an unrestrained communication between the settlers and the stranger. It
was some time before my suspicions were entirely
removed; but after he had invited me to take some
dinner, had saddled his horse, and had ridden through
the woods with me in free and friendly discourse, I
could no longer withhold my confidence from him,
when I saw him received in a familiar, yet respectful, manner by the sable inmates of the log-hut we
stopped at. It was a wretched cabin, with little or
no furniture, beyond a bed or two, and some chairs
of the meanest kind. Every thing about the room

and the inhabitants, bore the marks of extreme poverty. We were soon surrounded by people of all ages and of both sexes. An old man, between seventy and eighty, and his wife, the parent stem of no less than seventeen branches, with their collateral offsets, were the chief speakers ; and, as in the lower Camps, the old lady had most to say, and was most ready to say it. Four years had elapsed since they left Virginia for the place where I found them. When the other party, who now occupy the Camps, were sent off, against their consent, by the agent, William Wickham, about seventy remained behind in concealment. They were subsequently collected together by the authorities, and carried into the northern part of Ohio ; and being left there, without provisions, to shift for themselves, they dispersed,—some into Pennsylvania, and others into Canada. The rest found their way back, about a year after, to the plantation in Virginia. Here they maintained themselves on the land which they had formerly cultivated as slaves, as it was untenanted at the time, and belonged, they conceived, to them by their master's bequest.

When I questioned these people, they gave the same account of the manner in which they first heard of the death and the donation of Samuel Gist,—of the cruelties and vexations they underwent during their efforts to obtain their freedom ; and of the suspicious circumstances which attended the death of the Englishman who came over to see them. None of them could tell when Gist died. The old man said that he had made many fruitless attempts to find out the contents of the will; and had often expressed his surprise to Woodrow, that any one should undertake to carry into effect the object of a man's last wish, without knowing what it was. Joshua had told me, a few hours before, that he had never seen a copy of the document in question. As he was induced, according to his own statement, to befriend these unfortunate people from motives of pure benevolence, it is certainly strange, that he should not have thought it necessary to inquire what their rights and claims were; and whether the pittance, he was to dole out to them, was all they were entitled to. When they quitted the plantation, they were accompanied by three armed men, and two of them were hand-cuffed with irons, because they were unwilling to go. This, they declared, was done by Wickham's order. Here I interrupted the narrative, to ask how the slaves were treated in that part of the country. They threw up their hands, and exclaimed, " we cannot give you any idea of it: they are treated worse than dogs—they are cut to pieces." " That poor girl," said the old woman, pointing to a young person present, " had her back broke by a blow she had from a man, who knocked her down with a rail." The poor creature's appearance testified to the truth of what her grandmother had said.

When first they arrived, they were allowed five

acres to each person. They had one plough for two
families, and, subsequently, when the women were
anxious to earn something by spinning, they could
get from Joshua but two wheels for the whole party,
and were obliged to borrow the remainder of what
they wanted. They shewed me a miserable blanket
and a pair of trowsers that Joshua had given them,
—the latter of the coarsest material, and totally unfit
for the winter dress of an infirm old man. The
blanket was on one of the beds. When contrasted
with the clothing which their kind old master was
in the habit of sending them from England, and of
which I saw a specimen, it was too plain that they
had lost by the freedom they had obtained, and
would have been happier as slaves—if their benefactor had lived. And here is the worst part of
slavery; since the continuance of good treatment is
uncertain, while its remembrance embitters the evils
that follow its removal. They were told, when they
left Virginia, that they would have as much land,
where they were going, as they might want; but
now, that their numbers are increasing, they are unable to procure a further supply. What little there
is, is of a good quality; but there is not enough
(and my companion assented to the assertion) for
their support. They occasionally get a job in the
neighborhood; and some of them go to Cincinnati
for work: but they complained that they were often
defrauded of their wages, without a chance of re-

dress under a system which encourages roguery by
pinioning its victim. They had been urged to give
up their lands and go to Liberia; but they returned
the same answer to the importunate proposal, that
all make, who have a particle of free choice left
them. They are in fact in a state bordering upon
destitution; and to use their own words, do not
know what to do. I endeavored to console them
by assuring them that I would use my utmost efforts
to assist them—that I would publish a statement of
their case on my return to England; and that I
would, in the mean time, write home for a copy of
their master's will, if it could be procured in London,
that it might be sent over to America. That part of
the document, which I had afterwards copied out at
Doctor's Commons, will be found in the Appendix.

The poor creatures were much pleased with the
promise, thus held out to them; but I reminded
them that the difficulties which arose from lapse of
time, claims of relatives—the tricks of agents, the
decisions of the Virginia courts, and the distance
between the two countries,—these considerations
should check their expectations, and make them re-
signed to their fate. I inquired how many there
were of them; and, after counting the families, and
the individual members of each, they agreed that the
sum total was forty-two—just twelve more than
Joshua had reckoned when I was with him. Yet
he was present, they assured me, when they had

made the same calculation on a former occasion. They said, they had always understood there were 340 or 360 in the lower Camps originally, exclusive of those in the upper; though the agent had told me there were not more than 300 in both. They were loud in their complaints against the agents. When they succeed in obtaining relief from Joshua, it is given not in money, or raw material, so that they might purchase or make their own things with advantage to themselves; but they must take what they want out of his store, or employ Enoch's daughters to work up the clothing they require. It was some time before I could comprehend what they meant—when, at last, I said: " you mean that your agent is your tradesman, and puts what he pays you with one hand into his own pocket with the other; charging what price, and making what profit, he pleases?" They all smiled; and the old woman, clapping her hands and striding across the room, cried out, " You're right!—you're right! that's it exactly."

There was no school for their children, and no religious instructor among them.

The farm was in good condition—an excellent crop of wheat in the field adjoining the log-hut; two pretty white ponies, and a cow with a calf in another; and the whole as skilfully and industriously cultivated as the narrow means of the occupants would allow. The cow had just been obtained by one of the daughters who had received it in lieu of wages from a neighbor she had worked for—a source of great delight and comfort to them, as they could get no milk before. My guide said they would do well, if they had more land, and pointed out to me, as we reached and as we were leaving the farm, the neat and thrifty appearance of the fields. This, however, was the best managed allotment in the colony, and formed an exception to the general distress of which I have spoken; — though I question whether the owner had any thing beyond the bare necessaries of life for the support of his family. Speaking of the "black law" of Ohio, my companion declared his determination to remove, if he could, from its statute book, an enactment which he had always thought unconstitutional, and which is a disgrace to a free country, in an age fast verging towards the middle of the nineteenth century.

The sun was now declining; and we took our leave of these persecuted helpless people, and terminated a visit, which, I trust, has thrown a few gleams of hope over the gloomy path of their earthly pilgrimage.

Such are the people who are held up to the scorn of mankind by British statesmen as idle vagabonds —fit only " to point a moral " in a senatorial speech, " or adorn" a protest. Such are the people who supplied the Duke of Wellington, Lord St. Vincent,

Lord Penshurst, and Lord Wynford with a Christian argument against the abolition of slavery—from the bill for which they declared themselves dissentient, because, among other equally valid reasons, " the experience of the United States — a country but thinly peopled, in proportion to its extent and fertility, and always in want of hands, has shewn that, even in more temperate climates, the labor of emancipated negroes could not be relied on for the cultivation of the soil ; and that the welfare of society, as well as that of the emancipated negroes themselves, required that they should be removed elsewhere." Between whig and tory what is the black refugee to do ? The one would send him away because he enriches the country—the other because he impoverishes it.

As I had declined the farmer's invitation to dinner, I thought I could not do better than partake of his evening meal. On our return to his house, he introduced me to his sons—two sturdy strapping youths, with good looks and good appetites. One of his daughters made the tea, while the other drove away the flies. As soon as we had eaten and uttered as many good things as we could, (for the whole party was merry as well as hungry,) the lookers on sat down to their repast. This, as far as I had opportunity to observe, is the usual order of things in the houses of the middle class. The masculine is

more worthy than the feminine; and the feminine
more worthy than the neuter.   Hence the women
eat after the men; and the blacks after the women.

It was now time to "be off."   I had finished my
mission and my meal: so I shook my worthy host
by the hand, cracked a parting joke with the young
people, and mounting my horse, returned to Hillsborough.

The next morning, when I asked for my bill, the
landlord (Mr. Miller) refused to take any thing for
the hire of his horse; and I could not prevail upon
him to alter his determination.   Both he and his
wife had been extremely obliging and desirous of
contributing to my accommodation in every respect.

As the stage for Chillicothe would not arrive from
Cincinnati till Monday, and would travel all night,
I determined to walk on, making Bainbridge (about
half way) my resting place for the night.   I was
unable to procure a vehicle, and unwilling to borrow
Mr. Miller's horse without paying for it.   I set off,
therefore, on foot, and reached Bainbridge in the
evening.   Entering the first tavern I saw, I inquired
of the landlord if he had any meat in the house.
He was a mighty consequential sort of a personage.
He seemed highly offended at the imputation the
question conveyed to his mind.   " Sir," said he, in
a voice that preserved his dignity, while it indulged
his displeasure, " I should not be fit to keep a tavern if I had not."   " Pray ! what kinds of meat

have you?" "Why! bacon, Sir!—bacon!—bacon! bacon!" There were fortunately some eggs too in the house, and I was perfectly satisfied with my meal.

On being shewn into my bed-room, I found the chambers above as well furnished as the larder below. Those I passed through, as well as that destined for myself, had nothing in them but beds— beds—beds, while each bed had but one sheet. As my room was double-bedded, as well as single-sheeted, I soon borrowed what I wanted, and gave my feather bed as a security. No water was ever allowed up stairs, lest it should injure the furniture below. He must be difficult, indeed, to please, who could grumble about his toilette, when so much care was taken of the ladies in the parlor. There was a well in the yard; and he might shave and wash his face in the same tub.

The next day was rainy, and the heat very oppressive. After proceeding four or five miles, I stopped at a farm-house to get a glass of water; and, finding the owner inclined to be sociable, I sat some time conversing with him. He had been settled on his land about twenty years, and had come from Pennsylvania. He had given three dollars an acre for 260; and, now that his neighbors were becoming, as he said, too numerous, he was about to "sell out" and move further westward—though an old man of sixty or seventy, with a large family. He expected

to get twelve or fifteen dollars an acre in return for
the improvements he had made. About two-thirds
were in wood-land, and the soil very good. It is a
common thing, in this part of the country, for the
settlers to help one another in getting in their grain,
raising their log-huts, or cutting down the trees.
They assemble together for the purpose, and are fed
by the proprietor of the land, who is ready to take
his turn when called upon, and repay the obligation
by a similar mark of good neighborhood. When
this system is continued for any length of time, it
may be inferred that the population is scanty, and
the farms nearly equal in extent.

This way of realizing the profits of industry, by
selling the farm on which they were made, and bettering one's condition by investing the proceeds in
the purchase of land more remote from a settled district, and therefore cheaper, is the usual mode of
proceeding in the West. A regular succession of
cultivators is thus created, corresponding to the
quantity of labor bestowed on the land they have
selected, from the scientific agriculturist in the old
settlements, to the rude squatter on the virgin soil
of the wilderness. In the old world a man generally
carries his savings to the city; in the new, to the
woods. Labor follows capital in the one, and capital
follows labor in the other.

There is a sort of analogy between the geological

structure of the old, middle, and western States, and the people who respectively inhabit them. The latter, as well as the former, may be said to be of primary, secondary, and recent, formation. Having finished my chat with the Pennsylvanian, and declined his hospitable offer to sit down and partake of his dinner, I renewed my journey.

On entering Chillicothe, I had reason, for the first time, after having travelled so far, and seen so much of taverns and hotels, to complain of ill-treatment at one of these houses. I stopped to inquire at Watson's whether the Hillsborough stage was to be there the next morning. The book-keeper replied, that if I would remain where I was, he would send the next day for my luggage to Madeira's, where the passengers were to breakfast. On this condition I agreed to stay. The next morning, two hours had elapsed after the departure of the coach, before the man went to inquire; his object being to detain me two days longer, as he boasted to Madeira that he had intercepted one of his customers. This piece of roguery placed me in an awkward predicament, as my portmanteau had no address upon it. The fellow's civility when I remonstrated with him, was on a par with his honesty. I met, however, with great attention at Madeira's, to whose house I immediately moved, and all seemed to be heartily ashamed of their countryman's conduct to a stranger. My landlord's wardrobe consoled me for the loss of my own, which made its appearance with the next stage from Hillsborough.

Chillicothe is a flourishing town on one of the great links of that chain of water communication which connects New York with New Orleans. It contains a population of four or five thousand people, of whom the colored portion forms about one-tenth. The latter have two churches and a school, consisting of thirty-five scholars of both sexes. The teacher, who is of the same race, is a graduate of the college of Athens (Ohio). Though they are taxed to the poor fund, they derive no benefit from it. Whatever is done to instruct the ignorant or relieve the indigent, is exclusively derived from their own resources. They complain bitterly of the many discouragements to which their legal disqualifications expose them. There is scarcely one who has not suffered from want of evidence to prove a pecuniary claim upon the whites. One man, who had been a tanner, and possessed property to the amount of 10,000 dollars, is now reduced to a state of poverty, from the frauds that have been practised upon him with perfect impunity. Another had his house pulled down, in sight of himself and his family, and was forced to quit the place, as no legal proof could be obtained of an injury which was well known to the whole town. A third, who was a barber, happened to owe a physician, who died in Kentucky,

seven dollars and three quarters for taking care of
his health, while the doctor (Webb) owed him
eighteen dollars for taking care of his beard. Me-
dicine, being a necessary, must be paid for; shav-
ing, being a luxury, may be had for nothing at Chillicothe. The executors could prove he was a debtor,
and he could not prove he was a creditor. It is
lucky for him that the two trades are no longer
united, or he might be made to cure diseases as well
as cut hair gratis. One of these persecuted men
told me, that they were sometimes in such a state
of despondency, that they felt inclined to give up
the struggle, and descend to the level of those who
are to be found in many places, the victims of vice
and crime; and who, though discountenanced by
the rest, bring discredit on the whole race.

About 100 families had lately been driven, by religious intolerance, into the State from North Carolina, where they were prohibited from meeting together to pray. They had suffered infinitely more
for conscience sake than the Momiers of Switzer-
land, about whom so much was said a few years
ago. But where is the De Staël who will espouse
their cause, and expose the iniquity of their oppressors? Yet these people have contrived to
realize a good deal of property, though they dare
not engage extensively in business, while there is no
security for obtaining what is due to them.

They have houses and real estate in the town,

worth at least 10,000 dollars, and farms in the county worth about 30,000 more. One man alone has, within four miles of the place, an estate, the value of which may fairly be estimated at 5000 dollars. There is a considerable colony of them in Jackson county, at the distance of thirty or forty miles from Chillicothe. Some of these settlers have farms of 200 or 300 acres, and even more. There is another near Gallipolis that contains about 200 people, who are doing well, in spite of every obstacle. A Presbyterian minister, (a white,) assured me that they were an honest, industrious, and orderly people. The church to which he belongs, has declared itself most decidedly and unequivocally against slavery. The following is extracted from "the Minutes of the Synod of Cincinnati."—"Resolved, that the buying, selling, or holding of a slave, for the sake of gain, is, in the judgment of this Synod, a heinous sin and scandal, requiring the cognizance of the church judicatories." Two years ago, the Synod of Kentucky negatived similar resolutions by a majority of four only, at a meeting of upwards of 100 members. It is expected that the majority will shortly be on the other side.

On the 26th of June, having got my portmanteau, I proceeded with the stage that brought it, to Zanesville, about seventy miles from Chillicothe. I regretted much that I had not time to go round by

Jackson and Gallipolis, and visit the blacks who are settled in the neighborhood of those places. There are ten or twelve families in the first named colony—with farms of 250 or 300 acres. One man whom I saw at Chillicothe, told me his father had a farm there of 275 acres. The year before he had raised 1100 bushels of corn, besides sufficient hay to form several stacks. They have established a school among them, and are in a prosperous condition.

I had, however, during my tour, been thoroughly convinced, from the best evidence, that this unfortunate race of men are fully entitled, by their conduct, to the same rights and privileges as those who have robbed them of both, and have added insult to injustice. Their errors and their vices are the unavoidable consequence, and not the cause, of their proscription and persecution. The condemnation that has been wantonly and wickedly passed upon them, is as unwarranted by the condition to which they have raised themselves, as it is irreconcileable with what we know are the characteristics, and what we may believe are the destinies, of the human race. I think I had sufficient acquaintance with them to form an opinion, as correct and as unbiassed, at least, as that of those who revile and ridicule them ; and I can truly and honestly declare, that the orderly and obliging behavior I observed among them —the decent and comfortable arrangements I wit-

nessed in their houses—the anxiety they expressed
for the education of their children and their own
improvement—the industry which was apparent in
all about them, and the intelligence which marked
their conversation—their sympathy with one another, and the respect they maintain for themselves
—the absence of vindictive feeling against the
whites, and the gratitude they evinced towards every
one who treats them with common civility and regard,—far surpassed the expectation I had formed, of
finding among them something more elevated than
the instinct of monkeys united to the passions of
men. They are " not only almost, but altogether,
such as " the white man—except the bonds he has
fastened on their bodies or their minds.

Zanesville, which is divided from Putnam and
West Zanesville by the river Muskingum, contains,
with them, a numerous and industrious population,
among which are to be classed 400 or 500 persons
of African descent, distinguished by the various
tints that the white man's disregard of " Nature's
impassable barrier " has produced in the original
shade. The latter have a Sunday school, attended
by seventy pupils, chiefly adults. They have also
established a day school for children ; and, like their
brethren elsewhere, are eager for knowledge, and
anxious to improve their condition. From an Englishman (Mr. Howells) who is resident here with
his family, and from whom I experienced great civility, I received a very favorable account of their

conduct. From an extensive acquaintance with them, he is of opinion that their attainments exceed the common standard that white persons, under similar circumstances, might be expected to acquire. Evidence to this effect was so frequent from the most competent witnesses, that its repetition must, I fear, be tedious. The reiteration of charges, which become more virulent as they are refuted, gives calumny a great advantage over truth.

Though less harassed than their brethren at Cincinnati and Chillicothe, these people have not escaped the inflictions of the Ohio-justice code,—the fruitful parent of violence and villainy. An instance not long ago occurred at Marietta, where a colored man had his house attacked and his daughters insulted before his face by a drunken white, who stabbed a young man while he was attempting to rescue the females from the assault. Their protector died of his wounds; but the murderer escaped punishment; no one but a half-caste Indian among the many who were present could enter the witness box against him; and his evidence was set aside on the plea of a previous quarrel with the prisoner. Numerous instances of the cruel operation of this iniquitous enactment might be given; but the very existence of the disqualification marks the character of the country, and evinces a spirit of injustice as ready to apply the law as to make it.

There is an anti-slavery society at Zanesville. Its object is to rescue the freedman from obloquy as well as the slave from his chains. After little more than a year's duration, the original number of its members (four) had increased to nearly 200 at the time of my visit.

This place is well situated for trade ; both iron and coal, in abundance, being found at no great distance. It has several flour-mills, iron founderies, two glass-houses, and a cotton factory, with two small woollen factories. It appears to be an eligible place for the investment of capital, as good mortgages can be had at ten or even twelve per cent. If we compare the progress that the State has made with that of Virginia and Kentucky, from both of which it is separated by the river from which it derives its name, we shall see at once that " the battle is not to the strong" when they contend in chains against the free. In the year 1800, Ohio contained 45,365 inhabitants, while Virginia had 880,200, and Kentucky 220,959. At the next census, (1810,) Ohio had increased to the amount of 230,760, while the corresponding numbers for the other two States were 974,622 and 406,511. The succeeding census presented a still greater disparity; and the last, in 1830, exhibited Ohio in close approximation to Virginia, and triumphant over Kentucky.

The relative population was as follows :—

Virginia 1,211,375

Ohio   937,903

Kentucky   688,844

The rapidity with which new States are formed and forwarded, may be seen from the great addition which the public treasury has recently received from the sale of the public lands. The proceeds from that source amounted, in the first quarter of the year 1834, to 1,398,206 dollars; while for the corresponding period of the preceding year, the receipts were 668,526. The demand for the public lands increases at the rate of twenty-three per cent., while the population advances in a ratio of three per cent. per annum. The proceeds are about three millions of dollars a year. The quantity of land unsold within the States and territories amounted, in 1832, to 340,871,759 acres, and there were, beyond those limits, about 750 millions more belonging to the Union.

I left Zanesville on the 28th, between seven and eight in the morning, and arrived at Wheeling (about seventy-five miles) at nine in the evening. The great Western or Cumberland road, over which we travelled, was not in such good condition as the vast sums of money, that had been expended upon it by Congress, would lead one to expect. It seems bad economy to delay repairs till ruts become holes, and holes become pools of water. We passed through several small towns—the first of which (Norwich) contains about 500 people. Six or seven years ago the place, where it now stands, was covered with trees. It was purchased by an Englishman, who

sold it out in lots; and, having realized a considerable sum by the speculation, returned to Europe.
The neighborhood is now thickly settled.

While the stage, which happened to be before its
time, stopped for half an hour, I entered into conversation with the landlord of the hotel. He had
not long changed his religion, and abjured Calvin
for the Pope. His conversion was brought about
entirely by what he considered a misrepresentation
of the primitive church; the tenets of which had
been described as intolerant, exclusive, and impious.
Like all new converts, who are anxious to shew their
sincerity by their zeal, whether in polemics or in
politics, he had been plying his neighbors with
arguments and pamphlets, till he had succeeded,
with the assistance of a priest, who had given a
public lecture on the subject, not only in cooling the
heat of their hostility to " the scarlet lady," but in
extracting from their pockets the proofs of a changed
mind, in the shape of a contribution for building her
a temple in the town. Though there were but two
Catholic families among them, he had contrived to
raise 555 dollars. From one store alone he got
sixty; one man having given twenty-five and another
ten. They all declared they had been completely
deceived, and were now convinced, that the thunders
of the Vatican had ceased, and that they would
neither be broiled alive, nor condemned, when dead,
to eternal perdition.

That the number of Catholics is increasing in the
United States, cannot be disputed—whether the
cause is to be found in conversion or emigration from
Europe. The Papal Church has probably gained
by the rancorous abuse and animosity with which its
doctrines, real or imputed, are assailed by almost all
other sects, who agree in nothing but in hatred of
a common foe. A clergyman in Ohio warned his
congregation from the pulpit not to support a Roman
Catholic candidate for office, claiming for himself
the infallibility he denounced in the Pope, and
shewing his hatred of persecution by persecuting
his neighbor. Such bigotry defeats its own object,
and communicates by the reaction of its opponent,
the power it loses by its own violence. As men are
naturally lovers of justice, they are apt, when their
prejudices are once removed, to embrace what they
before shunned; and to make amends for the previous wrong by doing more than an indifferent
person would consider strictly due.

The narrow strip of land which runs on each
side of Wheeling, for thirty or forty miles, between
Ohio and Pennsylvania, though part of Virginia,
contains but few slaves, and those few are said to be
well treated: the facilities for escape to the neighboring States being such as to render that sort of
property too precarious to be profitable. The inhabitants of Wheeling appear to be less infected with
the feeling of caste than any place I saw. Both

races may be seen there in friendly communication; and, at an establishment kept by a person who would be treated with contempt elsewhere, blacks and whites sit at the same table together.

The system of slavery is becoming every day more odious to this part of Western Virginia. Not long ago, a poor fellow who was a great favorite with every one, was sold by his master at Wheeling to a trader, when the indignation of the people was such, that they assembled in great force and threatened to rescue him. Had any one offered to lead them on, they would have carried their resolution into effect. He was, however, taken off and separated for ever from his wife and children. The scene was described to me as one of the most heart-rending and horrible.

On the 30th, I went from Wheeling to Pittsburg in Pennsylvania; where I had the misfortune to put up at one of the worst hotels I was in during my stay in America. The sheets on my bed were wet, and under the window was a large mass of matter abounding in animal and vegetable putrefaction— the refuse of a tobacco factory that had been carried on next door. On my applying to the street commissioners, it was removed both promptly and effectually. A populous town at the point of junction, where the Alleghany and the Monongahela are lost in the Ohio, surrounded by hills that prevent a free current of air, and rivalling Birmingham in smoke and filth, had thus for a long time been exposed to the infectious atmosphere of an accumulation that seemed purposely created to convey cholera to the predisposed.

The heat of the weather was so oppressive, and I felt so unwell, that I was unable to visit the curiosities of this celebrated place. I was gratified by hearing that an abolition society existed in the town, and already counted 300 members, though, at its commencement a twelvemonth before, it had not more than half a dozen. It had, within the last ten or twelve days, established a school for the free blacks, of whom between sixty and seventy had entered their names as pupils. There are about 1200 of these people in the city. Nothing had been done before to improve their condition, beyond a small school which they supported themselves. They evince a great desire to receive instruction. One of the boys, about ten years of age, had been studying Greek about four or five months, yet he construed part of one of Æsop's Fables, and answered the questions I put to him, with regard to tenses and numbers, much better than many boys of longer standing in years and study. He was a very sharp little fellow, and went through his task without conceit or hesitation. They all read in the English Testament very fairly. Their instructor spoke of their docility and capacity in the same terms that all do who have seen as much of this injured race. I observed that more than half the children were mulattoes. So much for amalgamation ! They have a church of their own, and an association for mutual instruction.

The next morning I took the stage for Philadelphia. There were but three or four passengers inside. The first day we went to Ligonier, a small town about fifty-two miles from Pittsburg. Here we met with excellent fare and great civility. Nothing occurred during the day worthy of note, but a little incident which exhibited the " discretion" of my fellow travellers in a very commendable point of view. We met several vans containing wild beasts, followed by a camel and an elephant on foot. As soon as the caravan approached, the whole of *our* live-stock hurried out into the mud. There were three young men headed by a female. Dux fæmina facti—an appropriate leader of such an exploit. Upon inquiring the cause of this sudden step, I was informed that they were alarmed lest the horses should take fright and run off with the stage. One of these youths appeared to have been smitten in another way. According to the account he gave me, he had left his heart at Pittsburg. He could not shew me the lady's portrait, but he put her card into my hand. Another was laboring under the same complaint, and exhibited the same symptoms. The way in which they spoke of their Dulcineas was highly amusing. The female passenger was an old acquaintance, and a confidante of this interesting secret, if there could be anything like secrecy in such an affair. The former youth was reading his love-letters to her in the stage; while his fair friend, who was a spinster, listened with becoming attention to the story of his woes and his wishes.

The next day we proceeded to Bedford—43 miles. The road was hilly, and in some places, particularly about Laurel Hill and the Alleghany mountains, very picturesque :—not, however, presenting such fine scenery as may be seen from the same range in Virginia. Many of the farmers in this part of Pennsylvania had moved off towards the West. One man took with him fourteen or fifteen laborers into Illinois. He had them previously bound to him for two years. Their claim for wages would be contingent upon the performance of their part of the contract, and he would have the best security for their services ;—a matter of great difficulty with settlers in a new country. He was well provided in other respects for the undertaking, having materials with him for a saw-mill as well as for a grist-mill, with the requisite instruments of husbandry. Most of those who had passed this way, were bound for Illinois, which is now what Ohio was a few years back—the great point of attraction. There is a sort of fashion in these things that varies with the state of the public mind, as it is affected by reports of fertile soil, vicinity of markets, and other considerations, that are ever changing with the interested views and sanguine hopes of former emigrants. The third day brought us to Chambersburg, a pretty busy-looking town of three or four thousand inhabitants. The journey was not so long or fatiguing, as the roads were in better order, and the country less mountainous, than what we had passed over before. The rain, which fell in torrents, and a thick fog, allowed us to catch but a few glimpses of the beautiful scenery that presented itself on each side, as we ascended, and came down the hills, during the former part of the day.

At three the next morning the stage resumed its route, and completed the first ten miles to Shippensburg, in an hour and ten minutes. A piece of information I had from the driver explained the relation in which this class of men stand to their employers, and the motives they have for good conduct. He had been several years in the " profession," and was well known on the road. He had recently visited Pittsburg with twenty dollars in his pocket to pay his expenses, and had returned, after travelling 300 miles, without having disbursed a cent. As soon as the innkeepers on the road became acquainted with the nature of his employment, they refused to take anything for his board, though he lodged two or three days with some of them; and he was "franked" by every stage he went by. He said he believed a respectable man in the same occupation might travel in this way through the Union. The proprietors of the stages and of the hotels would recommend him to one another; and he would be charged nothing during the whole journey.

After passing through Harrisburg, (fifty miles from Chambersburg,) which is the seat of government, and is a handsome town on the Susquehanna, we arrived at seven P.M. at Lancaster, a place containing 7000 or 8000 people. The next day brought us, by the rail-road, to Philadelphia, which it connects with Pittsburg, by means of the canal at Columbia, twelve miles beyond Harrisburg. Philadelphia is thus brought into closer contact with the great Western market, and becomes a formidable competitor with New York for its favors. While goods were sent from the latter city by the Erie canal to Cincinnati for two dollars forty cents the cwt., they could be imported into the same place, from Philadelphia, for one dollar thirty cents.

CHAPTER XXVII.

Friendly Reception.—" Immediate "and " gradual " Abolition.
—Deplorable State of Liberia.—Amalgamation-mob versus
the Blacks.—Outrages encouraged by the Press.—Dr. Cox
threatened with indelible " Blacking."—Episcopal Interference.
— Indelicate Delicacy. — Heterodox Marriages. — History of
James Forten.—Fair Mount Water-works.—Hospital.—Penitentiary.

I was very fortunate, while at Philadelphia, in
meeting, through the introduction of a friend, with
a private boarding-house, where I received every attention that the most polite and obliging disposition
could bestow.   The apartment assigned me was
spacious and well-furnished, a cold bath in an adjoining room supplied a welcome remedy for the
lassitude produced by an unusually sultry season,
and a very agreeable society completed the sum total
of my " comforts."

The next morning, the man, who had waited at
table, was missing ; and the lady of the house ex-

pressed her apprehensions that he had been kidnapped,—an event of too frequent occurrence to be
thought improbable. I was on my way to the poor
fellow's lodging in search of him, when he made his
appearance and accounted for his absence by an
indisposition which had seized him. He soon overtook me, and I returned with him to the house.
Like so many others I had seen, he had been indebted to himself alone for his freedom, and that of
his wife, whom he had left in Virginia, and who
would, if she were delayed or detained there but a
short time longer, exceed the term allowed by law
to the emancipated, and again become a slave.

From some letters put into my hand by his present employer, I found his character for honesty and
industry stood as high as that of any one in any
sphere of life. The attestations to his respectability
were evidently unbiassed opinions, and reflected as
much honor on the writers as on the subject of the
testimonials. In one of the letters I read, the writer
declared that he was willing and ready to perform
his part of the engagement which had been entered
into between his father and the slave; and that he
trusted in the "integrity" of the latter, that he would
fulfil his part also. The writer of another certified
that he had known him for fifteen years, during
the whole of which time he had sustained an irre-
proachable character. "His reputation," he added,
"in the place of his residence, is that of being a

man of honesty, probity, and good demeanor."
" Since he has obtained his freedom, he has resided
in Charleston, Jefferson County, and by his correct
deportment and industry, he has secured the respect
and esteem of all the inhabitants, and has been
enabled to pay two-thirds of the purchase money—
which he realized by his energy, frugality, and
application to business."

I obtained a great deal of information from this
man on the subject of slavery; which he painted
exactly in the same colors as those employed by all
who have seen or felt it.

I may here state that I was cautious in be-
lieving any thing on " hearsay," though the good
character of the witness was not always so easy to
be ascertained. He came from the western part of
Virginia, where, as I have before said, the system
is less severe than in the rest of the State. When a
master is dissatisfied with his slave, he · generally
threatens to sell him to the traders; the fate that
impends over the victims of this infernal traffic being
well known to be of the most dreadful description.
" I'll put you in my pocket" is the phrase on these
occasions. The horror they feel in moving further
to the South, may be seen even in the ballads they
are said to sing before the whites. The following is
an extract from one of them, in the mouth of an
emigrant slave from South Carolina:—

" I born in Sout Calina,
    Fine country ebber seen,
I guine from Sout Calina,
    I guine to New Orlean.
Old boss, he discontentum—
    He take de mare, black Fanny,
He buy a pedlar wagon,
    And he boun' for Lousy-Anna.
        He boun' for Lousy-Anna,
        Old Debble, Lousy-Anna !

" He gone five day in Georgy,
    Fine place for egg and ham ;
When he get among the Ingens,
    And he push for Alabam.
He look 'bout 'pon de prairie,
    Where de hear de cotton grow ;
But he spirit still contrary,
    And he must fudder go.
        He boun' for Lousy-Anna, &c.

" He look at Mrs. Seapy [Mississippi],
    Good lady 'nough dey say ;
But he tink de State look sleepy,
    And so he 'fuse to stay.
When once he leff Calina,
    And on he mare, black Fanny,
He take not off he bridle-bit,
    Till he get to Lousy-Anna.

CHORUS.

" Old debble, Lousy-Anna,
    Dat scarecrow for poor nigger,
Where de sugar-cane grow to pine-tree,
    And de pine-tree turn to sugar," &c.

This threat of selling a discontented or refractory slave to those who are sure to treat him cruelly, is practised in the French colonies, and in fact wherever the system that gives it efficacy exists. M. Tanc, formerly a magistrate at Guadaloupe, (see Revue des Colonies, No. 7, p. 17,) says, speaking of one of the planters, that the dread of being sold to him was employed as a motive to obedience throughout the island. "Cet homme est si connu par son humeur féroce, que deux ateliers se sont révoltés pour ne pas lui être vendus. Quand on veut effrayer un nègre dont on est mécontent, on le menace de le vendre à cet habitant; cela suffit pour le corriger." Hence it is, perhaps, that the perpetrators of the most brutal atrocities are protected by slave-owners from punishment: they are "scarecrow for poor nigger."

The separation that takes place between the objects of a mutual affection—whether wives and husbands, or parents and children, is attended with circumstances of distress and despair, that no one can look upon unmoved, whose heart has not been hardened by familiarity with such scenes. Cases sometimes occur of what may be literally termed "broken hearts"—instant death from the shock of contending emotions. Other facts I became acquainted with must be suppressed from a regard to decency. I have alluded to them in reporting my conversation with Mr. Rankin at Ripley. It is well known that slavery injures the morals of the master:

delicacy has hitherto concealed its effects upon those who are most nearly and tenderly connected with him.

Forged papers of freedom are often obtained from white men, who make it a business to sell them to the slaves. Detection is impossible, as the matter is arranged through the medium of free blacks, who take care never to be seen by any other white man than the scrivener. All other evidence against the latter would be rejected; and every attempt to prevent or punish these practices serves only to increase their number, by binding still closer the tie that connects the offender with his clients. It is, in fact, a regular profession, carried on by men who thus endeavor to extract some profit from the system which has impoverished them—making the oppressor himself heal some of the wounds he has inflicted.

It is to freedom that the slave looks, amidst the toils of the field, and the torments of the lash. This is a refuge from his griefs and his wrongs, that he never loses sight of, however difficult of attainment; —a hope that " quits him but with life". Hence it is, that when he has at last obtained his object, he proves more industrious than many who, born free, have no inducements to exertion; because they are deprived of those motives which the prospect of rising inspires. I could generally distinguish, among the free blacks, those who had inherited, from those who had acquired, their freedom. The latter had a much quicker perception, more energy of character, and a more anxious wish to rise in the world.

The inference that is commonly drawn from the condition of the slave, is extremely fallacious. A little reflection will detect the error; and a slight acquaintance with the emancipated will confirm its condemnation. That labor with wages would be hated by those who have been forced to work without, is a conclusion unwarranted by reason and experience. The facts that seem to support it may be explained by others that are purposely kept out of sight. How far the policy adopted or suggested, of introducing large masses of European labor into our West Indian colonies *,—for the purpose, or with the effect, of keeping down the rate of wages by which the blacks would and ought to profit,—may be classed among the facts alluded to, I leave to the conscience of every honest man to decide. This importation is worse than the statute of wages; because it is encouraged by those who formerly made its supposed inefficiency a ground for refusing the very measure which, they now tell us, imperatively calls for it. It is easy to say that the manumitted black will not work; and the most effectual way to prove the assertion is, to lessen the inducement, by lowering the remuneration. Freedom is a mere name, where the buyer of labor is to decide upon its price,

* The Jamaica legislature has granted a bounty of £15 per head to laborers from Europe—a measure of which the results are more doubtful than the motives.

on the plea that the seller asks too much: and slavery still continues, if a man is to be punished because he will not submit to be cheated.

There are many persons who object to "immediate" emancipation, from a misconception of its purport. They are not, perhaps, aware that the term is used in contradistinction to " gradual" abolition; and is no more open to the charge of precipitancy, than the other of endless protraction. It simply means, that the slave should be placed under the protection and control of the same government to which other men are subject, and should be transferred immediately from the power of the master—who makes the law which he enforces—to that of the magistrate, who enforces the law which the general legislature makes for the whole community.

The American abolitionists have no intention to follow the example of England. They do not acknowledge a right in any community to compel men, by the terrors of the cart-whip, to toil for the benefit of those who have been already " compensated" for the loss of that power by which they plundered and tortured them. They cannot see why any one who has been exposed, against his consent, to the burning rays of the sun, should have half as much more injustice done him than another who has been sheltered from them, and be compelled to toil six years while the other toils but four. They think there is but little difference between the slave and the apprentice; and that both have the same rights, whether they be "prædial" or "non-prædial". In fine, they would blush for their country, if she boasted of having abolished slavery, while such paragraphs as the following appeared in any journal in any part of her dominions:—

"On Thursday last, when Mr. Jerdan, the special magistrate, was speaking to the apprentices on Golden Grove about taking off the crop, the women, as usual, made a great noise; and after being repeatedly told to be quiet, without effect, Mr. J. ordered one, who seemed most clamorous, to be put in confinement; on which the whole gang declared ' they would go in the dark room too'. When they got near it they rescued her; and, to shew their defiance of the king's magistrate and of the law, they gave three cheers, and continued ' hurraing' for some time. After this, they all went to their work; but as it was necessary to put a proper check upon such rebellious conduct, the magistrate brought thirteen of the police and seven soldiers to the estate that evening. On the following morning the whole of the people were assembled, when nine men were flogged; and two of those, with six women, were sent to the house of correction."—Jamaica Royal Gazette, October 25, 1834.

There are others who recommend some modification of the feudal services in lieu of compulsory labor. There is not sufficient analogy, however, between North American bondage and the feudal subjection, to warrant the experiment. The serfs have never been robbed of their property, or deprived of their inheritance: the land they till is the country of their ancestors: their claims are rather the claims of humanity than of justice: their situation is diversified by an acknowledged scale of services to be rendered: their servitude is in some measure political as well as personal, and varies with the varying legislation of the country. As they emerge from their hard lot, they are imperceptibly absorbed into the social mass; and no brand remains upon them, to remind them of their former degradation, and rivet the chains of their former associates. While in a state of vassalage they are human beings, not mere cattle, in the eye of the law: enumerated as " souls", not as fractions of men: every one an integral, not three-fifths of an unit. The American slave, on the other hand, presents a picture the very reverse of the one just described. He possesses not one solitary " incident" on which the superstructure of free action can be legally erected. He bears to his owner the relation of unqualified, unlimited submission. All that his friends demand for him at present is, that he should be to his master what the laborer is to the employer in every free country. His condition is not the result of that natural development which civil society has undergone everywhere, but has arisen from the forced union of barbarism and civilization,—the result of that power which unprincipled knowledge has obtained over helpless ignorance, by subjecting the physical force of one race to the ava-

rice of another more enlightened. All that is required is, that these unfortunate beings may be
allowed to employ their own limbs for the promotion
of their own happiness; that they may be as free to
sell their labor, as their owner is to use it without
paying for it; and that wages may take place of the
whip. No more is wanted than the application of
that principle which stimulates industry by connecting it with profit; and which may be seen in full
operation, wherever those who have been used to
work "by the day" undertake to work "by the
piece". Let but the slave-owner give signs of the
will, and the slave-legislature will find the way, to
emancipate the bond from his wrongs, and the master from his fears. The matter would easily be
settled, if the oppressor were as ready to grant freedom as the oppressed to receive it; for as a French
writer (M. de Passemans) says of the Russian serfs,
" Un peuple est toujours mûr pour la liberté; mais
les hommes qui oppriment le peuple, ne sont pas
toujours mûrs pour la justice et l'humanité."

I had another opportunity, while at Philadelphia, of
ascertaining the true state of Liberia. From Mr. Temple, who had been sent thither as a missionary by the
western Presbyterian board of Pittsburg, I received
an account that fully confirmed what Jones had told
me. He had resided there four or five months, and had
not long been returned when I saw him. His health
had suffered so much from the effects of the climate,

that he was compelled to quit the colony. Of six others, who went out with him, all died, in addition to two of the Methodist and Presbyterian persuasion who had arrived previously. In fact, all the missionaries, who had gone from the United States to that part of Africa, had died, with the exception of one who was then on his way home. The conduct of those colonists who were employed in the interior as religious teachers was highly blameable. They had all become traders, and were carrying on a traffic, the profits of which were at the expense both of the natives and the settlers. They supplied the one with goods at their own prices, as they had obtained them from the other, by imposing upon their ignorance. The whole settlement was one mass of chicanery and corruption, extending even to the aborigines, as far as they had the means of retaliating on the strangers, or of practising the same frauds on one another.

Temple drew the same picture as Jones, of the idleness that had neglected agriculture, and transferred all the hard work of the colony to the natives. Two thirds of the inhabitants at Monrovia were in a state of starvation; no statistical return was made of deaths to the local authorities; and the decent performance of funeral rights was often denied. With the exception of eight or ten recaptured slaves, no conversions had been effected among the native tribes. Temple, though he had suffered so much

from the climate, and was fully resolved to have no
kind of connexion with the colony, was willing, he
said, to go as a missionary into the interior. The
Colonization Society, to whom he had communicated
his wishes, had taken no public notice of his offer.
They were highly offended with him for having
given, in his letters from Liberia, such a discouraging representation of what he had witnessed. They
urged him to contradict it by the publication of a
more favorable statement, alleging as a reason for
the request and a motive for compliance, that their
funds were exhausted, and little hope of a further
supply remained, till the distrust in the public mind
was removed. Every artifice that cunning could
suggest—every inducement that might be likely to
work on a timid or a mercenary disposition, was used
to enlist him in their cause. Though worn down by
illness, and exposed to all the obloquy which hatred
of color can inflict, he firmly refused to participate
in the guilt of deceiving his fellow countrymen, in a
matter involving their health, their comfort, and
their lives.

His description of the emigrants, who went out
with him, was truly distressing. Some of them
were in a complete state of destitution—without a
blanket to lie on, or a change of clothes. They had
left many things behind, having been assured that
they would get every thing they might want during
the passage, and on their arrival. There was one

woman without her husband, and a little girl who
had neither parents, nor relatives, nor friends to take
care of her. On his return, the scene he witnessed
was heart-rending : the colonists imploring the captain on their knees to take them with him. Though
he wanted hands, he was not permitted to give them
a passage. A passport was necessary; the Governor
was applied to : but he refused one on various pre-
tences, and at last concealed himself to escape im-
portunity. Such is the condition of this " flourishing
settlement"—grass growing in the streets of Monrovia—vermin destroying the vegetation—the settlers
dying and desponding—unprotected from foreign
vessels that intercept their trade with the native
tribes—a prey to every sort of abuse, without a possibility of removing the impressions which the suppression of facts and the fabrications of falsehoods
have produced at home :—a colony without a mother-
country—a horde of semi-civilized helpless beings,
without an acknowledged government—a mere band
of buccaniers, with no regular commission to make
peace or war with the nations around, and without
any security against the vengeance or justice of
barbarous or civilized communities—a set of intruders on a foreign soil, living under the hybrid and
anomalous rule of a pseudo-philanthropic society, in
conjunction with a hypocritical congress of States,
which distrusts the power it grants and doubts its own
privileges—liable to be exterminated by the savages

in the neighborhood, or to be dispersed by the first
maritime power of any part of the globe, that may
call in question the title-deeds of its possessions,
and the charter of its political incorporation.

While the rival societies were carrying on their
literary warfare with all the zeal and energy that the
importance of the cause could inspire, the mob at
New York took up the cudgels in good earnest on
one side, and gave convincing proofs that the friends
of the Colonization Society are not always the
friends of those whose welfare it professes to promote. They attacked the churches and houses of
the colored people, and demolished both to an extent
of damage, which, according to the lowest estimate,
could not be repaired for less than 20,000 dollars.
Many of these unfortunate people, who were afterwards acknowledged, even by their enemies, to have
been as patient during these outrages as they had
been inoffensive before their infliction, were compelled to remove their families and furniture, and
seek refuge in flight. For three days the city was
completely at the mercy of these marauders, who
were each day becoming more formidable by
their numbers, and the audacity which the con-
nivance, if not the co-operation, of the more opulent
classes, had instilled into their minds.

According to the Courier and Enquirer, there
were not above ten or a dozen men and twenty or
thirty boys, that committed all the mischief. " It is

true," adds this firebrand, " that, whilst the acts of
the mob went to shew an abhorrence of the conduct
and doctrines of the immediate abolitionists, they
were encouraged by the general voice of those present; but the majority, and, indeed, almost all of
these were of too respectable a character, to take
part themselves in any act of violence." The three
days, during which Bristol was given up to fire and
plunder, do not reflect more disgrace on the authorities of that place, than the same period of time
which the magistrates of New York permitted to
elapse, while their fellow citizens were suffering in
their persons and property for no offence political or
religious. There was no excuse for the outrages
that would not have involved the apologist in greater
criminality than the perpetrator. The only crime
imputed was an excess of charity and liberty, beyond
what a superstitious tyrannical people had been accustomed to; and the only motive for violence was
the dread of an event, which had been passing before
their eyes to a much greater extent, and with more
disgusting accompaniments, than the doctrines imputed to their opponents could by any possibility
bring about. With all this the chief sufferers were
the innocent; and vengeance fell upon those who
had done nothing to excite it.

A silly cry of "amalgamation" had exasperated
the public mind; and so completely obstructed the
perception of truth, that it was believed, not only

that the abolitionists wished the two races to mingle their abhorrent and abhorred embraces, but
that the instrument of their unhallowed project, was
to be the adoption of measures which would necessarily set limits to the dreaded evil, by raising both
master and slave from the vices of their condition ;
while they would rescue the one from violence and
the other from a brutal and factitious passion. Never
was any nation exhibited in a more contemptible
light! Never did pride, and prejudice, and pre-
sumption gain more thorough mastery over the heart
and the intellect. It makes one blush for the inhu-
manity and folly of mankind. We are lost in astonishment to see how little influence either religion
or philosophy is able to exercise over men who
boast of their attainments in both ! How slow is
the progress of truth even among the most favored
people! We look back to the kindred superstitions
of past ages, and we can scarcely believe that civilization could ever have overcome such obstacles
to its advancement.

While these disgraceful scenes were going on, the
daily press was adding fuel to the flame it had
created. The Times of New York said, " The
spirit which pervaded the throng had been
aroused into action by a long and aggravating course
of reckless proceedings, contrary to the first principles of public justice."—" In our judgment," said
the Albany Argus, " the abolitionists, by their mad

measures and insane obstinacy, are endangering the peace and safety of the country. In this view, we regret that the laws have not armed the executive with authority to banish them from the country, upon the same principle that dogs are muzzled in hot weather, and foreign voyagers compelled to undergo quarantine."

The New York American, the editor of which acknowledged to Lewis Tappan that the abolition cause was a just one, thus expressed himself,— " They (the rioters) did, indeed, in their proceedings at the Chatham Chapel, shew that they were actuated by a spirit which one cannot help admiring; and their conduct, considering all the circumstances, would be contemplated with more pride than blame by their fellow citizens : but this spirit, so admirable, is a most delicate spirit to deal with; and the conduct, so laudable in one instance, most dangerous as a precedent." A whole book might be filled with similar quotations from the journals of the day.

When at last an effort was made to save the city from pillage and conflagration, the mayor thought fit to act the partisan as well as the magistrate ; and to rebuke the philanthropists while he denounced the incendiaries. In the first proclamation issued by this equitable functionary of the first city in the Union, the good people under his care and control were told, that, " however repugnant to the good sense of the community are the doctrines and mea-

sures of a few misguided individuals, on the subject
which has led to the existing excitement of the
public mind, their conduct affords no justification
for popular commotion. The laws are sufficient to
restrain whatever is subversive of public morals, and
to prevent all violation of public decorum. On
them alone must the citizen rely; and misjudging
and imprudent men, as well as the most temperate
and discreet, must be protected in their undoubted
right of persons and property." In his second proclamation he said: "I caution, in the most friendly
spirit, all those who, to resent an offensive difference
of opinion, have allowed themselves to usurp the
authority of the laws, against inciting or abetting
further commotion." This was the "*pulveris exigui
jactus*" of Cornelius W. Lawrence, Mayor of New
York!

Many estimable and harmless blacks were most
cruelly beaten during these disturbances, by men
who make it a matter of boast that they have got rid
of slavery themselves, and yet are incensed against
those who would have the Southern States follow
their example: men who vent their anger against
the mere accident of an accident,—a participation in
the color of an oppressed race. What was the persecution of the Salem witches, of the Jews, of the
Protestants, compared to this indiscriminate hatred
of a people, whom no peculiarity, religious, intellectual or political, has separated from their savage tor-

mentors? To call any country, where such abominations are perpetrated, encouraged, and defended, as
far as commendation openly bestowed on the spirit
from which they sprang, can encourage and defend
them,—to call such a country free or enlightened, is
an insult to the common sense of mankind.

The rioters, not contented with destroying the
furniture of Lewis Tappan's house, threatened to dip
his brother Arthur and Dr. Cox in indelible ink. It
was generally believed that they had prepared a tub
for the purpose,—a method of curing the abolition
mania highly applauded by all, who thought the
disorder required a strong remedy,—on the Homæo-
pathic principle—" Take a hair of the animal that
has bitten you". This is " going the whole hog"
with a vengeance!

Among those who lost their little all on this melancholy occasion, were two colored females, who
lived together; one of them the widowed mother of
a young man of the name of Smith, who has distinguished himself at Glasgow by his literary acquire-
ments and exemplary conduct; having won one
prize, and contended for another, if not for more, and
being highly respected by every one who knows him.

When the mayor ordered the rioters to disperse,
they shouted out, " Three cheers for James Watson
Webb, of the Courier!" The Board of Managers of
the Colonization Society of New York published certain resolutions disapproving of these tumultuous

assemblages, which they declared " were held without any previous knowledge on their part." Dis-
avowal does not always exonerate. " Qui s'excuse
s'accuse". The objects of the Society had been favored with the formal approbation of these disowned
coadjutors in the " good cause". The daily papers
announced to the public the intention of the Anti-
slavery Society to meet, and pointed out the time
and place, though no such intention existed as to
either. The Courier and Enquirer is the organ of
the planters, who know full well what string to touch,
when they would rouse the great " leviathan".
" Amalgamation" is the cry in the North ;. and " the
rights of property" in the South. Each is admirably
adapted to its purpose ; while neither would succeed
out of its appropriate sphere. The slave-owners
must laugh in their sleeves, to see how easily their
dupes are led to do their bidding, whether on the
floor of congress or in the streets of New York.

" Admit Missouri as she is into the Union", says
the slave-breeder, who is looking out for a new market, to the manufacturer, " and you shall have the
tariff." " Mob and muzzle the fanatics", says the
slave-owner, surrounded by his tawney brats, to the
sensitive Caucasian of the North, " or your women
will undergo the fate of the Sabines, and darkness
will cover the land." The appeal succeeds in both
cases, and the national welfare is sacrificed to mean
avarice and meaner pride. Plectuntur Achivi!—

" Uncle Sam" pays for all.   He struts and talks big, while he is paying a double price for the coat he wears, and is laughed at by the whole world for the care he takes of his skin.

It is supposed that 20,000 persons had collected together, in various parts of the city, for the purposes of mischief and plunder.   Of the rioters, 150 were committed to prison for want of bail.   Three were subsequently condemned to one year's imprisonment, with hard labor; and five to six months', in the penitentiary.

" We trust", said the Courier, " the immediate abolitionists and amalgamators will see, in the proceedings of the last few days, sufficient proof that the people of New York have determined to prevent the propagation among them of their wicked and absurd doctrines,—much less to permit the practice of them.   If we have been instrumental in producing this desirable state of public feeling, we take pride in it."   Singular state of public feeling, that is " much less determined" to " permit the practice", than to " prevent the propagation", of certain doctrines!   That there should be any determination to permit what was never contemplated, is as remarkable as the resolution to stifle opinions that were never taught.   Such are the instigators of an insane populace.

> " They praise, and they admire, they know not what,
>   And know not whom—but as one leads the other."

When order and tranquillity were restored by the presence of the military, so little were the inhabitants disposed to investigate the cause, or prevent the recurrence, of the danger from which they had just escaped, that they threw the whole blame upon the Anti-slavery Society, rather than confess that it originated in the wish they felt to answer argument by force. They urged their opponents to recant their humanity, instead of repenting and reforming themselves. What took place afterwards reflected more dishonor on the nation than all the violence which had marked the exploits of the memorable three days. Charges were laid against the leading members of the emancipation party, that never would have been thought of by men of ordinary candor, and could not have gained credence with any one not prepared to believe the most preposterous accusations. What motives could the Tappans, or Dr. Cox, have had for increasing the number of mulattoes in the United States? Was it likely that Arthur Tappan, a man remarkable for his piety and benevolence, had resolved to marry his daughter, against her consent, to a negro; or, that Dr. Cox, when he said in the pulpit, that we could not be certain what were the form and color of that body in which the Lord of life appeared on earth, meant more than that the distinction of caste had no existence in the divine mind?

Yet it was imputed and believed that these men

had entered into a conspiracy against the human species, by promoting marriage between the blacks and whites! The intention was taken for granted, and condemned as a crime! The population of a vast city arose in their might and majesty, to protest against a scheme so wicked and unnatural! and the accused, in deference to this monster of folly, entered a public disclaimer of the unpopular proposition! The advocates of slavery, under which the two races are fast blending their distinctive colors, proclaim their abhorrence of an intermixture which they are striving to perpetuate; while the friends of freedom think fit to disavow a project which the measures they recommend are the least calculated to promote!

The disgusting and indecent discussions with which New York is agitated and inflamed, are extended to the remotest corners of the Union; and the peace of a whole community is disturbed, because the earthly tabernacles of our immortal souls have not been cast in the same mould, and covered with the same clay! Even the Church steps forward to support the State in this emergency; and religion is called in to heal the wounds she ought to have prevented. Bishop Onderdonk invites Peter Williams, whose church had been damaged in the late shock, to come out from the evil thing; and Peter Williams, in obedience to the injunctions of his diocesan, disconnects himself from the managing committee of the Anti-

slavery Society, and places himself, by his moderation and Christian feeling, far above the authors and
abettors of the outrage which had separated him
from his congregation. Whether the Bishop exceeded the limits of his spiritual authority on this
occasion, remains for future discussion: but he certainly had no right to mutilate the letter of his sub-
ordinate; and, by omitting some of the most important passages, make the writer appear in a character
the very reverse of that which he had assumed. He
had no right to place an amiable, but timid man,
in such a position that he could not vindicate his
character without offending either the church of
which he is a minister, or the congregation of which
he is the pastor. The result has been, that he has
sacrificed his personal feelings to what he considers
the welfare of his flock; and is now abused by his
former friends, because the Episcopalians are too
strong or too cunning for him.

I was astonished that the young women would not
see, if they could not feel, the indelicacy of discuss-
ing the subject of " amalgamation." To found
objections to the matrimonial union on physical,
not on moral grounds, betrays an impurity of ideas
which could never gain admittance into a well-
regulated mind. Swift says, " the nicest people
have the nastiest ideas;" and what I witnessed in
America bears out his assertion. The same people,
who scrupulously avoid the use of certain innocent

words, because they are sometimes applied in an
indecent way, were talking, from morning to night,
about the sexual passion, with a vehemence of
manner, and in a tone of earnestness, utterly abhorrent from the generally received notions of propriety.

I had always thought that there was something
dignified and decorous about marriage,—something
in the intercourse between the sexes, to raise it
above the grovelling appetite of the brute creation,—
some little admixture of mental and moral qualities,
to charm the imagination, and give play to our love
of the gentle virtues;—but, from all I could make
out of the innumerable debates I heard on the subject, it appeared to be almost an universal feeling,
that the whole matter was to be decided upon by
physical considerations alone; that the sole avenue
to the heart was through the eye, as it rested on the
skin; that the circle, within which the taste and the
affections were suffered to range, was circumscribed
by boundaries, from which it is exempt when applied to other objects in all their diversified forms
and colors; and that, in short, the whole affair was
purely sensual, in its most disgusting and degrading
grossness. This may, for aught I know, be very
true; but the opposite error is at least complimentary to our nature, and may elevate where it fails to
enlighten.

What are we to think of a country, where concu-

binage is considered less criminal than marriage; and
where a preacher of the gospel can declare publicly,
that neither the victim nor the offspring of an illicit
intercourse shall ever be protected against injustice
and want by the civil power, or rescued from demo-
ralization by the sanction of religious rites?   " The
fact", says Dr. Reese, of New York, in a pamphlet
on this subject,—" The fact, that no white person
would consent to marry a negro, without having previously forfeited all character with the whites; and
that *even* profligate sexual intercourse between the
races everywhere meets with the execration of the
respectable and virtuous among the whites, as the
most despicable form of licentiousness, is of itself
irrefragable proof that equality in any respect, in this
country, is neither practicable nor desirable."   He
goes on to say, " Amalgamation may and does exist
among the most degraded of the species: but Americans"—(in the name of the Prophet!)—" will never
yield the sanction of law and religion to an equality
so incongruous and unnatural."

The reverend author, it may be observed, asserts, in
the one place, that equality cannot exist, because the
Americans will not sanction it; and, in the other, that
the Americans will not sanction it, although it *does*
exist. The holy man turns away his face from an " incongruous" equality, because it is " impracticable".
Silly as the objection to abolition is, from its supposed tendency to amalgamation, one feels at a loss

how to answer it properly: for whether, as an abolitionist, you profess to prevent, or promote an intermixture, you give up the very principle for which
you are contending; and admit the inequality, while
you deny its existence. Why, indeed, should you
trouble yourself about the matter? Indifference is
the natural state of mind in contemplating a contin-
gency in which you can have no interest, and ought
to have no influence.

In the Philadelphia Directory, the names of the
colored inhabitants have a cross prefixed to them.
In the Boston Guide you may hunt a long time for
them in vain: they are placed at the end of the book
by themselves. No place is too high or too low to
shelter them from insult. If the European blood
were really purer than the African, there ought to be
a graduated scale of dishonor corresponding to the
degrees of intermixture, and apportioning to every
tint, whether full or fading, its appropriate place in
public estimation. Such is, or was, the rule in other
countries, where human rights were invaded or cur-
tailed. But here the low-minded, vulgar pride of
the whites defeats its own object, and tumbles into
the ludicrous by leaping at the sublime. How can
one fluid be superior in quality to another, when the
smallest quantity of the latter can totally destroy its
virtues? If Folly ever took counsel of Common
Sense, she would not give such an advantage to her
adversary. She would tremble for herself, when she

saw every feather, plucked from her cap, turned against her, shorn of its beauty, and disfigured by the very thing she abominates.

It appears, by an act of the Maryland legislature, passed in 1663, that there was less sensitiveness on this point formerly than at present. The second section says, " Forasmuch as divers free-born English women, forgetful of their free condition, and to the disgrace of our nation, do intermarry with negro slaves; by which also divers suits may arise, touching the issue of such women, and a great damage doth befall the master of such negroes; for preservation whereof, &c., be it enacted, that whatsoever free-born woman shall intermarry with any slave, from and after the last day of this present assembly, shall serve the master of such slave during the life of her husband; and that all the issue of such free-born women so married shall be slaves, as their fathers were." The planters took advantage of this law, to compel those white women they had bought as redemptioners to marry their slaves, for the purpose of adding the wives and the children to their live-stock.

Among the numerous colored citizens, whose respectability is " the glory and the shame" of Philadelphia, is one who is well known throughout the Union for the wealth he possesses, and the probity and urbanity which mark his character, in public and private life. The history of James Forten, such as I had it from his own lips, while sitting at his hospitable board, is somewhat remarkable. He is descended from a family that has resided in Pennsylvania 170 years; and does not, as far as he has been able to ascertain, number one slave among its members. He himself took an active part in the revolutionary war, and fell into the hands of the enemy, while serving in the Royal Louis, under the father of the celebrated Decatur. It was in 1780 that this vessel was captured by the Amphion, commanded by Sir John Beazley. Sir John's son, who was then a midshipman, about the same age with young Forten, was one day playing at marbles on the deck, when the latter, who had been employed to pick them up, exhibited such superior skill, after the game was over, in " knuckling down" and hitting the object aimed at, that the young Englishman was delighted with him. The acquaintance soon ripened into a sort of intimacy; and his generous friend offered, if he would accompany him to England, to provide for his education, and assist him in procuring some respectable occupation. The young Africo-American, however, preferred serving his country, small as the chance was that he would ever recover his liberty, to the brilliant career thus placed before him; and he was ultimately transferred to the prison-ship, the old Jersey, of sixty-four guns, then lying in the East river, where the New York navy-yard now is. Sir John's son was so affected at parting,

that he shed tears; and having obtained from his
father a protection for him against enlistment, saved
him from the wretched fate which befell many of his
brethren, who were carried by their captors to the
West Indies, and sold there as slaves. He remained
in confinement seven months, till he was sent home
in exchange. During the period of his detention, no
less than 3500 prisoners fell victims to an epidemic,
which the crowded state of the vessel occasioned.
The average number on board was 1500.   When the
war was over, Forten went to London, where he remained a year; and, on his return to his native land,
obtained employment in the sail-loft which is now
his own property, and which has witnessed his industry and enterprise for upwards of forty-six years.
In his business, as a sail-maker, he is generally considered to stand above competition.

No citizen ought to be more honored in his own
country than James Forten, if to be instrumental in
saving human life give a title to respect. No less
than twelve fellow creatures owe their existence to
him; for that is the number of persons he has saved
with his own hands from drowning—I believe they
were all whites. That circumstance, however, would
have had no influence upon his humanity. His
work-shop being on the banks of the river, he has
frequent opportunity of exercising his philanthropy
at the risk of his life. There was hanging up in his
sitting-room, in a gilt frame, an honorable testimony

to his successful efforts in rescuing four men from a
watery grave.   This heir-loom, for which he would
not take a thousand dollars, was presented to him, in
1821, by the Humane Society of Philadelphia.   It
consists of an engraving, in which is represented the
rescue of a female from the waves, and a written
attestation, signed by the President and Secretary,
with the dates of the cases, which the Society thus
thought deserving of its " honorary certificate."

Mr. Forten, while I was in the city, gave a strong
proof of his disregard for self-interest, in a case
where the happiness of his fellow-man was concerned.
He refused a commission to supply a ship in the
harbour with sails, because it had been employed in
the slave-trade, and was likely to be engaged again
in the same abominable traffic.   He is now a wealthy
man; and has given his family, consisting of eight
children, an excellent education, adapted to the
fortunes they will one day have, and (I hope I may
add) to the station they will one day fill:—for the
time cannot be distant, when virtues and accomplishments, that would be respected in every other
part of the world, will raise their possessors in
America above the insults and vexations of the
Pariah State.

I was anxious to see the water-works at Fair
Mount, of which I had heard so much ; and my
visit was productive of great pleasure to me from the
beautiful scenery, in the midst of which they are

placed, and the ingenuity displayed in supplying a
populous city with the means of providing for its
health, its cleanliness, and its security against fire.
The Schuylkill, on the banks of which the buildings
are placed, is raised twelve feet at low tide above its
natural level by means of a dam; and the power
thus obtained, acting on a series of wheels, puts
into motion a corresponding number of double hori-
zontal forcing pumps, and throws up into two basins
that are elevated ninety-six feet above the river,
more than a sufficient quantity of water to meet any
demand that may be made upon it by the population of the city below. There are at present five
pumps of sixteen and a half inches diameter each;
and another is about to be laid down. Each throws
up 1000 gallons of water in a minute; and all are in
operation except at high tide, when a cessation,
averaging two hours, takes place.

Nothing can surpass this contrivance in beautiful
simplicity of principle. The waters of the Schuylkill, in seeking, through the pipes from the reservoir,
the level to which they have raised themselves by
their own weight, find their way into every house,
that chooses to pay for the accommodation. During
the summer about four and a half millions of gallons
are used by the city in the course of twenty-four
hours. The pipes, already laid down, exclusive of
the collateral branches introduced for private purposes, are eighty-three miles in extent. Every fa-

mily pays five dollars yearly for the supply its domestic wants may require, and three for the additional privilege of a bath. The net annual revenue derived from the water rents exceeds 30,000 dollars. The cost of these admirable and useful works, which have been in operation about twelve years, was, in 1830, 432,512 dollars; which sum, added to the previous expenditure occasioned by the steam engines and apparatus before employed, amounted to 1,443,585 dollars. It is supposed that the Corporation, under whose control it is, will in a short time derive from the establishment a revenue of 100,000 dollars a year. Great difficulties were experienced in carrying the plan suggested into effect, from the opposition, which the fear of incurring an unprofitable expense, created against it in the public mind; and the resolution to complete the design was carried, in Common Council, by a majority of one only.

The various districts that enjoy their own charters, and are not incorporated with the city, refused to contribute their share towards its completion, and are, in consequence, charged higher prices for the benefit they derive from it, than those who co-operated with their money, and have a share in electing the officers entrusted with its management. The great utility of these works was seen during the oppressive heats of last year. While twenty-five persons died in New York from the effects of drinking cold water from the springs, there were but three cases of the same kind in Philadelphia, where the fluid was at a higher temperature from its previous exposure to the sun and air.

Of the public institutions I visited at Philadelphia, none afforded me a higher gratification than the hospital and the penitentiary;—practical testimonies to the deep interest felt by its inhabitants, in the misfortunes and crimes of their fellow-men, and to the successful exertions they have made in alleviating the one, and reforming the other.

The Pennsylvania hospital, to which I was conducted by one of the physicians, (Dr. Parrish, jun.,) is a handsome building, presenting, with the wings and the principal edifice, a front of 281 feet. The centre is appropriated to the female patients; the western wing to the insane; and the eastern to the men; with the addition of a ward for surgical cases. The spacious garden that surrounds it, with its venerable trees, its well-trimmed parterres, and its neat walks, gives an air of cheerfulness and salubrity to the establishment, with which the cleanliness of the apartments within, and the well-contrived arrangements throughout, for light and ventilation, and the comfort of the inmates, fully correspond. Below is a medical library; while the room opposite is occupied by a dispensary. The former is kept up, as it was originally endowed, by the fees which the students pay for the instruction they receive from the

physicians, who not only attend the institution gra-
tuitously, but thus make their disinterested charity
contribute to the improvement of their profession;—
setting an example of liberality which is more likely
to find admirers than imitators elsewhere. The establishment is under the care of a Board of Managers,
who are chosen annually by the contributors, and
who are invested with the power of appointing the
officers and servants. With them also rests the
election, annually, of the medical and surgical attendants, the number of each being three, as well as
two for the lying-in department;—a regulation that
seems less liable to abuse, than where the governors
have votes in proportion to their subscriptions, and
where the success of a candidate for office depends
more on his skill in canvassing than his professional
qualifications. It is generally found that the responsibility of an improper choice is in an inverse ratio
to the number among whom it is shared; while those
who are most likely to practise intrigue or corruption
themselves, are least likely to overlook it in others.

Of 983 patients admitted in 1833, 500 were foreigners. This proportion is nearly the same with
that between the " pay " patients and the " poor "
patients; as, out of 31,641, (the total number admitted from 1752, the year of its establishment, to
1834,) 16,469 were maintained out of the funds of
the hospital.

The first object of the institution is, the accommodation of the poor. Those who can afford it pay from three to six dollars a-week. The receipts from this source form part of the revenue of the establishment; admittance to which, on these terms, must be obtained under the guarantee of some respectable resident of the city. There were 235 patients in the house in April 1834. The number of insane was 120, of both sexes. The treatment they receive is mild and conciliatory; coercion being rarely used, and then with great precaution and prudence. They have a garden for recreation, but no ground for work. A room is set apart for manual labor; but it did not appear to afford occupation or diversion to many. I was informed by the attendant, that the proportion of insane among the society of Friends was supposed to be greater than in other sects. This peculiarity has been found, or said, to prevail in England, and has been attributed to the custom of confining matrimonial connexions within their own society. In the rules of discipline for the American Quakers, " Friends are advised to be very cautious in changing their places of residence, it having been observed that the dissolving of old, and the forming of new, connexions, have, in many instances, been attended with effects prejudicial to a growth in the truth and service thereof, both in the heads and younger branches of families." He was of opinion, that intemperance is not often the cause of mental aberration. A contrary belief is generally entertained.

The Scotch seem to take it for granted; for they call a drunkard by the same name that the French bestow upon a madman. They say he is " fou".

There is one feature observable in almost every case of insanity, that the patient is more irritated by the presence of a relative than by that of any other person. Care is taken to limit or exclude the visits of such persons; as experience has shewn that the disorder is usually exasperated by them. This is easily accounted for,—not by the vulgar notion, that the affections are influenced by the imagination, and the objects most beloved and trusted become the most hated and suspected,—but because the sympathy which is sought for in the early stages, is refused by those who are expected to afford it, and are most able to exercise it beneficially: because the complaints of the patient are met with ridicule or indifference: because the daily intercourse, that might soothe and solace, is employed to upbraid and annoy: because the forbearance, which the rules of courtesy impose upon strangers, is little practised where habits of familiarity have blinded the parent or the brother to the symptoms of a disordered mind, or have rendered him insensible to ailments which impatience and despair are gradually converting into confirmed mania. The querulousness that accompanies excess of suffering, deadens the sympathy of the spectator, who in his turn affects incredulity, as an excuse for indifference, and thus adds to the

sense of pain the bitter feeling of injustice and unkindness.   Hence, perhaps, it is, that dyspeptics
often recover when removed from home.

To leave his home is recommended to the hypo-
chondriac by the very persons who send its inmates
to comfort him when he is in confinement.   While
he is nervous—i. e. while he is but half insane—he
is to quit his family and get rid of all the associations that are connected with it; and, when he is
altogether deprived of reason, he is to be reminded
of them by the presence of those whose ignorance or
inattention has been the chief cause of his irritation
and wretchedness.   If we took as much care of our
children as of our dogs and horses, fretfulness would
be ascribed to the right cause, and the bodily health
would be restored by the same hand that now converts indisposition into chronic disorder, and drives
the patient, through the various stages of suspicion
and resentment, into insanity.   Who ever conversed
with a dyspeptic that he did not perceive, in the
narrative of his griefs and grievances, the marks of
alienated affection, and the bitter remembrance of
unkindness, real or imaginary, received from his
family?

The popular prejudice against dissection is less
prevalent in Philadelphia than probably in any other
city in the Union.   Subjects can easily be obtained
for about eight dollars each, by means of the public
institutions, from which the bodies of those who die

unclaimed, may be had through a channel that is well understood by the parties interested, and need not be more particularly described. The surgical schools at New York and Boston are occasionally supplied from this quarter. But two cases of exhumation have been publicly known for the last seven years; and they were both the acts of professional men, who were anxious to get possession of bodies that had been committed to the grave from the effects of some peculiar disease.

The Penitentiary at Cherry Hill I visited, in company with two Canadians, who had been commissioned by the government of the Lower Province to inspect some of the prisons in the United States. The arrangements of this establishment are made upon the most simple principles; the corridors, into which the cells open, radiating, to the number of seven, from a common centre; and the discipline to which their inmates are subjected, having unity of design for its object. As each convict is to be completely separated from the rest, sufficient room is allowed him both for work and exercise. The former is considered as an indulgence, the privation or suspension of which is imposed as a punishment for insubordination. As the county, however, by which the prisoner is sent to the penitentiary, is, in order to exclude idle or impotent persons, debited with his board at the rate of twenty cents per day, including all expenses, he must perform a proportionate quantity of work, or be contented with a diet of bread (eight ounces per day) and water.

Attached to every cell on the ground floor is a small yard, where exercise is allowed for one hour in the day; the summit of the pavilion in the centre enabling the warden, or any one of the keepers, to see that the indulgence is not abused. The rooms are well ventilated, and supplied with water from the Fair Mount works, by means of pipes. Each is provided with a bible and religious tracts. At stated times divine service is performed in such a manner, that it can be heard along the corridor through the open doors of the cells; while a curtain that traverses the passage, prevents the convicts from seeing their opposite neighbors. Occasional visits are also paid by ministers, as opportunity offers.

As no remission of the sentence is granted for good behavior, no hope is entertained or encouraged of shortening the term of confinement by increased assiduity to work, or a display of devotion and reformation. Time is given for reflection: but no bounty is offered to hypocrisy.

If the duration of imprisonment were to depend upon conduct, the rule should be applied both ways. Confinement should be lengthened to the refractory, whose bad actions cannot have good motives, while it is shortened to the obedient whose good actions may have bad motives. Reformation should be suggested and rewarded by conscience alone. Both its purity and its permanence will be affected by any induce-ment or expectation from other sources. Professions of amendment, like professions of faith, are less to be relied on in proportion to the worldly advantages they bring with them. " La sauce vaut mieux que le poisson."

Of all those who have completed their term of confinement in this prison since the year 1822, but three have been recommitted for crime ; and of these two were old offenders, and were sent to other establishments. A very fallacious test, however, is afforded by this fact of the state of crime in a com-munity under the jurisdiction of independent govern-ments. There are altogether 560 cells. The whole, however, is not finished. There were several work-men employed while we were there. The number under confinement was 180. Three of the corridors have one story only—the others have two ; and, as there is no yard attached to the cells above, they are generally occupied by prisoners who have been sen-tenced for short terms, or whose work is light. While there are so many spare cells, two might be allotted for each convict, who would thus be able to work in the one and sleep in the other, and enjoy the advantages which a change of objects as well as of air would thus afford. No injury, however, to health has occurred to those in the upper story for want of a yard in the open air.

Out of the whole number (averaging 124), but one

death had occurred during the past year. There was not one in the infirmary at the time of our visit. The mean number of deaths in the city for ten years was, annually, one in 42.3, according to Emerson's Medical Statistics.

No chains, or whips, or armed guards are employed. It is on the mind alone that the discipline employed operates; and its instruments are all those considerations which can be suggested by kindness, and may work on the conscience. The prisoner can see nothing vindictive in the sentence that condemns him, and nothing suspicious in the system that confines him. Those who approach him, exhibit neither fear nor secrecy. His confidence is gradually won by the sympathy expressed for him; and the better part of his nature has room to develop itself—while the indulgence of his evil propensities would carry its own punishment with it, without the possibility of inflicting pain or gratifying resentment. Two or three, with whom I was left alone, assured me that they were well treated and contented; that they had sufficient to eat, and were in good health; and that they trusted the leisure they had for repentance would conduce to their welfare both here and hereafter. One of them said he should return to his former place of abode, where the crime he had committed was known, that the consciousness of being watched might be an additional motive to good conduct. As the offence was of a minor nature, he hoped he should regain the good opinion of his neighbors, and wipe away the remembrance of his guilt by an honest and virtuous life. All of them attributed their misconduct to habits of drinking, which had led them into bad company; where gambling—a vice that seems to be on the increase, accelerated their ruin. Intemperance, they said, made a man indifferent to character.

They spoke in the highest terms of Mr. Wood, the Warden, whose mild and kind manner had removed from their minds those angry feelings which had been engendered by a residence in other prisons, where mutual corruption is suffered to go on to a frightful extent.

Mr. Wood sometimes sends meat to the sick convicts from his own table. It is much to be feared that party intrigue, which has driven, so many good men in this country from the public service, will not much longer permit these well-merited eulogies to be heard within the walls of the Cherry Hill penitentiary.

As it is impossible for the prisoners to hold any kind of intercourse with one another, they are neither diverted from thoughts of repentance by the hope of conspiring together, nor deterred from honest industry, on their release, by the fear of recognition. If this good effect alone resulted from the system pursued here, its superiority to the Auburn plan would be at once apparent.

Amendment of life is no easy matter to a man, whose good resolutions are thwarted by the solicitations of his former associates in iniquity, and their threats to expose him as a "jail-bird" if he refuses compliance.

Much of the success that has attended the "Philadelphia system," may be traced to this suppression of the name. The convict feels, on his discharge, that he is unknown; that the tie which bound him to his fellow-man is not entirely broken by scorn or distrust: and that he may yet be a respectable and useful member of society. A contrary sentiment in the French convicts who are subject, when released from prison, to the surveillance of the police, has been productive of great evil. It is difficult for those, who have undergone the reformative process, according to the Auburn plan, to obtain employment or escape the discouragements that await them. While it is deemed disgraceful to work or associate with a reformed criminal, the progress of social improvement must be retarded. With desperate offenders, and an unforgiving world, how is crime to be arrested in its career? Yet where is he who might not say with Boërhaave,—"That man, who is going to his execution, is perhaps less guilty in the sight of God than I."

At Singsing the chief object seems to be, to extract the greatest quantity of labor out of its unfortunate inmates, and to swell the profits above the expenditure.   At Cherry-hill the physical exertions of the prisoner for the benefit of the community are less attended to than his moral efforts for his own.   The good of the individual is the good of society; but it may well be questioned whether the pecuniary interest of the latter may not be promoted at the expense of the former; whether the list of criminals is not enlarged with the revenue derived from their compulsory labor.   The cat-o'-nine-tails is an equivocal preventive of crime.   The recollection of its infliction, for transgressing an arbitrary rule, serves but as an incentive to a breach of moral duty.   The enforcement of silence by stripes, prepares the mind for any delinquency that want or vice may whisper.   The whipped convict returns to a scornful world with the scars of his dishonor on his person, and the determination to be avenged in his heart.   He has lost all feeling of self-respect; and his only security against crime is his dread of detection.

At the Philadelphia penitentiary any inclination, after the first few days, to communicate with the occupants of the adjoining cells, is likely to be given up, except in very bad cases; the discovery being soon made, that the interests of all are better promoted by concealment and privacy.   At their discharge, the convicts receive four dollars each, to provide for their immediate wants.   Their names are unknown to the officers of the establishment; as they are designated in the register, on their entrance, by numbers, which with the letter indicating the gallery, are placed over the dormitories. The manufactures carried on in the prison are shoe-making, iron-work, &c. The proceeds are not disposed of by contract, but are sold on the spot to any one who is disposed to purchase them; the price being regulated by the competition of the buyers, so as to be pretty much on a level with the market value. No complaint has been made on this head by the mechanics, as in the State of New York, where the ignorant prejudices of the working classes are likely to obstruct, if not to destroy, the operation of a system which depends for its success on the quantity of goods it sells.

When the French Commissioners (Messrs. de Tocqueville and de Beaumont) visited this place, they told Mr. Wood, that they should have limited their inquiries to the first inspection, had they not been permitted, and even solicited, to view the cells and converse alone with the convicts. Having been refused this indulgence at Singsing, they felt little anxiety to prosecute an investigation, which could have led to few practical results under similar restrictions.

An attempt was once made to bribe the physician, by the father of one of the prisoners. He had been condemned for forgery; and a thousand dollars were offered for a certificate, declaring that his life would be endangered by the confinement. The fact became known on the refusal of the bribe.

Admirable as this system appears to be, it may be doubted whether the principle, on which it is founded, would not require considerable modifications, when applied to an old country; where the restraining influences of self-respect have been weakened by the habit, or the example, of receiving parish relief; where liberty, with potatoes and water, has less charms than incarceration with bread and meat; and where total solitude and seclusion would be thought by many a relief from sorrow and suffering. A different treatment must be adopted, according as the disease has been brought on by vice or by poverty: and the chances of a relapse must mainly depend upon the patient's constitution, and the atmosphere he breathes.

I should have observed, that five days are found sufficient to reduce the most refractory to obedience, by the discipline generally employed. To active minds, solitary confinement, without work, is found to be more irksome with light than without it.

This institution is popular with the legislature, who are disposed to grant whatever may be required for its completion. 200,000 dollars were expended before a cell was made. Each of these cost 500, on an average, including water-pipes, &c. There will be sufficient accommodation for 586 convicts, when the whole is finished. There are ten acres within the walls, and three outside, belonging to the establishment.

It is supposed that the whole cost will be half a million of dollars.

While I was at the penitentiary, one of the discharged convicts called to pay Mr. Wood part of some money (five dollars) he had lent him, on his leaving the prison, three weeks previously. Another had borrowed ten dollars on a similar occasion; and the warden had no doubt he would discharge the obligation, as soon as he could. He was gone to Cincinnati. I conversed alone with eight of the colored prisoners. The greater part had fallen into crime through want and ignorance. Two of them had taken no more than was necessary to satisfy the exigencies of the moment. One had been convicted of receiving goods, knowing them to have been stolen. His account was, that he had been requested by some strangers, to assist in carrying a bundle. He owned he had committed petty depredations occasionally; so that he was condemned, in all probability, in consequence of his bad character. He seemed fully aware of this, and promised, without any canting professions, to amend his life. He was a mere boy, deprived of parental care—his mother being dead, and his father at a distance. Another had been sentenced to eight years' imprisonment for an offence, which any unprincipled woman might fasten on any man. He declared his innocence, and ascribed his misfortune to a spirit of revenge in his master's wife, whose bad character he had exposed. If it was true, as he asserted, that his master owed him 150 dollars for work, a better reason might be found for the charge. It is hardly probable, however, that the jury would come, unbiassed by prejudice, to the examination of a question, involving considerations peculiarly odious to their feelings. Mr. Wood, who had known him from a boy, spoke very favorably of his character. One young man had been committed for cutting and stabbing, when detected in an attempt to steal. He seemed an old offender, and a bad subject. One, an elderly man, had passed a considerable part of his life in different gaols. He had, however, had " a call," and was sure he should be preserved in future from temptation. Though he stuttered very much, he had made up his mind to turn preacher, on his discharge. He seemed to think the Lord would open his mouth. Whatever the amount of his own faith might be, the keepers had but little in his sincerity. Another of these convicts, who had been a slave, declared that he had been so much insulted in the North, that he would rather return to his former condition, than again undergo so many mortifications. Another was a runaway slave, who had stolen a suit of clothes in the depth of winter, to supply the place of the worn-out garments he had on at the time.

Such is the history of these cases, as they presented themselves indiscriminately to my inquiries. Most of them were, I believe, as they were narrated. One or two, the keeper, to whom I repeated what had been told me, declared to be falsely stated. In general, however, there was an air of candor and sincerity about the men, that could not well have been assumed. At least it was unaccompanied with canting or professions. One of them corrected me when I said to him—"This, then, is your second offence." "No, Sir!" was his reply—"it is my third." The keepers spoke well of them. The colored prisoners, he told me, were generally quiet and well-behaved. From what I saw on this occasion, I am led to believe that want of work, ignorance, and the difficulty of finding unprejudiced witnesses and juries, are the chief causes that have led so many of this unfortunate race to the prisons and penitentiaries of the country. I would not draw a hasty or sweeping conclusion from the few isolated facts thus brought under my notice: but I would submit it to the consideration of any candid man, whether it is just to ascribe any given circumstance to a physical peculiarity, when the common motives that actuate human beings are sufficient to account for it.

CHAPTER XXVIII.

Infant Schools.—State of Education in Pennsylvania.—Alms-house.—Increase of Pauperism.—Institution for poor Children.—House of Refuge.—Hackney-coachmen and Barbers in Philadelphia.—Quaker schism.—Elias Hicks.—Generous and affectionate Character of the Blacks.

THE public schools in Philadelphia are nearly on the same plan with those at New York. At one of the establishments I visited, the infant school, which is preparatory to the others, was on the ground floor; and the apartments, appropriated to the girls and to the boys, were in regular succession above. The average number of pupils in all was about 700. The salaries of the instructors are 800 dollars a year for the masters, and 400 for the female teachers, besides 200 a year for assistants to the latter. The infants were all neatly dressed, and appeared to take great pleasure in the exercises.

They were asked a few questions in astronomy and in numbers; a small planetary, to represent the solar system in action, and the usual arithmetical board, being placed before them. They seemed to answer mechanically. When they are receiving instruction in natural history, or other subjects that can be illustrated by reference to familiar objects, their attention is directed to those facts that are suited to their tastes and capacities. Very little difficulty is experienced in preserving order and good temper among them. They belong to that class, who are too much occupied to spoil their children. Three days are generally sufficient for the mistress " her statutes to maintain " by taming the most rebellious who enter, and recommending obedience to the most refractory new comers.

The teacher, who was a remarkably intelligent young woman, and devoted to the occupation she was engaged in, observed that she found the girls more quick and docile than the boys, during the early periods of life; whereas, when both had arrived at the age of fourteen or fifteen, there was a greater degree, she thought, of judgment and steadiness on the other side.

The parents are so satisfied with the improvement their children derive from these schools in disposition and intellect, that they are anxious they should attend regularly and properly dressed; while the little things themselves are never so happy as when they are surrounded by their school-fellows, under the eye of their teacher and friend. Those who live at a distance bring their dinners with them, and

nothing like discord or discontent is to be seen while
they are at their meals. I took particular notice of
this, as I had seen a remarkable instance at Paris of
the tractable disposition, to which children may be
habituated in these establishments. All the pupils
of an infant school there voluntarily laid down what
they had begun to eat, and ran to their places, to
resume their exercises. It is here that the benevolent affections may be cultivated, and self-control
acquired, when impressions are most easily made
and most durable. It is here that the gratification
of the intellectual appetite is felt by the young mind
to be above those pleasures in supplying or promising which, the senses and the passions degrade
or delude.

The system of infant schools is not so popular in
the United States as it was at its introduction, and
might be again, if more attention were paid to its
original object. Intellectual cultivation has unfortunately been more thought of than the improvement
of the disposition; and the faculties of the mind are
prematurely exercised, while those of the body are
comparatively neglected. The Sunday School Union
seems to have mistaken both the means and the end of
these institutions. " In accordance" (it says in one
of its reports,) " with the resolution passed at the last
meeting of the Society, particular attention has been
paid to the preparation of manuals and forms of
instruction for infant schools. The series of lessons

and lithographic prints in natural history has been continued; and a volume of lessons has been prepared with great care for the instruction of very young children in the fundamental doctrines and duties of our holy religion. We know not that the attempt has ever before been made to state such doctrines as the incarnation and atonement of Christ; the nature and evidences of regeneration; the resurrection of the body and the retributions of the world to come,—in such language and with such illustrations, as are intelligible to a child of five or six years of age. It has been done, however, in our ' first lessons on the great principles of religion,' and with so much success, as to place teachers of infant schools, and classes, under great obligations to the author for her valuable services in this behalf."

A better understanding, however, of the end these places are calculated to answer, seems to prevail. A writer in the " American Annals of Education" for July, 1833, says: " Never were the infant schools of this country in a better condition, than at this moment. They may, indeed, be fewer in number than formerly; though we are not sure that even this is the fact. But they are better organized—their purposes better understood—the intellect is cultivated less in proportion, and the affections more:—teachers are becoming better qualified—the methods of instructing and educating are becoming less mechanical—and the school-room and its inmates, in appearance and influences, are daily assuming a stronger resemblance to the parlor and the domestic circle."

It is to be hoped that these schools will become more general throughout the Union—and, indeed, throughout the world:—for a more charming picture of human nature as it is, or a more promising prospect of what it may be, than they present, cannot any where be found.   In Europe, the delight we receive in visiting them is unalloyed by the intermixture of painful reflections.   In America, we are reminded of the base antipathies that have separated the two races.   Were they to associate together in the early periods of life, no room would be left for those feelings of arrogance and contempt that now step in to divide them.   What is now called natural repugnance would be seen to be nothing but an artificial affection of the mind produced by the conjunction of two   ideas   that   have   no   necessary   connexion.   In the South, where children of both colors are brought up together, and the white infant is often suckled at a black breast, the link that unites the prejudice of the mind with the visible object, is supplied from a different source.   It is not the color, but the condition that qualifies the sentiment.   It is the idea of servitude, which inseparably accompanies that of the complexion, and produces an abhorrence, not so much of the person, as of his occupation.   There is something even honorable to our nature in the feeling; as it is associated with contempt for those who degrade it, by submitting to oppression.   In the North it is unmixed absurdity and wickedness—gross and grovelling—with nothing generous to redeem it, and no misconception to excuse it*.

Pennsylvania, though one of the wealthiest and most populous States in the Union, has done much less for the education of her people, than others that are inferior to her in both respects.   The legislature has recently passed an act for supplying this defect in her policy.   The Committee on education thus expressed themselves in their report on the subject. "Assuming the last census as a basis, we have 637,849 children under the age of twenty ; between four and five hundred thousand of these are, by the constitution, placed under the guardianship of the legislature; of which [of whom] by official returns made last year to the Secretary of the Common-wealth, only 17,462 are now receiving—and that nominally, perhaps—instruction gratis.   Here then are 400,000 at least wholly without any kind of school-

* In Martinique, a white man (Bardel) a year or two ago, sent a challenge to a colored man (Frotté)—an honor which we sometimes see refused in England to a candidate for a patrician death, though the distinction of rank in the one case is so much less than that of complexion in the other, that a plebeian eye cannot see the difference, and a generous mind would not make it.

ing: yet we now only begin to hear a murmur of discontent." " A citizen," they observe, " who pays a tax of a few cents only, can go to the election with power equal to [that of] him who pays a tax of many hundred dollars, and by his vote directs the public weal with the same authority as the wealthiest citizen. It becomes necessary, therefore, to give the man of humble means an opportunity of understanding the advantages in which he so largely shares."

There is a large number, according to their evidence, of voters who cannot read the tickets that are handed to them at the polls; and their number is increasing. A legislative enactment has now provided for the more effectual education of the good people of Pennsylvania. Two inspectors are to be appointed for each county, to visit the schools once at least every three months, to inquire into the character of the teachers, and to give certificates to such as, on examination, shall be found properly qualified. Without such certificate, which is to last one year, no compensation is to be paid for their professional services. Another act, passed the same session, shews that capital punishments are either odious to the people, or considered injurious to public morals when openly inflicted. Executions are, for the future, to take place in the gaol-yards belonging to the county where the conviction took place. The sheriff, or the coroner, is to attend and depose on oath, or by affirmation, to the due execution of the sen-

tence. Immediate relatives, and two, but not more,
ministers of religion, may be present—but no minor
of either sex, " on any account."

While the penitentiary is elevating the criminal, the
almshouse, it is much to be feared, is degrading the
unfortunate; and the demoralisation that is checked
among the prisoners, is spreading among the paupers. On the other side of the Schuylkill, and about
a mile and a half from the city, a vast and splendid
edifice rears its head, and attracts the curiosity of the
passing stranger. He is informed that the palace he
sees before him, is destined to the reception of the
city poor ; that the establishment they formerly occupied in the town is for sale, as too small or badly
situated for its object; and that they have just entered their new abode. Formerly it was the custom
to relieve them at their own homes, where something
like self-respect might survive their calamity; and
the bread of honest industry be still sweet on the
restoration of health, or better days. This system
has now ceased; and the casualties to which the
poor are exposed, are to find, with some exceptions,
relief or remedy in the lazar-house—where the idle
and the industrious, the sober and the intemperate,
are to seek an asylum, and mix with people of the
most uncongenial and opposite habits.

A committee, appointed by the Guardians of the
Philadelphia Poor to inquire, &c., reported, in 1827,
as the result of experience, " that of all modes of

providing for the poor, the most wasteful, the most
expensive, and the most injurious to their morals
and destructive of their industrious habits, is that of
supply in their own families." Is not this because
the relief given is "seen of men?" Let a distinction
be made between crime and misfortune, by a well-
organized system of domiciliary visits. Let the names
of the indigent be studiously concealed, as among the
Quakers of Philadelphia, and assistance bestowed "in
secret" with such delicacy as may snatch the sufferer from the dangers of self-humiliation; and it will
be found that the vis medicatrix of the mind, like
that of the body, will aid the prudent physician in
his efforts to remove the disorder or relieve the
patient. Why, indeed, should not every religious
sect imitate the example of the Friends, and provide
for its own poor? It may be said that they have
their preachers to pay—a tax from which the others
are exempt. That is the very reason why the public
should not be saddled with their paupers. They
would take good care to appoint no minister, the
effects of whose negligence in inculcating habits of
economy and prudence would fall on themselves.
Such a regulation would afford a criterion of their
relative value to the State. There would no longer
be a fashionable religion. The poor would naturally
be attracted to the rich; and the same wealth, which
is now heedlessly employed in encouraging mendi-
city, would soon find some plan to prevent it.

The new building consists of a square, that encloses within its sides about ten acres of ground, to be appropriated to such purposes as the wants of the establishment may require. Each side is 500 feet in length, and three stories high, in addition to the garrets above. Those which contain the infirmary and the work-shops, are opposite to each other, as are the sides inhabited respectively by the men and the women.

There are 187 acres of land attached to the house. Fifty are to be reserved for meadow, and 100 for arable. In the centre of the area stands the washhouse, communicating with the different offices into which the space included within the square is divided. The sale of the old premises will, it is thought, realize 200,000 dollars, and reduce the debt upon the new to six or seven hundred thousand.

The infirmary is divided into two departments, for the male and the female patients; the wards having each two windows looking towards the outside of the building, and two folding doors opening from the cieling to the floor, into a lofty and spacious passage that runs along the side, and commands a view of the court-yard. The arrangements above correspond with those below. At each end of the infirmary is a ward for lunatics, the sexes being separated by the hospital. On each story are private cells or dormitories for the patients, opening into the passage, and kept in a very clean and comfortable condition. This part of the institution appears to be the best both in its construction and its management. The whole building is supplied with water by means of pipes communicating with pumps, at which the paupers are employed to draw water from wells below. There is a shower-bath attached to the insane department, where the shock is employed both to subdue the violent and punish the disobedient. Opposite the cells, and in that part where light cannot be obtained except through the door, are small rooms where delinquents suffer solitary confinement. Upon asking the keeper whether the inmates of these wretched holes did not disturb the patients, I was told that the addition of a few tongues was hardly perceptible in this nocturnal Babel. Had I reversed the question, the answer would have shewn less regard for the prisoners. He wished that the patients were not allowed to see their relatives, as they were generally worse after such visits.

There were seventy women and forty men among the insane. The latter I did not see. Among the females were several colored persons. The two races agree together pretty well; though some repugnance is at first expressed by some of the " more worthy." Habit, however, reconciles them to an unavoidable necessity; and more rational conduct is exhibited by those who have lost their reason, than by those who are supposed to retain it in all its vigor.

Mania à potu is much more common among the white than the black women. The same may be said generally of inebriety. Dr. Parrish, jun., who was with me, confirmed what the keeper said on this subject. The year before, 123 persons, of whom twenty were women, died of this complaint in the city and liberties of Philadelphia.

A fact equally honorable to the African race, was mentioned by the matron of the female infirmary, where one or two were employed at the side of a sick relative in keeping off the flies, and assuaging the heat of the day with a fan. She said that there were but few of them in the establishment, their aversion to enter its walls being as strong as that of their white fellow-countrymen. To many of both death would be preferable to the disgrace of living in the almshouse. The second report of the Ladies' Branch of the Union Benevolent Association, pays an honorable and a well merited tribute to these people. " Nine colored families have agreed to make deposits [to the Fuel Saving Society]. They reside in one court, and might be held up as patterns for habits of order, industry, and regularity."

The proportion of Irish paupers in the house is very great. Out of 1,500 inmates, 500 only had a legal settlement in the State. Of 2,396 females, who were admitted into the almshouse during two years and a half from May 1828, no less than 550 were foreigners: of these, 450 were from Ireland,

while England sent seventy-five, and Scotland sixteen. The whiskey is to the roast beef, like Fal-
staff's sack to his bread. Of 3,197 out-door poor,
who received relief in wood in 1831-32, there were
950 foreigners. Here again the Irish came in for
their share; their number being 491, while that of
the English was 157, and that of the Scotch thirty-
eight. Pat prefers the "house" to his home.

There are generally from three to four hundred
Irish, who have been working on the rail-roads
during the summer, and who come in a complete
state of destitution, approaching to nudity, into
the house, till the return of the fine season allures
them to their former haunts, where they find the
tools, and clothes, and money they had secreted
during the period of their hybernation. These mi-
gratory movements are as periodical as the visit
and the departure of the swallow or the wood-
cock.

There is room, in this enormous asylum, for 3000
paupers; and even more might easily be accommo-
dated within its walls. The average number is
about 1400. They prefer their present quarters;
as each has a separate dormitory, instead of being
crowded together in the same room. The aged and
infirm are distinct from the rest. There is no arrangement for the cruel and demoralizing separation of husband and wife. The building is well
contrived; the wards and dormitories being on one

side of the passage, and the windows, looking into the court, on the other. By opening the doors, a thorough ventilation is produced, the construction resembling that of the infirmary. The chief cause of pauperism is drinking. Seventy-five per cent. may be attributed to that alone.

When the workshops are completed, it is expected that there will be less inducement to seek refuge within the walls; as a certain quantity of labor will be exacted from every able-bodied man. Every sort of work, that the place will admit of, will be carried on there. The cost of each, including all the expenses of the establishment, is one dollar and eighteen cents per week. It is thought it will be somewhat greater in future. At the Baltimore alms-house a debtor and creditor account is opened against every pauper, on his entrance; and the work he has to perform, if able-bodied, must balance the cost of his keep. Should he abscond, before this is cleared, he is liable to an imprisonment of twelve months. Whatever property he may have about him, is set aside as an additional pledge against his running away.

It will be an arduous task to prevent corruption in the managers, and enforce discipline among the objects of such an establishment as the Philadelphia alms-house. Any vigilant and systematic plan of superintendence is liable to be thwarted by those party predilections that influence official appoint-

ments and removals, while every regulation that
evasion or disobedience gives birth to, will be the
parent of new frauds and irregularities. Nine
tenths of the inmates have lost all feeling of self-
respect. Every day sufficient liquor is introduced
to inebriate forty of them. There appears to be
little or no effectual discipline, whether punitive or
reformatory. Solitary confinement, for twenty-four
hours, is scarcely any punishment to a drunken man,
who sleeps the time away, or loses all consciousness
of its duration. Two-thirds come out worse than
they went in. The " black book" exhibits numerous instances of relapses into misbehavior; and
the register shews that attachment to the place still
clings to those who have left it. It may be considered an unfortunate circumstance that the alms-
house should be situated in the immediate vicinity
of the city; as the temptations to abscond are mul-
tiplied by all the attractions that old acquaintances
and old haunts can offer, in addition to the shelter
and encouragement that vice and crime can always
find in a mixed population.

But the effect produced on the honest and industrious outside is still worse, as they become gradually familiarized with the conduct and sentiments of
those, who are living on the public bounty, with no
sensible diminution of cheerfulness and contentment,
—with no marks of self-abasement, and no signs of
inferiority. The relief of which any pressing emerg-

ency may compel the acceptance, will spread the contagion of vice and improvidence, and gradually undermine that honest pride, which shrinks at the approach of an humiliating charity. No permanent preventive of distress can be depended on, that appeals to the worst part of our nature.

Every nation has its own standard of respectability; to descend from which is much easier than to preserve its level, or recover it when it is lost.

To foreigners this place will offer an attractive asylum on their arrival; and they will have little objection to hard work, till they can procure an eligible situation. As for applicants from other States, they cannot gain a settlement in Philadelphia, except on the same conditions as at home,— a retaliatory law having been passed to meet those cases, which the former facility of obtaining relief from the public fund, had rendered a serious evil.

There are eight medical students resident in the house. They pay 200 dollars a-year for board and lodging, in addition to the privilege of witnessing the practice at the hospital, and enjoying the benefits of the library. This sum is paid into the funds of the institution. There are four physicians, four surgeons, and one accoucheur, who visit it in turns, and the fee (ten dollars) which is paid for attendance on their lectures, is made over, as at the Pennsylvania hospital, to the establishment. The services of the medical officers are thus altogether

gratuitous. They have no reason to complain of
the fare they meet with at table; for, if I was not
misinformed by one, who had occasionally partaken
of it, every eatable is in profusion,—bottled porter
ad libitum,—and such a repast, as is to be found in
few private houses.

The cost of this institution will, when completed,
amount, on a moderate calculation, to eight or nine
hundred thousand dollars. A committee of twelve
managers, chosen by the corporation, visit the house
once a week, and four of them visit it twice in rotation during the same time.

Philadelphia, like New York, finds the increase of
pauperism going on in a greater ratio than her population; and there is little reason to hope it will
be checked by the judicious application of charity.
The Union Benevolent Association, the object of
which is to prevent misery by the encouragement of
prudential and economical habits among the poor,
complains that the principles on which it acts, are
not well understood, even by its members. " The
questions—' what is the use of visiting in the summer?'—' How would you get at people who ask for
nothing?' are not uncommon." The " Provident
Society for employing the poor" promises work to
all who will apply for it, without regard to those
wants in the community which can alone supply it
beneficially. " The consequence of this free delivery of work to the poor," says one of its reports,

"has occasioned a large accumulation of goods; and it has unfortunately happened, that we have experienced greater difficulties this season, than we have before known in disposing of them: in addition to which, we had a considerable quantity at the commencement of the last year, remaining unsold in the hands of our correspondents. The demand for such goods as we have to sell is in this city very limited, and our shipping merchants are discouraged, by the results of former shipments, from making further purchases from us. We have, therefore, been put to the necessity of shipping for sale on our account the bulk of the shirts made during the last season."

The Society expected that the goods thus sent out, must be sold at reduced prices—unconscious, it appears, of the injury it was inflicting upon trade. Though its resources were inadequate to its objects, it still hoped for "further remittances," and "benevolent contributions," and added, that the people whom it had set to work, had expressed their thanks, when the usual demand for hands had arrived, "hoping to be employed again on the return of another season." The promises of assistance are not likely to be lost upon them: for who will lay by for a rainy day, when the hand of mistaking kindness thus offers him a shelter?

The principle upon which this well-meaning association proceeds, inverts the natural order of things. It attracts labor to an overstocked market, and diverts capital from its appropriate channels. It places between demand and supply an artificial interloper, that lessens the former while it increases the latter. The result corresponds with the tendency. Prices that were already below the remunerating level, sink still lower; and a course of action is continued which enlightened self-interest, if left to itself, would have shewn to be ruinous to the individual and to society. Were the acting committee composed, in part, of sensible persons from the working class, more judicious measures would be adopted, and the experiment might act as an example to the mother country; where it seems to be an acknowledged maxim, that those alone are qualified to prevent or provide for " adversity," who have neither known its " sweet uses," nor dreaded its bitter inflictions.

If these good people, instead of detaining labor in the cities, where it is not wanted, and where it is too much disposed to linger, would find some way to forward it to the west, where it is so scarce, that the most iniquitous means are often used to obtain it, they would rescue the distant States from slavery, and their own from pauperism. The Virginia " breeders" ought to subscribe to the Provident Society, as it indirectly creates a demand for their " stock" in Indiana and Illinois.

That the " good cheer" to be had at the alms-house is such a bounty on improvidence, as the ordinary motives to the opposite virtues will hardly be powerful enough to resist, will appear from the following facts:—During the year ending on the 20th of May, 1833, there were, on an average, 1010 paupers upon the establishment. The whole cost of their support was at the rate of one dollar $18\frac{4}{5}$ cents per week for each. Among other items of expenditure for the year, there were 173,329 pounds of beef, and 23,116 of mutton, 1900 barrels of wheat flour, and $224\frac{45}{70}$ bushels of Indian meal; 1,163 pounds of tea, and 10,352 of coffee; 17,937 pounds of brown sugar, $1,347\frac{1}{2}$ of lump sugar, and 1,172 of white Havaña, and $12\frac{1}{2}$ boxes of segars. The expenses of the steward's table for the same period, amounted to 2,137 dollars, 96 cents; of the whole 1010, 499 were men, 443 women, and 68 children. The proceeds arising from the sale of manufactured goods, amounted to 949 dollars, 14 cents, while the value of what was consumed in the house, was 5,484 dollars, 6 cents; leaving in raw material, machinery, and goods on hand, 4,138 dollars, 18 cents. The amount received in fees from resident students, &c., was 3,461 dollars, 45 cents. This last sum was paid into the treasury by the steward. In the winter of 1831–32, 3197 out-door poor received relief in wood; of these, 950 were foreigners; 2794 were whites, and 403 blacks. Of the whole number, 438 were on the regular list of paupers. As many of these had families, the aggregate of persons, including children, thus relieved, was 11,538. Among them were twenty between ninety and 100; three between 100 and 110, and one whose age exceeded the last mentioned period. The number who received wood next winter, was 3175; of whom 478 were on the regular list. There were 158 between eighty and ninety years of age; fifteen from ninety to 100; five from 100 to 110, and one above the last period. Of the whole number, 888 were foreigners—493 from Ireland, 103 from England, twenty-two from Scotland, and 195 Germans. The latter, as well as the Irish, are in the habit of begging their way, having frequently money concealed about the person. Wherever I went, I heard complaint of German meanness. Some emigrants of that class are accustomed, I was told, to send out their children to beg, while they themselves are living in comfortable houses. One family, consisting of eight or ten, with the parents, passed through a town, and stopped to ask for money at every door. Having gone along the principal street, the father, with the boys on one side, and the mother, with the daughters, on the other, they crossed over, and returned on each other's path. This is the general character of the Dutch or German laborers, as these emigrants are indiscriminately called. All those with whom I conversed on the subject, concurred in the same description of them.

The out-door expenses for the poor, during the preceding year, amounted to 33,551 dollars, 54 cents, including medical treatment, salaries of visitors, &c.

By the register it appears, that there had been admitted into the house,—

for the 2d time 312
　　3d 157
　　4th........ 79
　　5th........ 53
　　6th........ 31
　　7th........ 37
　　8th........ 25
　　9th........ 21
　10th........ 14
　11th........ 10
　12th........ 9
　13th........ 4 ;

five had been admitted fifteen times, six no less than sixteen times, two for the eighteenth, twentieth, twenty-first, and twenty-second; and one for the twenty-fourth, twenty-sixth, and twenty-eighth time.

While the cholera was raging at Philadelphia, eight Sisters of Charity were sent, at the request of the managers, from Emmetsburg, to the alms-house. They were subsequently withdrawn by the superior of the order; their continuance not being, as was stated in a letter to the Board, " in accordance with the charitable end of the Society, and with the religious retirement, and the exercises of piety peculiar to its members." Any thing like a well regulated discipline among such a mixed and lawless medley, can hardly be expected to be kept up. "With all the good-will and kindness," says the writer, "which you, gentlemen, have manifested in their regard, I do not perceive that, consistently with the principle on which the institution is founded, supported, and governed, it is in your power to secure to them those opportunities of practising the duties of their state of life, according to their rules;—that protection of their feelings from the rude assaults of such persons as are necessarily in your institution, and who regard it as their own, whilst they look upon those who minister to their comfort, as servants paid for doing it;—or that security from misrepresentation of motives and of actions, to which a few retiring and timid females are necessarily exposed, labouring amidst such a population of paupers."

At each end of that side of the square appropriated to the workshops, is an asylum for children —one for each of the two races, which, while they are destined to inhabit together the land of their common inheritance, are studiously separated in infancy and in manhood—in sickness and in old age— in the manufactory and the poor-house—in the school and the hospital—in the house of prayer, and in the house of mourning—in the public festival, and in the private assembly—in the day of battle, and in the hour of death—in the funeral procession, and in the grave itself.

While the cholera was raging, the only ministers who attended at the hospital to afford religious consolation to the patients, were the Catholic priests, whom no personal considerations could prevail upon to quit the post assigned them by their sense of duty. It was the same at the time of the yellow-fever. I have both facts from one of the physicians who attended. On the former occasion, the only spiritual aid the Protestant sick received, was from a black man, who prayed by their bed-side, and some women of the same race, who were employed to wash the linen, and who sang hymns to the poor sufferers. Similar desertion, and similar devotedness, were remarked in other places. Who are the persons most respected in the city? Those who abandoned it in its affliction! Who are most reviled as religionists and despised as men? The very people who exposed their lives in smoothing the path of death to its inhabitants!

In the establishment, appropriated to the children of the white paupers, an old building in Philadelphia, formerly the scene of a fête given by the "Tory party" to General Howe, in honor of the short-lived trophies he had gained, there are one hundred and twenty-six inmates, ninety-eight of whom are boys. The age of admittance is from eighteen months to eight years. Some, however, exceed the latter age. More than three fourths are of foreign parents, chiefly Irish. Formerly they were liable to be removed by their family or friends. To remedy the evils, that had arisen from thus affording a temporary retreat to the victims of want or caprice, a regulation was made, that none should be withdrawn, except on payment of their board during their residence. This demand, though estimated at a low rate, had the effect of checking a practice which was as injurious to the discipline of the institution, as to the economy which the state of its funds required. The children are, in general, very reluctant to return home, or to be put out as apprentices : and, indeed, if an opinion could be formed of their treatment from what I saw of the matron, I should conclude they had good reason for the feeling. Their education, their morals, and their comfort seem to be zealously provided for. The apartments are well adapted, from the cleanliness in which they are kept, and the cheerful aspect around, to the purposes for which they are destined. There was something melancholy, however, in the appearance of the inmates. Many of them were stunted and squalid, with every indication of having been neglected in infancy, and exposed to the most vicious and unhealthy habits.

The parents have, in nearly every instance, been reduced to pauperism by intemperance; and many of the children have shared in the vice as well as in its consequences. A child, about five years of age, was brought into the house, two or three years before, a confirmed drunkard. She had been in a state of intoxication for six weeks. Her constant cry was " give me whiskey—give me whiskey." She is now thoroughly reformed; and her health, as well as her morals, in a sound state. The parents and friends of the children are allowed to visit them once a month. More of the boys are bound out, in proportion to their numbers, than of the girls, as their services are available at an earlier age. On their first arrival, nearly all are subject to sore eyes ; a complaint that has been observed to prevail in most institutions of the kind. It is soon relieved by proper medical treatment. It seems to be the result of the sudden change they undergo of air and diet—a restorative process of Nature.

A satisfactory recommendation is required to obtain apprentices from the institution. It is found that those parents, who stand most in need of relief, are the last to avail themselves of that which the asylum offers—not from any feeling of shame, to which they have long been strangers—not from affection to their children, whose welfare has long been indifferent to them—but from some unaccountable caprice, that urges them to retain what has ceased to be an object of endearment—beings whom they can neither protect nor provide for; and who can no further administer to their gratification than in partaking of their vices, and submitting to their humors.

The more one sees of paupers, and pauper establishments, the deeper is the conviction, that the distresses of the laboring classes are chiefly, if not entirely, owing to intemperance, or want of foresight; and that the remedies, usually employed for their relief, are better fitted to increase, than prevent, the evil, by weakening the chief check to indulgence in removing the dread of its consequences. This asylum, however, does honor to its benevolent founders and conductors. They have been peculiarly fortunate in the choice of a matron, who understands the disposition of children, and of parents, and is equally successful in managing the one by mildness, and the other by firmness. Harsh treatment never does any good with the former, while good humor and a little tact keeps the whole body in order. Falsehood and tale-bearing are discouraged; and every thing is done to make the flock as kind, as happy, and as fat as the portly shepherdess.

The Philadelphia House of Refuge is similar in its object to the institution which bears the same name at New York; being established for the reformation of juvenile offenders of both sexes; who, though under the same roof, are separated from each other—not, however, so completely as they are in the latter place. The matron regretted that the sexes had not, as in London, a distinct building allotted to each.

Sufficient provision has been made, in the disposition of the dormitories, for the free admission of air, and the complete separation of their inmates. They run the whole length of the building in front; those for the girls being on one side of the entrance, where the superintendant receives visits and applications, and those for the boys on the other. This is an injudicious arrangement; as communication can, unless constant vigilance be exercised, take place through the windows or apertures with persons on the outside.

The State makes occasional grants in aid of the institution; and the subscriptions are still further increased by bequests from benevolent individuals. A legacy of 100,000 dollars was left to it not long ago—contingent on the life of the testator's widow. 25,000 dollars have been raised upon this security.

The room, in which the girls work and dine, looks into the court, where the boys are allowed, when their task is done, to amuse themselves by play, or in reading the books, with which a well-stored library supplies them. The windows happened to be open on account of the hot weather. The matron, when I made some remark upon the inconvenience of such a vicinity, said, that the shutters were generally closed. Still the place was ill-chosen for its purposes, as whatever was said or done on either side of the partition, was liable to be heard on the other.

Every thing in this part of the building bore the marks of strict attention to order and cleanliness. The young women, who are sent into the country after their discharge, do much better than those who get places in the city ; where solicitation and recognition are more apt to undermine the resolutions of amendment, and weaken the hope of redeeming their character. The applications for servants and apprentices are too numerous to be supplied. This may arise as much from the scarcity of hands, as from the favorable opinion entertained by the public of the reformatory system pursued here. The latter, however, is known to be eminently successful, both from the annual reports of the Committee, and from the testimony to its excellent management given by a portion of the legislature, who had been appointed to examine it. It is very rarely that any allusion is made, in the way of accusation, whether by the boys or the girls, to the previous conduct of those with whom they may have any altercation. Disputes and quarrels seldom happen. Silence seems to be observed by common consent with regard to the past. The boys sometimes make their escape.

Shoe-making, book-binding, brass-foundering, &c., are carried on in the work-shops ; in each of which a list of the names is stuck up on a board. Attached to them, are movable pegs, by observing the situation of which the superintendant can see at a glance, on entering, how many and who have behaved ill. The foreman is not allowed to punish the offenders. The proceeds of their labour are disposed of by open contract. No complaint has been made, except by the shoe-makers, of being undersold by the establishment.

Each boy has a certain quantity of work to do for the day. It is divided into two portions; and the time that remains, after it is finished, belongs to himself. It was ten o'clock when I visited the workshops, and several of the inmates were already in the court below, having completed their half-day's task. There was one colored boy among them. His conduct was as good as that of the others, and his treatment the same. No contempt or aversion was manifested against him. The poor fellow had stolen a watch—an offence that his destitute condition might almost excuse. He had neither father, nor mother, nor friend, to advise and correct him. He was literally without a home, and did not know that he had ever had one.

There were 106 boys and fifty-eight girls—one-third vagrants. They are discharged, the former at twenty-one, the latter at eighteen—the legal ages of majority.

The dormitories are separate, and placed in three stories with corresponding galleries above each other. The highest are used for solitary confinement, in cases of misconduct. A watchman goes his rounds regularly every night, to prevent escape or communication.

The girls are employed in sewing and other work for the house. Their dormitories are neatly decorated with prints and paintings, and other ornaments, that shew at once, by the taste exhibited in their selection and distribution, that they are inhabited by the fairer and more fanciful portion of the species. The chapel is so arranged, that the boys sit below the gallery, where the girls are placed, and are not seen, except by the younger part of the former. The school-room, which is well supplied with maps and books, is common to both sexes, and affords facilities for correspondence by means of writing; the places of concealment being known to the parties alone. It is very difficult to prevent these practices.

Monitors are chosen in the school for good conduct. Would it not be better that they should become so by rotation? There would then be less jealousy and self-conceit. The duties of the situation would perhaps be more impartially performed, if they were *official* than if they were *personal*, and exclusion would be a punishment as well as a disqualification. The average work per day is eight hours—three hours and a half during the summer, and four in the winter, are appropriated to the school.

Here, as well as at the refuge in New York, the solicitude shewn for the welfare of the children ex-

tends beyond the period of their residence. Inquiries are made into their conduct at the places
where they are settled, and the results are, in general,
satisfactory. Some of them visit the house from
time to time, and one of them is now a life-sub-
scriber. The board of managers appoint the visiting
committees. Twelve ladies meet monthly, and appoint two of their number to visit the establishment
weekly.

A case of great hardship occurred while I was at
Philadelphia. A man of the name of William Hec-
tor was claimed as a slave by a person from Maryland. He had been resident ten or twelve years in
Pennsylvania:—the greater part of which time he
had passed honestly and industriously in the city.
Such at least was the testimony I received to his
character from one of his neighbors, who had long
been acquainted with him. There were 300 or
400 blacks present when the trial took place. The
judge decided in favor of the claimant (Southern);
having refused to allow sufficient time to procure
evidence that would have established the prisoner's
right to freedom. Three weeks were requested, and
three days only were granted. His mother was an
Indian; and his brother, it was said, had obtained
judgment against a similar claim, on that ground.
His wife, who was present, expressed her grief in a
way that would have melted the heart of any one,
but the administrator of the most cruel and unjust

code that ever disgraced a civilized community—the sole interpreter and agent of a slave-holding legislature's will—with no jury to direct him, and little conscience to restrain him. If a black man's cow is taken from him, twelve honest men assist him to recover his property; if his person is seised, a judge or a magistrate decides on his right to his own body. In New Jersey and in other States, a justice of the peace has summary and definitive jurisdiction in such cases. By the revised statutes of New York, a supposed fugitive might formerly take out a writ *de homine replegiando*, and obtain the protection of a jury. Such security is now denied; as the superior court have unanimously declared the law, under which he seeks a remedy, unconstitutional. " I would observe," said Judge Hoffman, " that, as far as concerns the southern States, without this provision, (giving exclusive jurisdiction to a single magistrate,) our present government would not have been in existence. I may say it was the price of that constitution."

The law, by which the liberty of a human being is placed at the mercy of one man, was passed by the legislature of Pennsylvania in 1826. By the sixth section it is enacted, that " a fugitive " (any colored person may be claimed as a fugitive) " from labor or service, shall be brought before a judge, and upon proof, to the satisfaction of such judge, that the person so seized or arrested, doth, under the laws of the State or territory from which he or she fled, owe service to the person claiming him or her, it shall be the duty of such judge to give a certificate thereof to such claimant, his or her duly authorized agent or attorney, which shall be sufficient warrant for removing the said fugitive to the State or territory from which he or she fled."

In many of the cities in the Union, the free blacks are hackney coachmen; and some of them drive their own carriages, which are usually the best and the neatest on the stand. I asked one of them, whether the whites did not prefer them. He replied that they did, and added, that there were three reasons for the preference;—because they had no fear that they would assume any thing like equality, —because they could order them about in the tone of masters,—and still more, because it might be thought they were riding in their own carriages— like our cockneys, who put a livery-servant at the back of a glass-coach, and then pass it off as their own. Hence it is that these men are more attentive to the appearance both of themselves and their vehicles, and elevate their condition by the means employed to degrade it.

It is highly gratifying to see the pride of man defeating its own purposes, and enriching the very persons it would impoverish and depress. It is the same with the barbers, who are almost entirely colored men. The whites are too proud or too lazy

to shave themselves; and one of the few employments they have left open to the despised race, has
given it both wealth and influence. The barber's
shop is a lounging place, and a reading-room;
where the customers amuse themselves with carica-
tures and newspapers; while the conversation that
passes makes the operator acquainted with the oc-
currences of the day. The information these men
possess is astonishing. Most of them take in the
abolition papers, which thus find a powerful support, and the best channel to convey their sentiments to the public. Were they to act in concert,
their numbers would enable them to exercise a sa-
lutary check upon a large portion of the periodical
press, by limiting their subscriptions to those publications that are friendly or less violent in their hostility to them. There are many who express themselves freely upon those topics, in which they are
personally interested, who, in handling a coloniza-
tionist, are as ready with their logic as their razors,
and can take off his arguments and his beard with
equal dexterity.

The respectability of this class was proved a few
years back, by a memorial they sent to the legislature of the State. According to statistical tables,
the accuracy of which could not be disputed, they
contributed 2500 dollars annually to the poor fund,
and seldom received more than 2000 from it,—while
but four per cent. upon the whole amount of pau-

pers, whether in or out of the alms-house, belonged to them;—eight and a quarter per cent. being, in 1830, their proportion of the population in Philadelphia. They were paying annually for rents 100,000 dollars, and had six methodist meeting-houses, two Baptist, two Presbyterian, one Episcopalian, and one public hall, all supported by themselves, and valued at upwards of 100,000 dollars. They owned two Sunday schools, two tract societies, two Bible societies, two temperance societies, and one female literary institution. " We have among ourselves," say these ill-treated men, " more than fifty beneficent societies, some of which are incorporated, for mutual aid in times of sickness and distress." The members were liable to be expelled or suspended for misconduct. Upwards of 7000 dollars, raised among themselves, were expended annually in the relief of sickness or distress. " It is worthy of remark," they add, " that we cannot find a single instance of one of the members of these societies being convicted in any of our courts. One instance only has occurred of a member brought up and accused before a court, but this individual was acquitted."

The Quakers in the United States are less noted for their co-operation in works of benevolence with the members of other religious societies than their brethren in the mother country. This difference is partly owing to the spirit of sectarianism; but more

particularly to the custom, which generally prevails,
of opening charitable meetings with prayer—an
observance, to comply with which would be inconsistent with the principles of many among the
" Friends." It was dispensed with on this account
at the convention for forming the National Anti-
Slavery Society; which thus adopted a rule that
has obviated any scruples or objections on this head
in England. It is a great misfortune that any obstacle of the kind should exist, to cripple the exertions of men, who would be able to act more
effectually in concert, and who are often defeated,
when isolated, where they might have been successful united. It would be highly honorable to the
society, if it were merely an adherence to principle,
and not a deviation from it, that distinguished them
from the parent stock. Had they, as a body, acted
up to the rule they profess as individuals; had they
publicly borne their " testimony " against the prejudice they condemn in private, and admitted their
sable brethren to that social equality which they
generally acknowledge is due to them, the national
character would never have been stained by such
cruel and cowardly proceedings as have lately taken
place; an appeal to their conduct would have been
an unanswerable reply to the charge of " amalgamation " (if the prejudice which gave it birth could
have survived the respect they had ceased to pay to
it). Instead of being stigmatized, by the victims of

this wicked antipathy, as hypocrites and time-servers, they would have been found the best friends and protectors of the free, as they have always been the unwearied opponent of the kidnapper. No one could have raised his voice successfully against a practice which they had sanctioned by their example. The followers of Penn would have abashed the apostles of mischief; and those who may now fairly lay their misfortunes at the door of Quaker apostasy, would have been indebted for their safety to Quaker consistency.

The sons of Africa are reminded, even in the Quaker meeting-houses, of the mark which has been set upon them, as if they were the children of Cain. Yet the rules of discipline particularly forbid such unchristian distinctions. Monthly meetings are desired by them, to exercise due deliberation, in consulting upon the qualification of applicants for admission; and to receive such as are found worthy " into membership, without distinction of nation or color." Who, on reading this injunction, would believe that " colored friends," when assembled with their white brethren to worship their common father, are obliged to sit by themselves; and that those attempts, which are now and then made, to join the excluded, or invite them to sit among the privileged, have been rewarded with remonstrance, reproach, and persecution? Even upon the subject of slavery, the Society is far from an explicit, or an unequivocal

denunciation of its injustice. Among the rules of
discipline, published at Philadelphia in 1831, is the
following:—" We earnestly desire it may become
the concern of our members generally, to use the
influence they have with those who hold slaves, by
inheritance or otherwise, that they may be treated with
moderation and kindness, and instructed as objects
of the common salvation, in the principles of the
Christian religion, as well as in such branches of
school learning as may fit them for freedom, and to
become useful members of society." What is this
but an encouragement of slavery? Talk of moderation indeed to a man, the very coat on whose back
you know to be purchased at the expense of the person
for whom you ask it! Tell him to be kind, while
you see he knows not how to be just! Advise the
open violator of religion to disseminate its principles,
among those, who would thus become the judges, as
they are now the victims, of his wickedness! Recommend the instruction of the very beings from
whose ignorance he derives his pelf and his power!
—and urge him to prepare his slaves for freedom,
when it is the want of that preparation that supplies
him with an apology for his guilt, and a motive for
its continuance! If it be a sin in Quakers to hold
slaves, they must consider it a sin in others; and
they are partakers of the sin, who employ their influence with the offender, to palliate its heinousness
with the suggestion of an amelioration, or to con-

nive at its enormities by their silence on the para-
mount duty of repentance and reparation. What
follows is little better: " Also, that friends in their
several neighborhoods, advise and assist such of
the black people, as are at liberty, in the education
of their children, and common worldly concerns."
Is there no better way, in which they can be assisted? Do they labor under no disabilities or
grievances? Will not the assistance thus recommended by " the discipline," make them feel more
keenly the pressure of their wrongs, and the denial
of their rights? The black man stands in need of
far other protection from the Quaker :—" Bear your
testimony, he would say, against the pride of your
white brother, by removing the barrier it has planted
between his children and mine. Shew your sincerity
by your humility, and let not the ill-treatment I
receive he sanctioned by your deference to the vo-
taries of worldly-mindedness. Let your practice
conform to your principles, and those common courtesies be observed, which you would not dare to
refuse me in any other country."

Nothing is said in the rules above quoted about
the sin of slavery. The slave-trade alone is condemned; and " hiring slaves " is called " an un-
righteous traffic." Its victims, however, are never
spoken of as men entitled to the same rights as every
other branch of the human family. Friends are exhorted " to educate those whom they or their prede-

cessors have released from bondage, that they may
become useful and respectable members of the community." They are described, whenever they are
named, as a distinct race,—as objects of beneficence
and condescension, destined to never-ending infe·
riority—doomed to experience, in the very kindness
they receive, the proofs of hopeless degradation, and
the sentence of unrelenting exclusion. What a disgraceful contrast does this apostate body of religionists exhibit with the Synod of Cincinnati, who, the
year before, had declared slavery to be "a heinous
sin and scandal!" Even the enemies of human
freedom—those who hold that emancipation would
destroy the constitution, and dissolve the Union,
have openly insulted the Quakers, by praising their
prudence and forbearance in this matter. The
"Friends" and the New York rioters have been
coupled together as sharers of that approbation,
which the "waiters upon" public opinion are so
skilful in applying.

Those who feel no abhorrence for the shouts of
incendiaries, may well be pleased with the canting
of time-servers.

It should be observed that a great schism has
separated the Society into two hostile camps. The
orthodox, who happen to be in the minority, are
naturally anxious to conciliate public favor, and to
obtain from without the power they want within.
To this cause may be attributed the retrograde move-

ment which has for some time characterised their " sayings and doings." Those who are abolitionists of the new school, who would take off the fetters from the white man's mind, as well as from the black man's body—veteres avias de pulmone—are chiefly of that party who are stigmatized as " Hicksites;" and, as the " orthodox " have ceased to hold communion with them in their schools—their places of worship—their almshouses—and, as far as they could, in the common intercourse of life, subjecting them to a degree of obloquy and persecution that is happily without a parallel among the Quakers of other countries, what was merely indifferent has become distasteful; and an approximation to the opinions and practices of new friends, has followed the desertion of the old. Thus, as is always the case where the passions have gained the mastery over reason, things which have no necessary connexion have been identified by juxta-position, and the " true believers" have adopted the observances of the world they have sought, and eschewed those of the brethren they have left.

So far have they carried their hostility, that they have prejudiced many " Friends" in England against its unoffending objects; who have in vain requested to be heard in their own defence, and solicited attention to a remonstrance which has been twice returned to them from that country unanswered. Even the grave cannot bury their animosity. The gate which leads to " the narrow house," must be forced by the living before the dead can find a place of repose. The whole country was lately scandalized by the sight of a Quaker litigation in a court of justice. A school in New Jersey, founded by the Society, was claimed by both parties; and they, who never had any articles of faith, and who deprecate appeals to legal adjudication in all disputes between members of the same religious family, called upon a legal tribunal to scrutinize the belief of their forefathers, and permitted the creed of another sect to be set up as a standard for their own.

Though the defendants in the suit, many of whom were subscribers to the school, proposed that the fund in question should be divided among the contending parties in proportion to their numbers, yet judgment was prayed for by the plaintiffs, and the decision was in their favor. It is singular that a similar trial was productive of similar results, about the same time, in England—a coincidence which the " orthodox" party were not slow to turn to their own advantage, though there was wanting, in the two cases, that analogy which might have afforded them some plea for their conduct. The possessors of the litigated fund in England were neither its founders, nor the descendants of its founders; while the creed of the donor was the creed of the claimants ; and no violation of principle was involved in the dispute or the decision. If the secular power is

thus to cut the Gordian knot of polemical controversy, and declare what is nonconformity with the
tenets it may in its wisdom think fit to ascribe to
any religious society, there will soon be an end of
sectarian equality, and the State may proceed to
celebrate its union with the Church upon its ruins.
The triumph will be the greater, as it will be owing
to the most zealous opponents of the connexion.
No persons have had a keener eye upon the various
sects into which the nation is separated, or seen
more clearly the efforts made by each for the ascendancy, than this society; and it is, in some measure,
owing to this jealousy, that the American Quakers
unite so seldom with other denominations in the
performance of " good deeds."

They are suspicious, and perhaps with good reason, that the ministers of some of the latter are
striving to prepare the public mind for a change in
ecclesiastical matters. Some of them, indeed, have
very unguardedly boasted of their numbers and influence, expressing a wish to spiritualize the body
politic, by making the profession of certain dogmas
the condition of obtaining a seat in the legislature.
Nomination to public offices would thus lead, by an
easy transition, to a command of the public treasury;
and fixed salaries from the government would render
the present stipendiaries of individual congregations
independent of all control, by dissevering the tie

that now binds together the doctrines of the one, and the interests of the other.

While the Missouri question was under discussion, a memorial was sent by the Philadelphians to Congress against admitting a new State into the Union with the curse of slavery upon it. I was informed that several Quakers affixed their names to it. I am unwilling to believe that any " Friend " would adopt or approve of such sentiments as the following :—
" Your memorialists will not deny that most of the slave-holding States are free from blame with respect to the introduction of negro slavery, and its continuance until the present time among them ; that its immediate total abolition is incompatible with their safety, and even with genuine benevolence to the blacks ; and that, in permitting its admission in the new States of Louisiana, Mississippi, and Alabama, Congress pursued a policy perhaps indispensable for the general security of our brethren of the South."

Elias Hicks, whose " heresies" are recorded in the appellation bestowed upon the Quaker " neologists", had so much influence with the monthly meeting, of which he was a member, that he prevailed upon all of them not only to manumit their slaves, but to pay them the arrears of those wages which would have been due to them if free. He abstained entirely from every article of food, or dress, or furniture, which had been produced by slave-labor. He evinced, in his last moments, how strong the ruling principle of his life was even in death. He was observed, by those who surrounded his bed at that awful moment, to push off, with what little strength remained, a cotton coverlid that had been put over him. As he repeated the effort three or four times in succession, some one remarked that it was probably on account of the material of which it was made, that he was unwilling it should remain upon him. He fixed his eyes upon the speaker, and, nodding assent, turned round on his side, and soon after, breathed his last.

An anecdote told me by Isaac Hopper, who has the active benevolence, as well as the religious opinions, of the heresiarch, throws some light on the relative characteristics of the two races that seem destined to share the new continent between them. It is seldom, indeed, that any one has an opportunity of ascertaining the validity of those opinions which ascribe generosity and high-mindedness to the owner, and the opposite qualities to his bondsman. A citizen of Delaware, of the name of Perry Boots, had allowed his slave, Daniel Benson, some twenty years ago, to reside in Philadelphia, on condition that he would pay him forty dollars a-year. The " rent" of his own body was punctually paid for some time, though the " tenant" had to support his own mother, as well as to provide for his own maintenance. Having, however, been told that he was free by the laws of Pennsylvania, he applied to Mr. Hopper for advice; and the latter informed his master, by letter, that he had no further claim upon his services. It was in vain that remonstrances were made, and lawyers consulted. The case was plain. His consent had been given for a longer residence than that within which his property in human flesh could be retained; and the man was declared to be no longer " bound to service". Disappointed and chagrined at the decision, the master upbraided the man with ingratitude for the kindness he had always shewn him. " It is true", replied the other, " that you have always treated me well; and I feel attached to your family, from having lived with your father: but the same law which gave you my labor, now gives me my liberty. You say you intended to grant me my freedom on some future day:—what price would you ask for me, were I still your slave ?" " One hundred dollars." " The money is yours," said the generous black, producing a bag of hard dollars that he had laid by; " and now that I am a free citizen of the United States, I hope you will do me the honor of dining with me to-day." Both offers were accepted: a receipt was given for the money; and the parties sat down together to as good a banquet as the remainder of the hoard could provide.

Another story I had from the same quarter, presents a melancholy picture of the attachment these

people possess for their children. A fugitive, who
had accumulated a handsome fortune in Philadelphia, was anxious, about fifteen years back, to recover
his family; and Isaac Hopper undertook to pay his
master 150 dollars for his freedom. The bargain having been settled, and the necessary papers completed,
the father went into Maryland in search of his little
ones. They were no longer there. He had been
promised them. They were sold. The shock was
too much for a parent's feelings. His wealth had
lost all its charms. He returned to Philadelphia,
and died of a broken heart.

Isaac Hopper assured me, that he never knew a
slave-owner whose word he could trust in any case
where slave-property was concerned. He has had
great experience in such matters; having rescued and
redeemed many from the horrors of slavery, and
being well acquainted with the tricks and treachery
of those who are engaged in this infamous traffic.
Yet these men frequently confide in the honor of
their slaves; allowing them to work out their own
emancipation, with no other security for their observance of the agreement than their integrity. The
servant at the house where I lodged in Philadelphia,
was 100 dollars in debt to his master,—having bound
himself to pay the purchase-money of his freedom
by instalments. He was without any incumbrance,
and might with ease have made his escape to Canada.

When I asked him why he remained, he replied that he had given his honor, and nothing should induce him to break his faith. Such instances are very frequent. He himself put to me a case of conscience, and asked my advice. A person, with whom he was acquainted, had been brought from Virginia by his owner, with the hope that some one would advance the price of his freedom, (400 dollars,) and, as the slave's wife, a free woman, and her children, were in Philadelphia, he had left him there, while he went on to New York. The slave had promised not to run away. I recommended that he should return to Virginia, and, taking the first opportunity of rejoining his wife, proceed to Canada.

Both master and man were disappointed at the result, the one of his visit to Philadelphia, the other of his application to friends. Such was the sense of honor, that restrained the latter from violating his engagement, that he went back to his chains. Masters often work on the compassion of benevolent men, and connive at the escape of their slaves, with the hope of obtaining their value, when they cannot dispose of them in the usual way. To purchase under such circumstances, or indeed under any, is doubly injurious to the interests of humanity; as it acknowledges the right of the master to sell, and enables him to replace his stock. The sum of human suffering is not in the slightest degree diminished. There is merely a change in its distribution:—for, while the system continues, the necessary instruments of its operation will be sought for.

A remarkable trait of generosity occurred about thirty years ago. Three men, who had concealed themselves in Philadelphia, fell into the hands of their master. A Quaker, whose name was Harrison, advanced, though he had never seen them, the sum of 250 dollars for them. In the mean time, two of them had made their escape; and a person, who wanted a servant, agreed to pay Harrison 125 dollars for the one that remained. When, at the expiration of five years, for which he had been bound, the man became his own master, he went to his benefactor, and offered to return him the remainder of the money; observing, that the whole debt had become his, by the flight of his comrades, and that it was hard upon Harrison that he should suffer from an act of kindness. I need not say what reply was made to the proposal.

CHAPTER XXIX.

Newhaven.—Cemetery.—Grave of Ashmun.—"Potter's Field."
—Yale College.—Hartford.—Christian Promise and Performance.—Liberty of Speech imprudent in the United States.—
Second Edition of "Canterbury Tale."—Bishop of Charleston's Letter to Daniel O'Connell.—Providence.—Interview
with Dr. Channing.—Philanthropy of the Unitarians, and Philanthropy of Moses Brown.—Contrasted Industry.

ON the 9th of August, I left Philadelphia for New
York, and proceeded from the latter place, on the
15th, to Newhaven, in Connecticut. This is one of
the prettiest towns in the Union; the streets being
shaded by avenues of trees, the tops of which, when
viewed from a distance, appear to be interlaced with
each other—presenting, at every turn, beautiful
and varied illustrations of those curves, which are
supposed to have suggested the Gothic arch. The
gardens attached to the houses are, in general, neatly
kept, and give an air of comfort and privacy to the
families of their proprietors; while they break the
uniformity which the too frequent recurrence of
straight lines produces.

There is a spacious cemetery near the town, or rather forming a part of it, where the inhabitants find a last home. The pride of caste, in pushing its folly beyond the grave, has effected an approximation, by attempting a disjunction between the two races. The ground is divided into two lots, each thirty feet by twenty, the price of which is about twenty-five dollars. A portion of these had been purchased by the " people called Africans," as Mrs. Child, in her very interesting work *, has appropriately termed them. In process of time, as the population of the town increased, more land was added to the burying-ground, and monuments were erected, beyond that portion appropriated to the " outcasts." So that they who were once on the outside, are now in the midst of their skin-proud revilers. Among the former, lies Ashmun, the first governor of Liberia; in death, as in life, the friend and the companion of the black man. Beyond is the Potter's Field, where the dead bodies of the poor are deposited. The paupers of Newhaven are reminded, when they visit the graves of their departed friends, that the purity of their blood is a matter of deep interest and concern to their " betters"; and that the contamination of " bad company" will not be allowed to " corrupt" their " good manners," while reposing beneath the few feet of sod allotted to them

* An Appeal in favor of that class of Americans called Africans, by Mrs. Child, &c., Boston, 1833.

by the hand of charity. It is thus that the earliest and the latest associations of life,—the first impressions of the cradle, and the last monitions from the grave, are made to perpetuate an antipathy, opposed alike to the innocence of the one, and to the humility of the other. The blood of the black man cries from the ground against his brother. The heart of the white man is hardened against him. May the Father of both look with pity and mercy upon them!

The singular distribution of the graves in the burying ground, was pointed out to me by the Rev. Mr. Jocelyn, of Newhaven—one of those who are pre-eminently entitled to the appellation of "fanatics";—men, who, in every age and country, catch, from the elevated situation they have assumed, the first rays of that divine light which has not yet reached the crowd below;—men who are honorably distinguished by the hatred and compassion of the wicked and the weak,—the enemies of that reform they will one day boastingly advocate * ; — men,

* The nature and progress of national reform, may be seen in the conduct of its opponents. They begin by stigmatizing its leaders as the vilest of the vile, that it may be thought bad advocates cannot have a good cause:—and they end by becoming its friends, that it may be thought a good cause cannot have bad advocates. Great men belong to the first period: great statesmen to the second. It is unjust to confound them, and to expect principle where there never has been any thing

whose zeal in the cause of humanity is at once the result and the reproach of the selfishness around them;—men, who, in the confederated republics of North America, are a butt and a by-word for the ribaldry of the vilest and most venal journalists in the world :

> " By whom to be disprais'd is no small praise :
> Their lot who dare be singularly good."

From this place Mr. Jocelyn accompanied me to Yale College; one of the professors of which (Mr. Goodrich) very politely took me about the building to shew me the library, the lecture-rooms, and the cabinet of mineralogy :—the latter of which contains a most valuable collection of specimens from all quarters of the globe; admirably arranged for the purposes of reference and study, and accompanied with models of the various forms which crystallization assumes in its development.

The college is under the care of the President, who is not exempted from the labors of tuition, six professors, and eight tutors.   Chemistry, with mineralogy and geology;—mathematics, including astronomy, &c.; rhetoric, divinity, the Latin and the Greek languages, have each its professor.   The whole course of instruction embraces four years, of

but expediency.   American emancipation is pure from all political taint.   She has had her martyrs : she is not yet disgraced by demagogues.

which each contains three terms. The average age
of admission is sixteen; the lowest being fourteen.
The period of residence for the year is altogether
forty weeks, at an average expense, for board, fuel,
&c., of 175 dollars. One sitting-room, with two bed-
chambers, is, as at Harvard College, appropriated
to two students; who take their meals at a common
table, with the rest of the community. There are
two halls, at one of which the board is about one
dollar, seventy-five cents per week—at the other,
one dollar, twenty-five cents. The number of the
under-graduates was 376; there were besides these,
fifty-five graduates who were studying divinity,
thirty-nine law, and about seventy-one medical students.

Having visited the establishment, we saw an exhibition of paintings by Trumbull—the subjects of
which are chiefly national. The proceeds from the
fees paid by visitors form an annuity for the artist,
and, after his death, are to belong to the college, on
the premises of which it is placed. In the afternoon
I went on to Hartford, and put up at the same hotel,
in which I was the year before—the first I had ever
slept in during my sojourn in America, and one of
the best for quiet, civility, and cleanliness.

Throughout the Union, there is, perhaps, no city,
containing the same amount of population, where
the blacks meet with more contumely and unkindness than at this place. Some of them told me it

was hardly safe for them to be in the streets alone
at night.   One man assured me that he never ventured out after day-light, without some weapon of
defence about him.   No young woman of that race,
if she would avoid insult, dare pass through the
town, in the dusk of the evening, without a man to
protect her.   To pelt them with stones, and cry out
nigger! nigger! as they pass, seems to be the pastime
of the place.   I had seen and heard so much of the
indignities and cruelties heaped on the heads of this
persecuted race, that I had ceased to feel surprise at
any thing I was told on the subject.   Indignation,
I trust, I shall never cease to feel; and I blame myself for not having spoken more strongly and more
frequently against these enormities.   I could perceive that I had given great offence in several quarters, by the expression of my sentiments.   It would
be more to my honor if I had given more reason
for it.

A stranger can declare his opinions on any matter
with much greater freedom in France or England—
I believe I might add in Austria or Turkey—than in
America,—the only country on the surface of the
globe, where philanthropy is persecuted or sneered
at, and where " high and low, rich and poor," have
conspired together to put down humanity.

At Hartford I was confined to my bed several
days by illness; during which I met with much
attention from the people of the hotel.   On the 26th

I went to Brooklyn, passing over the same ground I had travelled the year before.

I found, on my arrival, that " war had smoothed his wrinkled front" at Canterbury ; and that a more agreeable deity had been both there and at Brooklyn : that Miss Crandall had become a bride, and one of the young ladies whom I had seen on my former visit, was about to be married to W. L. Garrison.

The next morning one of the brothers of the betrothed, drove me over to the school.   Neither the late, nor the present, Miss Crandall was at home. Mrs. Philleo was passing the honey-moon at Philadelphia ; and Miss Almira was out on a visit. A young man, however, of the name of Burleigh, who assisted in teaching the pupils, received us very cordially.   In requital of his kind offices to a persecuted woman, he was then under an indictment, as an infringer of the same enactment under which she had been subjected to such unmanly and harassing proceedings.   His trial—if there is to be a trial—was to come on in December.   The object of the information was, most probably, to intimidate him, and deter others from taking any share in the tuition of a school, which had become more odious to its enemies in proportion to their failure in trying to put it down with or without law. Reflection had had time enough to see, that the Federal Court, as long as it had any regard for its own reputation, or any respect for the constitution

of the country, would never confirm the validity of
a law, that must strike a fatal blow at both.   If free
blacks be citizens,—and it will be no easy matter to
prove they are not so—they are entitled, in moving
from one commonwealth to another, to the same
privileges that are granted, by the terms of their
union with the rest, to the citizens of the latter *.

There were twenty pupils in the school—there had
been as many as thirty.   On the mantel-piece of the
room, into which we were shewn, was lying a stone,
twice as large as that I saw the year before.   It had
been used for the same purpose.   It was thrown
into the house through one of the windows.   The
weight of it must have been at least two pounds.
There were ten panes of glass completely destroyed
by a long pole, which had been left on the premises,
and which I saw.   Part of the window-sash had
been broken in.   There were two windows in this
state ; both in the sitting room.   On the table were
lying Baxter's Bible and Cruden's Concordance ;
beautifully bound in russia : the former in two
volumes octavo—the latter in one.   They had been
brought over from Scotland by Mr. Charles Stuart,
the great " malleus " of the Colonization imposture.
In each volume was the following inscription:
" Presented to Miss Crandall by the Ladies of

---

* The citizens of each State shall be entitled to all privileges
and immunities of citizens in the several States.—Constitution
of the United States, Article 4, Section 2.

Edinburgh, as a mark of the respect with which they regard the Christian courage of her conduct towards their colored sisters in the United States; and from a conviction that such consistent love and strength, could only be derived from the DIVINE AUTHOR of the SACRED VOLUME." Below were quotations from St. John xxi. 15, and Psalm xl. 1, 2, dated Edinburgh, March 5, 1834. The expenses of the prosecution had already cost Mrs. Philleo upwards of 600 dollars. Legal eloquence is by no means cheap—not that it is scarce, but that the seller too often puts his own price upon it. Mr. Ellsworth, of Hartford, the counsel for the defendant, charged 200 dollars for the last pleadings. Cheap law may encourage litigation : but dear law is undoubtedly a premium upon persecution. Il faut que chacun vive; and disinterestedness is not the characteristic of every profession. Till I visited Canterbury, personal experience had led me to think that physicians might fairly claim it as their own peculiar virtue. But the behavior of Dr. Harris, the opposite neighbor of Mrs. Philleo, dispelled this " amabilis error." When called upon to render medical assistance to one of the pupils, who was suffering severe pain, he flatly refused to cross the road; told Mr. Burleigh that he might publish his refusal to the whole world : and declared that he looked upon the request as a personal insult. No other medical advice was to be had within three miles!

Another information for harboring,—the former was for teaching colored children, was hanging over the head of this meritorious woman. It ought to be mentioned, that her sister had nobly supported her under her trials—had never shrunk from the task she undertook: and, though but twenty years of age, had remained firmly at her post, alone, and surrounded by enemies against whom even her life could hardly be considered safe.

Some time before, the house was discovered to be on fire; and a colored man, who happened to be there at the time, was accused, and tried for an offence which, if proved, would have subjected him to perpetual imprisonment. Not a particle of evidence, however, could be produced against him; and he was immediately acquitted. The poor fellow had to pay one hundred dollars for his innocence. There is every reason to believe that the fire was the work of an incendiary; as the "Windham County Advertiser" had, a short time before, informed the public, that Miss Crandall's school would soon be totally broken up. All attempts to obtain from the Editor an explanation of his mysterious words failed.

Though some of the young women had certificates from the congregational churches to which they belonged, yet they were not admitted to the Canterbury meeting-house, where the same religious society assemble. They were forced to attend worship at a place two miles off, and were frequently insulted on their way thither and on their return. The lapse of a year had not produced either a relaxation of persecution, or an advance towards a truce, on the part of the oppressor. The same dark and fanatical spirit still cast his baneful shadow over a village, that one would have expected, from its secluded and beautiful situation, to be the abode of charity and good neighborhood. The assistant teacher could scarcely walk out, without hearing something intended to wound his feelings, and provoke a retort. That manly calmness, however, which the noble task he had assumed demanded and supposed was never wanting; and the consciousness of a good cause tempered the zeal of youth with the composure of mature years. Visitors even were not secure from insult. The traces of the harness, when they were about to leave, were sometimes found to be cut; and practices were resorted to, that would have disgraced the most brutal tribe of savages.

When the day, on which Miss Crandall was to be married, had arrived, the minister of the place, who had published the banns, and had promised, " if Providence would permit him," to perform the ceremony, wrote her a note declining to officiate " under existing circumstances." He had that morning received a letter, enclosing some money, and requesting he would not unite the parties in matrimony. They were compelled to go to Brook-

lyn, where the marriage took place. He had bitterly repented his conduct, I was told; the majority
of his congregation having become displeased with
him. His mortification must have been great, as
he had been appointed just when former dissensions,
that had so far separated his flock into feuds, as to
occasion the dismissal of five or six pastors in about
twice as many years, had been merged in a common
feeling of animosity against the unwelcome institution for teaching A, B, C, to an outlawed race. Party
feeling had put its own construction on his proceedings.
In sooth, the little village of Canterbury contains within
its bosom a set of self-tormentors, that seem determined to sting every thing, and every body, that
comes near them. There was a little English girl,
of six or seven years of age, in the school. Her
aunt was staying there. She had been but two years
from the old country, and was much shocked at the
unnatural conduct she had witnessed in a Christian
people towards their fellow-men. The little girl had
been sent by her father from Utica (New York) to Canterbury; from a feeling of abhorrence to tyranny.

In the room where we were sitting, I observed a
lithographic portrait of O'Connell—a name that no
descendant of Africa can pronounce without feelings
of deep respect. That the expression is not too
strong may be seen in the following letter, as it was
published in America, the most honorable testimony
that could well be paid to the value of that influence

against which it was directed. The writer of this
" *verbosa et grandis epistola* " was lately sent, if
rumor is to be believed, on a spiritual mission from
the Pope to Hayti!

" Charleston, (S. C.) Dec. 8, 1829.

" Should any one have told me, that a day would
come, when a sense of deep and awful duty would
require of me to address you, as I this day do, I
would not have thought it possible.

" I wrote a few weeks since from Baltimore a
letter, which you cannot, I suppose, have yet received ; in which I alluded to the injustice which
you thoughtlessly did to a people, of whom you
know so little as you do of the slave-holding Americans. But this day I have had an imperfect view
of a letter, which you appear to have written from
Derrynane, in last September, upon the subject of
our cruelty and injustice. That view, imperfect as
it was, was to my eye more blasting than any I
have for years beheld. I now tell you that a more
wanton piece of injustice has never been done to a
brave and generous people than this, which you, ignorant of our situation, of our history, of our laws,
of our customs, and of our principles, have dared to
perpetrate. You have not only been guilty of gross
injustice to a people, whom you know not, and who
aided you with a noble and disinterested enthusiasm;
but you have heaped shame and confusion upon

your own countrymen, and those who were once
your admirers, and would still, if you permitted it,
be your friends.

" Do you believe that we, who love freedom and our
fellow-men, are the heartless wretches that you describe, because we cannot at once do all that your
imagination conceives to be perfection, and which
we, who have the experimental knowledge, have the
irrefragable evidence to be destructive folly? You
have, in the unfortunate moment when you sent forth
that document (if it be your's) done an evil, which
no contrition can repair, no service can redeem. As
a Carolinian, I cannot reason with you upon facts,
of which you are ignorant. As an Irishman, I
bewail your infatuation. And, whilst I am doomed
to meet a variety of trials, one of the keenest and
bitterest of my feelings will be, that the most con-
tumelious insult, which was flung upon the land of
my adoption, was ungratefully and wantonly given
in the moment when she was flushed with a victory
won by American aid, by one whom I once valued
as a dear friend in the country of my birth.

" Should the Derrynane manifesto against the proud
Americans and their slave-holding States be a forgery, I should rejoice to learn the fact from yourself.
Should it be your production, I would say—in me
you shall find one amongst thousands of your countrymen, who will not succumb to your insult, nor
quail before your threat.

"I shall make no parade of my love of liberty, nor send you homilies upon my humanity. But whilst, with every Carolinian that I know, I lament an evil, which Britain has superinduced, and which we cannot at once remedy, I deny your right to interfere; and I pray you might succeed in raising the ruined population of Ireland to the level of the comforts of the Carolinian slave. Should you live to behold this result of your labors, you will have accomplished more than is expected by

"JOHN, Bishop of Charleston.

"To Daniel O'Connell, Esq."

The Hiberno-Americans, though wedded to the land of their adoption, still look back with "longing, lingering" affection to the place of their birth. Their first-love is dead to them; but it is never forgotten. Uxorem vivam amare voluptas: defunctam religio. This is an amiable feeling; and no one would blame it, if it were pure, or properly directed. But how can the same man be the friend of liberty in one country, and trample upon it in another? Strange and mysterious is the state of things here! The victims of political and of commercial tyranny meet together on the common soil of a new continent! The descendants of Ireland and of Africa are contending for the possession of a foreign land! The present inhabitants affect to depise them both; yet they are outvoted by the one, and will be outnumbered by the other!

The day after my visit to Canterbury, I removed from Brooklyn to Providence, Rhode Island. I had received from Mr. May a letter of introduction to Dr. Channing, who was at his country seat about thirty or forty miles from the city. Thither I proceeded to visit him, entirely at the suggestion of others; for, though he had been represented to me as a man of an expanded mind, who would probably be desirous of hearing the sentiments entertained in Europe on the conduct of those Americans, who had restricted the blessings of freedom to mere physical enjoyment, " and despised others" on account of their skins, yet I thought it more complimentary to the Doctor, to apply to him what Dr. Bentley has remarked in the case of an epidemical illusion. " All honorable men and good citizens would prefer to be considered as participating in the excitement, than as having been free from it, and opposed to it, without ever daring to resist, or check, or reduce it."

After some common-place observations, which the ceremony of introduction drew on, I stated, in allusion to something in the letter I had brought with me, that I had, during my residence in America, felt deeply interested in the condition of a large portion of the community, who appeared to be condemned, from no fault or crime on their part, to a state of degradation, of which no one who has never been out of Europe, could form an adequate conception.

I referred, among other instances, to the separation at meals between the two races. The Doctor asserted, in reply, that the feeling, which induced the white man to reject his colored brother from his table, was the same with that which excluded the servant from his master's society; and that the prejudice, which the feudal lord entertained against his serf, was analogous to the antipathy of which I had given an example. To this I objected, that the distinction, of which I spoke, was that of color not of rank: that the qualification, required for admittance to equality, might be obtained by the domestic, or his descendants, but was out of the reach of the Africo-American, till the Æthiopian was enabled to change his skin; and that I could not admit the analogy, without admitting that the persons, to whom it was applied, were to remain and be treated as servants,—the very thing against which I was contending:—the end I had in view being to classify men according to their character and condition, and not to confound the learned with the illiterate, or the wealthy with the indigent;—an arrangement that would be sure to mortify one party and embarrass the other. As for the serf, he had none of those political rights which the free black possessed:—he had the advantages neither of property nor of education. He was not excluded from social intercourse with freemen of the same class, and was subject to no further disabilities than were to be found in most communities during their progress to refinement. He was not marked as an object of insult and contempt, wherever he went—he was as much a man as his lord—he was not an outcast—a Pariah.

There were other prejudices in the world, I was told, equally painful to their objects, and equally deserving of our attention. The answer was that *they* were neither permanent nor general—that they were neither so odious to those who suffered from them, nor so disgraceful to those who cherished them: that few would defend, and none were afraid to condemn them, and that little improvement of the human mind could be looked for, while a superstition so degrading was permitted to weaken its powers and sully its attainments.

I was assured, that all those colored persons, who had come under the notice of the Doctor, were men of indifferent character; that the whole race were remarkable for want of sympathy with one another's misfortunes: and that, according to the evidence of a correspondent in Philadelphia, the generality of those of African descent in that city, were degraded to the lowest state.

To the first assertion I could merely object, that the experience of one man ought not to settle a question, involving the character and condition of millions; and that a comprehensive conclusion could not be drawn from a few limited cases. To the second, I replied, that all I had ever heard upon the subject from men who differed widely upon other points, concurred in ascribing qualities directly the reverse of those imputed by him, and that a contrary opinion was so prevalent as to throw suspicion on the free blacks, as assistants or accessaries in almost every case of escape from slavery. As for the testimony of the Philadelphian, little credit is due to a man, who deposes to facts that may be proved to be false by official documents, to be ignorant of which, is to be guilty of injustice towards those he condemns.

The Doctor stated, that he entertained no prejudice himself, being willing to sit at the same table with any one, and having remonstrated with the driver of a stage for not admitting his colored servant into his coach.

I was at a loss how to express myself upon a general subject before a person, who thus, as he had frequently done before, applied my observations to his own conduct. I contented myself with assuring him, that I should not have entered so fully into the subject, if he had not said that he was exempt from the prejudice in question *; though I could not

* The Doctor must have deceived himself here, or forgotten what he said to Mrs. Child, when he pronounced his judgment of her work on the Africo-Americans. He agreed, he told her, with her sentiments on slavery, but he disapproved of what she had written about equal rights. Such a concession, he thought, would lead to amalgamation—an event which he was

but think, that a circumstance he had previously
mentioned, would have afforded the driver a recrimi-
natory plea, if not a justification. The Doctor had
acknowledged to me that his black and his white
servants were in the habit of eating at separate
tables. The driver might have fairly answered—
" I do no more in my coach, than you do in your
kitchen. I wish to please my passengers, you your
servants. I cannot live without white passengers—
you can live just as well as you now do with black
servants."

A hint was then given that there were different
races of men, with various degrees of intellect, according to the discoveries of phrenology *. I ob-

surprised she should view with no abhorrence. Dr. Beecher,
of Cincinnati, made a similar observation to me. " Would
you," said he, " have us sully the pure blood we have received
from our English ancestors, by such alliances as a closer intimacy
with the other race would produce ?"

* " We undoubtedly feel ourselves to be all of one race ; and
this is well : we trace ourselves up to one pair, and feel the
same blood flowing in our veins. But do we understand our
spiritual brotherhood? Do we feel ourselves to be derived
from one Heavenly Parent, in whose image we are all made,
and whose perfection we may constantly approach? Do we
feel that there is one divine life in our own and in all souls ?
This seems to me the only true bond of man to man. Here is
a tie more sacred, more enduring, than all the ties of this
earth. Is it felt? and do we in consequence truly honour one
another?"—Dr. Channing's Discourses.

served that this circumstance, if correctly stated, entitled the inferior race to greater indulgence, and called for increased efforts to supply the deficiency;—that the correspondence between the material structure, and the mental operations, was ascribed to the influence of the latter over the former; and would, consequently, lead to an inference directly the reverse of that implied;—that no one's reception in general society depended on the quantity or the quality of his brain;—and that the proscription, against which I protested, was directed exclusively against the complexion. To an observation that none but the uneducated classes were infected with this antipathy, I replied by quoting the literary productions of the country, the sermons and speeches publicly delivered by its most eminent men, and what I had myself witnessed.

My remarks were declared to be erroneous or irrelevant. There was no reason, it was added, to suppose that any pain or humiliation was inflicted by these national customs*. He had never seen any

* " We have spoken of the inferiority and worthlessness of that dominion over others which has been coveted so greedily in all ages. We should rejoice could we convey some just idea of its moral turpitude. . . . . . No outrage, no injury can equal that which is perpetrated by him who would break down and subjugate the human mind; who would rob men of self-reverence; who would bring them to stand more in awe of outward authority, than of reason and conscience in their own souls; who

indication of the kind in his own house. He denied that antipathy was the cause, and asserted that it was the effect of slavery. I qualified what I had said upon this subject by referring to that well-known operation of the mind by which a reciprocal action takes place between two ideas, and that which was prior in time becomes posterior in influence. I may perhaps be excused for offering further explanation of my meaning, that the opinion, if false, may be corrected. We all know that habits are continued and extended by the feelings they have created, and how much difficulty is experienced in subduing affections long after the motives that induced them have ceased. The negro intellect stands lower in the estimation of a Virginian, than it did in that of Las Casas, or whoever it was that first recommended the employ- ment of African labor. This, in one sense, is the result of slavery, while in another and in a much stronger sense, it upholds it*. The Ma- hometans enslave the Christians, because they

would make himself a standard and law for his race; and shape, by force or terror, the free spirits of others after his own judge- ment and will."—Dr. Channing on Napoleon Bonaparte.

* Negroes were once not only thought inferior to us, but excluded from the rights of humanity. Fuller, in his " Holy State," while drawing a picture of a religious sailor, says:— " In the taking of a prize he most prizeth the men's lives whom he takes; though some of them may chance to be negroes

despise them; and the debasement to which they reduce them, confirms their contempt. When the people of the same nation, as the Africans, make slaves of one another, the latter are better treated, and no reason against their enfranchisement and elevation exists in any disdain that is felt for their minds, or in any apprehension of an intermixture with their masters. I insisted upon this distinction, because I feel convinced that if there were no prejudice in the northern States, there could be no slavery in the southern, while their union continues. Hence I observed to the Doctor, that the Indians, who had never, or very rarely, been treated as slaves, were suffering under the same sort of contempt as the blacks; that in those States where slavery had been abolished, the prejudice was so much more intense than where it still existed, that the planters themselves complain of it when they bring their slaves with them to the north.

If, said I, a man is despised not for his crimes, but for his own or his father's misfortunes, such injustice ought not to go unpunished or unexposed. The Doctor thought the best way to combat the prejudice was to elevate its object. This method I

or savages; and it is the custom of some to throw them overboard. But our captain counts the image of God nevertheless his image, cut in ebony as if done in ivory."

conceived was impracticable, as the rejection of moral distinctions was the very evil complained of. No impression, I was told, could be made by entreaty or remonstrance on habits so long formed; and that, therefore, it must be left to time and the better conduct of the aggrieved, to convert contumely into respect, and obtain those rights which are now denied.

I could not see how the white man's mind was to be enlightened from without, when no corrective was applied within*. I thought it neither just nor judicious to wait till jealousy was subdued by the presence of the very attentions and accomplishments it dreaded. I alluded to a statement just made, that the poorer classes of whites had been much offended with the abolitionists for their civility to the colored people, and the pains they took to educate their children. A few minutes after, the conversation turned on the difficulty that was felt in

---

* " The energy which is to carry forward the intellect of a people, belongs to private individuals, who devote themselves to lonely thought, who worship truth, who originate the views demanded by their age, who help us to throw off the yoke of established prejudices," &c.—Dr. Channing on Napoleon.

" Among these will be ranked, perhaps on the highest throne, the moral and religious reformer, who truly merits that name; who rises above his times; who is moved by a holy impulse to assail vicious establishments sustained by fierce passions and inveterate prejudices."—Dr. Channing on Milton.

procuring work for the blacks, with whom the whites refused to labor. This was a fact, that the Doctor, with all his knowledge of the race, had never heard of before. " Why," he asked, " should we not encourage them by dealing with them for what we want ?" " That," I replied, " would be adding fuel to the flame. It has just been said that the whites are much displeased with the kindness shewn them —how will they feel when their bread is thus taken from them by the very people they are jealous of? They want no favor or preference. All they claim is a fair trial; and that the evidence of color may not be suffered to outweigh those testimonies from character and conduct, which decide the merits of other men. Society owes them respect in proportion to the services they render it."

I mentioned that I should probably publish an account of what I had seen of the colored race in America, as, now that our colonial system had been changed, the subject would be interesting to many in England. The Doctor observed, that he, for one, had not the slightest objection that Europe should be minutely acquainted with the condition of the United States, f the account were just and fair. He had just before remarked, that it would be as well if the zealous friends of the African race would bestow some of their care upon those whom difference of rank subjects to exclusion and mortification. I made no answer: I could not apply the charge to myself without being guilty of discourtesy by imputing it. A suggestion was then made that rather surprised me. The Doctor thought that if some great genius were to appear among the colored people, the reputation he would obtain might be extended to his brethren, and their lot be ameliorated through the admiration and sympathy he would excite for himself and his race. It seemed hard indeed that the destiny of nearly three millions of human beings should be contingent on the appearance of a miracle; and the redemption of a whole nation be made to wait for the Avatar of " a faultless monster."

The Doctor informed me he had just heard that what he had predicted had occurred in our colonies —that the transition from forced to free labor was likely to throw many persons out of employment; and that freedom would thus be an injury instead of a benefit to a large portion of its objects. I replied, that the event alluded to, if it should take place, would confirm what the abolitionists had asserted, and the planters denied; since it would shew that the labor of slaves was more costly than that of free men, and that the same quantity of work could be done with fewer hands under the stimulus of wages; that the evil, if it was one, would find its own remedy, as the surplus number would soon be provided for out of that increase of capital which the compensation money, as well as a more profitable mode of agriculture, will create. The difficulty, however, that was anticipated has no existence; for the planters complain that the apprentices demand too high wages—a proof that labor is not redundant;—and are absolutely importing European workmen,—a proof that they wish it were so.

In the course of our discussion, the Doctor declared it, as the result of all his reflections on the matter, to be his firm conviction, that the best, and only way to assist the colored people, (I am obliged to repeat this odious expression,) would be to educate them in separate schools—in other words, to destroy the distinction by continuing it; and that the abolitionists had injured their cause by their imprudence. It was hardly worth while to answer, that no reform, religious or political, had ever been carried on by the "meek and gentle": that the violence complained of was the result, and not the occasion, of the opposition the cause had met with; and that it would be unjust to punish the client for the faults of his advocate *. This view of the subject, indeed,

---

* " Men of natural softness and timidity, of a sincere but effeminate virtue, will be apt to look on these bolder, hardier spirits as violent, perturbed, and uncharitable; and the charge will not be wholly groundless. But that deep feeling of evils, which is necessary to effectual conflict with them, and which marks God's most powerful messengers to mankind, cannot breathe itself in soft and tender accents. The deeply moved soul will speak strongly, and ought to speak strongly, so as to move and shake nations."—Dr. Channing on Milton.

is hardly reconcileable with the natural order of
events; which, in questions that concern national
changes, usually run in the following train: violent
attack on existing practices—persecution—sympathy
with the sufferer—reaction in public opinion—reformation.   As error never gains firm footing in the
human mind, unconnected with the imagination or
the affections, it is hardly fair to expect that truth
shall prevail without borrowing the weapons of her
enemy.   To treat men as philosophers, in order to
teach them philosophy, is to be no philosopher
one's self.

Throughout the whole of this protracted discussion, my opponent seemed to take it for granted that
it turned upon the claims of a race naturally inferior
to our own,—a method of begging the question
more suited to the predilections of the disputant,
than the common rules of logic.   That they were
doomed to be " hewers of wood and drawers of water " appeared to be a reasonable postulate.   They
were invariably spoken of as " servants," whose
proper place was in the kitchen ; where they were
to take their meals apart, because they did not complain of a distinction, which complaint would render
more galling ; and because no white servant would
remain in the establishment, if it were otherwise arranged,—a determination so utterly unworthy of notice, that no man who wishes to be respected by his
domestics, would allow them to decide upon the

usages of his own house, and no great or good mind would for a moment place personal convenience in collision with a sense of duty, or sacrifice principle to vulgar malevolence.

When I was told that the prejudice was invincible, and that no effort, therefore, should be made to subdue it, I could not admit either the premises or the conclusion, unless it were demonstrated that truth and reason had lost their influence on the national mind; and that it was the result, not the motive, of human actions, that ought to determine the line of our conduct, and regulate the conscience *. If Luther and Calvin, I argued, had thus reasoned, the world might still have been groaning under the yoke of spiritual oppression. The Doctor said it was a hardship to be deprived of work by the refusal of mechanics to associate with men of a different complexion. This reluctance, I begged leave to say, was encouraged and supported by a similar refusal, on the part of the wealthier portions of society, to admit, under any circumstances whatever, the

* " It is an important branch of the minister's duty to bring home the general principles of duty to the individual mind; to turn it upon itself; to rouse it to a resolute impartial survey of its own responsibilities and ill-deserts. And is not energy needed to break through the barriers of pride and self-love, and to place the individual before a tribunal in his own breast, as solemn and as searching as that which awaits him at the last day?"—Dr. Channing's Discourses.

class excluded to a participation of the courtesies
and refinements they enjoyed themselves. The carpenter, or blacksmith, was not more aggrieved than
the clergyman, or the physician; while the former
might see in the ignorance of his brother workman
an excuse, which might be supposed to be wanting
in the other case. It was not the mere privation of
a privilege, but the utter hopelessness of ever attaining it, that was felt as a grievance. It was the condemnation to a state of inferiority and contumely
that was so galling; it was the unnatural association
in the white man's mind between an indelible mark
that Divine wisdom had impressed on the skin, and
the character of the wearer, that constituted the
wrong complained of;—a wrong that nothing could
ever compensate or soften, an injustice that must
necessarily expose the son of Africa to oppression
and opprobrium, and shut him out from the enjoyment of those rights, which the declaration of his
country's independence had solemnly promised to
assure to all within its bosom.

The Doctor alleged as a proof of his regard for the
swarthy part of his fellow-citizens, that the " African
schools" of Boston had originated with him—a mani-
festation of kindness little in accordance with a wish
to abolish distinctions which it is calculated to perpetuate *. As contributors to the common prosperity,

* A large majority of citizens, at a public meeting at Salem,
(Massachusetts,) lately resolved, " that the school committee

these people have a right to share in the common fund;
to be partakers of the national justice, not recipients
of the national charity ; to be treated as citizens, not
as aliens. Why should the schoolmaster make a
distinction unknown to the tax-gatherer? Why
should there be common duties and separate privileges for the great mass of the population, living
under the same government, speaking the same language, and professing the same religion? In every
other case, and in every other country, moral qualities, or their presumed signs, are the land-marks
between the various ranks,—while from the cradle
to the grave, the class in question find their physical peculiarities operating against them as a pre-
sumptive proof of demerit, and a verdict of guilty
to the good and the bad alike. " How can they

be instructed to provide a school in some convenient place for
the instruction of colored children, belonging to the town; and
to remove said children, now in the public schools, to said
school." In the cities, where this class of people are more
numerous, the schools they attend, are distinct from the rest.
Where, from reasons of economy, a different arrangement prevails, it seems that additional expense is to be incurred, with
the view of gratifying the abominable jealousies of the white
people. It is easy to see both the motives and the effects of
this public announcement. It encourages the evil-disposed by
the example it gives; and points out the intended victim of
their brutality, by driving deeper in the brand that marks him.
The " higher orders " are guiltless of the slaughter;—they
merely put up the game.

be our friends," they ask, " who select the most susceptible periods of life, to impress on the minds of both races, a feeling of hostility and estrangement, incompatible with benevolent and Christian affections? What cordiality could there ever be between orthodoxy and heresy, if their respective adherents were studiously separated in the cradle— the college—the convivial assembly—the council-room—and the cemetery?" This line of argument I could not of course take up in the presence of Dr. Channing, though, perhaps, it would be as well for him to remember that the Unitarians were persecuted because they would not change their creed; while the negro is persecuted because he cannot change his complexion.

The most striking feature in what passed, during this interview, was the attempt of a philosopher, to find in the extent and intensity of a prejudice a reason for its continuance,—to confound the subject of superstition with its victim, (as if the best way to cure Cotton Mather of witch-finding would have been to teach the old women of Salem divinity, or as if a monomaniac could be restored to reason by placing the object of his illusion in a new position,) and to leave the task of correction not to the conscience of the proud man, but the conduct of him whom he scorns for not having the "wedding garment" he wears himself. " I should be sorry," said the reverend Doctor, " to say any thing that may

lessen the sympathy you feel for the blacks." I
assured him that I did not feel for them, because they
differed from me in complexion, but because they
resembled me in mind. As one branch of the human family, they are entitled to my sympathy, as
much as any other. The humblest of them is one
of those "little ones," to offend whom, is to offend
the great Father of all. The conversation concluded
with an observation, from the other side, that prejudices and follies existed in every country, and that
this was one of the consequences of the existing
state of society:—a truism I was so little inclined to
controvert, that it had formed the ground-work of
all that I had been saying.

As for the inequalities which prevail in the world,
whatever grievances may attend them fall indiscriminately on all, as the wealth, and rank, and vanity,
and ambition, in which they originate, change hands.
One evil can never sanction another; nor is it a valid
objection to the reformation of an abuse, that it cannot embrace all. I had spoken with considerable
warmth and earnestness; but, I trust, without forgetting what was due from a stranger to a distinguished man in his own house. I thought it right,
however, to apologize for the excess which had appeared on my part, both of zeal and of loquacity. I
should probably have exhibited less of the former, if
there had been more of the latter on the other side.
But the Doctor throughout was extremely cold and

reserved, and seemed to weigh every word before he gave it utterance;—urging me to continue, as if to take time for reflection. Having declined to partake of the refreshment which was politely offered me, I took my leave of this celebrated writer.

I have related the details of what passed on this occasion with the same object that would lead an Eastern traveller to record the opinions of a high-caste Brahmin. What an humiliating contrast does the acknowledged cradle of civilization present with its boasted asylum! How great is the difference between the convert to Unitarianism in the east, and its champion in the west!—between Rammohun Roy and Dr. Channing! The Shaster could not take away moral courage from the one, nor the Bible give it to the other. In the darkest ages of cruelty and ignorance, the cause of truth and justice has found its friends and martyrs. But who, in the whole compass of American literature, has stood up against the brutal superstition of his country? What will posterity say, when they see, among the most distinguished of her writers, not one solitary instance of a man who was willing to sacrifice the paltry ambition of the hour to principle;—not one who could rise above the infected atmosphere around him;—not one who had mind enough to perceive the gross idolatry of his contemporaries, or heart enough to denounce it?—while the few who are destined to take the lead

as moral teachers, have been reproved for their bold-
ness by those who have usurped the throne, and are
repelled from a nearer approach by the very persons
who ought to have honored them with their applause,
and aided them with their co-operation.

A few days after my visit to Dr. Channing, I was
informed by one of his friends, who had just seen
him, that he had called me an " enthusiast ":—an
appellation that implies the same difference between
his feelings and mine, that the word " heretic " does
between his opinions and those of his orthodox opponents.

Before I left America, the Doctor preached a ser-
mon against slavery,—in consequence, I was told, of
what had passed between us. But that could not be
the case, as I had said nothing to him on the subject; having purposely separated the question as it
bears on the South and on the North, and confining
my observations to the prejudice that prevails in the
latter,—a point, I think, of greater importance, because I believe the other hangs upon it. The distinction was well drawn by a Haytian, while conversing with an American, from whom I had the
anecdote. " If I were a white," said he, " I would
submit to treatment from the Algerines or Tripoli-
tans, from which neither William of England, nor
Louis Philip of France, would be exempted : but I
would rather die than suffer the infliction of chains

on account of my skin." The first case he viewed as a chance of war—a right of conquest: the other an outrage to humanity—a personal insult.

An incident that occurred some years back in Kentucky, shews how completely the very existence of American slavery depends upon the prejudice against color,—diverting the sense of justice, and the sympathy due to human suffering, from their natural channels. " A laudable indignation", says the Emporium of Louisville, " was universally manifested among our citizens, and even among our blacks, on Saturday last, by the exposure of a woman and two children for sale by public auction, at the front of our principal tavern. This woman and children were as white as any of our citizens: indeed, we scarcely ever saw a child with a fairer or clearer complexion than the younger one. That they were not slaves, we do not pretend to say; but there was something so revolting to the feelings at the sight of this woman and children exposed to sale by their young master,—it excited such an association of ideas in the mind of every one,—it brought to recollection so forcibly the morality of slave-holding States,—that not a person was found to make an offer for them."

The account of this interview, which I had read from my journal to some of the Doctor's friends, I was particularly requested not to publish; as they thought it might injure our cause, by exciting a feeling of hostility to it among those who are attached to him. This consideration, if it be valid, affords an additional reason why I *should* publish it ; as it shews what are the chief obstacles that obstruct a fair and impartial inquiry into this momentous subject. If friendship is to stand in the way of justice, and humanity wait upon personal feeling,—let it be known, that we may not over-rate our forces. I replied, that I never would admit such a principle : we must look to Truth, and not to Socrates. The greater part of my manuscript was seen by several of my American friends, and they approved of it. Any alterations it may have undergone, were made with a view to soften what might be thought harsh. I mention this to prove honesty of intention. I insist on it no further. If I am to lose their respect, be it so. I shall at least retain my own. If I have done any man injustice, the same motive which led to an unintentional wrong, will prompt a free and an open reparation.

That the Unitarians, as a body, should, while they profess to be the fearless and unbiassed advocates of freedom, have as yet done nothing to shew their sincerity, by putting into practice those principles which have cost nobler men their lives or their fortunes, is, however discreditable to America, no matter for surprise. What Jew will admit ham to his table, when the High Priest will not eat pork ? Parties, coteries, and sects are governed by their leaders. Whether in politics, literature, or religion, " man-worship," as it is termed, seems to be the fashion of the country. People admire the dial-plate, and forget the works which alone give it value. The Unitarians know their duty, but they dare not act up to it *. In the Christian Examiner, one of their periodical publications (1830), is the following passage: " There is nothing more humbling than the history of prejudices, when they have ceased to awaken any feeling. . . . . We feel that there must be a want of generosity in the breast that harbors and defends them, and that nothing can be done for moral or intellectual improvement till they are done away. But such prejudices become alarming, when they come armed with the authority of numbers. Then truth lies brow-beaten and still, leaving its wrongs to be redressed by the reformer, Time. The

* The Pope at Rome was more liberal two hundred years ago, than the " liberals " at Boston are now. The Catholic missionaries in Africa received instructions from home, in 1633, requiring them to put a stop to the slave-trade. " Les missionaires Capuçins reçurent une lettre du Cardinal Cibo, au nom du sacré college. Elle contenait des plaintes amères sur la continuation de la vente des esclaves, et des instances pour faire cesser enfin cet odieux usage. Mais ils virent peu d'apparence de pouvoir executer les ordres du Saint Siege, parce que le commerce du pays consiste uniquement en ivoire et dans la traite des esclaves."—Prevot. Histoire Générale des Voyages, 12. 186.

The missionaries succeeded in excluding the English from the trade.—The latter " made up " for the interruption afterwards.

prejudice passes from breast to breast, and from generation to generation. Though in the hearts of a few, it was an obstinate and passive affection, in the hearts of many, it grows savage, blood-thirsty, and revengeful." A recent number of this journal contains a defence of slavery, or such a palliation of its guilt, as amounts to a vindication. Not long ago a promise was made to Mr. May, that an article he had written in favor of emancipation, should be inserted in its columns. It was not, however, admitted; the refusal being accompanied with this observation. " It would be against the interest of the work to publish such an essay in it."

Before I left Providence, I had the pleasure of being introduced to the venerable Moses Brown, then in his ninety-sixth year—a consistent member of the Society of Friends, who, when the rights of the negro were little known and less cared for, carried out into unrestricted practice, more than sixty years ago, the great principle that " all men are to be protected in the possession of personal liberty and the pursuit of happiness." Not only did this upright Quaker emancipate his slaves: he scrupulously paid them the difference between the value of the labor he had drawn from them, while in his " service," and the food and clothing he had given them. I was presented by one of the most active abolitionists in the city (George Benson) with a copy of the manumission papers, drawn up by him and properly attested, on this occasion. The document is dated the 10th of the 11th Month, 1773.

In the preamble the writer says: " Whereas I am clearly convinced that the buying and selling men of what color soever as slaves, is contrary to the Divine mind, manifest in the consciences of all men, however some may smother and neglect its reprovings, and being also made sensible that the holding negroes in slavery, however kindly treated by their masters, has a great tendency to encourage the iniquitous traffic and practice of importing them from their native country, and is contrary to that justice, mercy, and humility, enjoined as the duty of every Christian, I do therefore, " &c.

Speaking of one, a child of two years of age, he says: " She having the same natural right, I hereby give her the same power, as my own children, to take and use her freedom, enjoining upon my heirs a careful watch over her for her good, and that they, in case I be taken hence, give her suitable education; or, if she be bound out, that they take care in that and all other respects as much as to white children, " &c. Addressing the objects of his kindness, he thus expresses himself. " For the encouragement to such sober prudence and industry, I hereby give to the first six named, the other three having good trades, the use of one acre of land, as marked off on my farm, as long as you improve it to good purpose.

I now no longer consider you as slaves, nor myself as your master, but your friend; and, so long as you behave well, may you expect my further countenance, support, and assistance," &c.   " Receive your liberty with a humble sense of its being a favor from the great King of heaven and earth, who, through his light that shines upon the consciences of all men, black as well as white, thereby sheweth us what is good, and that the Lord's requiring each of us to do justice, to love mercy, and to walk humbly with our God, is the cause of this my duty to you.   Be therefore watchful and attentive to that divine teaching in your own minds," &c.

Moses Brown was a member of the Pennsylvania Society, incorporated by the legislature of the State in 1789, for promoting the abolition of slavery.   His name appears on the list among those of Franklin, Rush, Jay, Benjamin West, Granville Sharp, Thomas Day (author of Sandford and Merton), Thomas Clarkson, Richard Price, David Barclay, William Pitt, J. C. Lettsom, l'Abbé Raynal, and le Marquis de la Fayette.

The act which passed, in 1780, for the gradual abolition of slavery in the Commonwealth of Pennsylvania, has this sentiment in the preamble.   " Weaned by a long course of experience from those narrow prejudices and partialities we had imbibed, we find our hearts enlarged with kindness and benevolence, towards men of all conditions and nations; and we conceive ourselves at this particular period extraordinarily called upon by the blessings we have received to manifest the sincerity of our profession, and to give a substantial proof of our gratitude." *

Rhode Island, while yet a colony, prohibited slavery so early as the middle of the 17th century. This fact was discovered among the records of the State, and communicated to the public through one of its journals, by the benevolent father of the abolitionists. The document is as follows.

" At a general court, held at Warwick, the 18th of May, 1652. Whereas there is a common course practised among Englishmen to buy negroes to that end they may have them for service or slaves for ever : for the preventing of such practices among us, let it be ordered, that no black mankind, or white being, shall be forced by covenant, bond, or otherwise, to serve any man or his assignees, longer than ten years, or until they come to be twenty-four years of age, if they be taken in under fourteen, from the time

---

* Henry the Eighth of England, in emancipating two of his villeins, made use of an expression closely resembling what may be found in the above document. " Whereas God created all men free; but afterwards the laws and customs of nations subjected some under the yoke of servitude, we think it is pious and meritorious with God, to manumit Henry Knight, a tailor, and John Herne, a husbandman, our natives, as being born within the manor of Stoke Clymmysland, in our county of Cornwall," &c.

of their coming within the liberties of this colony;—
at the end or term of ten years to set them free, as the
manner is with the English servants. And that man,
that will not let them go free, or shall sell them away
elsewhere, to that end they may be enslaved to
others for a longer time, he or they shall forfeit to
the colony forty pounds." Moses Brown gives the
names of the members from whom this memorable
enactment proceeded. It appears, from it, that
whites as well as blacks were slaves, and distinguished from the " redemptioners." It was at that
time, and long after, the policy of European govern-
ments to prohibit the emigration of mechanics and
artisans. Labor was therefore extremely scarce
in the new world; and its high price led to the
enormity, which the law thus attempted to prevent.

Though Rhode Island was the first to abolish
slavery, it was the last to give up the profits of the
slave-trade, and still encourages the system by punishing, with a fine of 300 dollars and five or three
years' imprisonment, any one who assists a slave to
escape. The citizens of this State carried on the
abominable traffic long after it had been declared
illegal by the general government. About ten
years ago, a vessel belonging to a Rhode-islander,
was seized and condemned for having been engaged in the slave-trade. No buyer, however,
could be found, when the sale took place, among
his fellow-citizens; till the confiscated goods were

at last purchased by a Bostonian, who had come from Massachusetts for the express purpose. Such was the general indignation against this man for daring to brave public opinion, which had manifested itself so strongly in favor of the slave-trader, that he was seized by the people, who had assembled on the occasion, and his ears were cut off. This anecdote was told me by Mr. Peter A. Jay*, of New York,—a man little inclined by sympathy with the blacks to exaggerate on the subject, as he remarked, at the same time, that the slaves were generally well treated, and that he had never known one, who had been manumitted and turned out well. As he had not been into the South, he probably spoke the sentiments of others. He added that his country had done itself honor by abolishing slavery in so many States. If the humanity, for which Mr. Jay vouched, be like the justice, of which he boasted, the poor slave has but a sorry protection. The colored man owes nothing to the Ma-

* Mr. Peter A. Jay, who is descended from a Huguenot family, which the fame of his father, during the struggle for American liberty, has rendered illustrious, is well known in New York for the active aid he affords to its numerous charities. His brother (Mr. William Jay) has just excited an extraordinary interest in America, by a work entitled " An Inquiry into the Colonization and Anti-Slavery Societies ". It will probably be republished in this country; and the proceeds of the sale will form a scholarship for a colored student at the Auburn Theological Seminary.

numission Society or his country's legislature. His master's whip was more tolerable than the finger of scorn now pointed at him. An American citizen has as much right to social equality as an American bondman to personal freedom. In denying the former, the North has lost what little merit there was in granting the latter.

The following is extracted from a memorial presented to the legislature of Connecticut in 1834, and signed by a long list of its most distinguished constituents. "The white man cannot labor upon equal terms with the negro. Those who have just emerged from a state of barbarism or slavery have few artificial wants. Regardless of the decencies of life, and improvident of the future, the black can afford his services at a lower price than the white man. And as he is, in caste, below the influence of public opinion, he seldom hesitates in supplying any contingent wants, without the ceremony of contracts, or the efforts of toil. If native indolence should deter him from this course, he has no compunctions in supplying himself from the public store-house, as a legal pauper. Whenever they come into competition, therefore, the white man is deprived of employment, or is forced to labor for less than he requires. He is compelled to yield the market to the African, and, with his family, ultimately becomes the tenant of an alms-house, or is driven from the State, to seek a better lot in

Western wilds. Thus have thousands of our most valuable citizens been banished from home and kindred, for the accommodation of the most debased race that the civilized world has ever seen, and whom the false philosophy of enthusiasts is hourly inviting to deprive us of the benefits of civilized society."

The above picture will be rather a " poser" to our protesting peers.—Instead of the whites driving away the blacks, the blacks are driving away the whites. What a curious country! the same people are driven from the South because the negro is a slave, and from the North, because he is free. The West, however, gains by it. Here they may mingle their tears together, and exchange consolation. But they will not escape, even in the wilderness; the horrid black man will find them out some day. It is a hard case:—the African is the evil genius of the American.

CHAPTER XXX.

Boston.—Blind distinguishing colors.—Judge Story's Charge.—
" Row" at Harvard University.—Nunnery burnt down by Boston Mob.—Brotherly Love between Protestants and Catholics
mutual.—Lowell.—American Manufactures.—School at Canaan.—Daniel Webster.—Students driven from Lane Seminary.—Academical " Gag-laws."

At Boston, to which place I went on the 1st of
September, I saw a cousin of Peter Vicey. She
gave the same account of what passed in Virginia,
on the establishment of their claim to liberty, as
was given me by the colonists in Ohio. She was
married to a man, of whom I heard a very favorable report from Mr. Child. She stated that she had
had great difficulty in obtaining her papers of freedom from the agent, William Wickham, as he refused to let her have them, because she would not
accompany the party who had gone into Ohio.
When she had at last succeeded in her object, he
told her there was money due to her, and he would
remit it to her at Boston, whither she was going.
She applied for it several times, through a lawyer;

but not one cent did she ever get from William Wickham. Her husband informed me that a friend had once seen a copy of Mr. Gist's will in Virginia, but had forgotten the contents.

Among the many instances which I was doomed to hear of the national bigotry, were one or two particularly deserving of notice. It is an established fact that blindness is more prevalent among the blacks than the whites; yet none of them are allowed to partake of the benefits which the asylum, lately established at Boston, affords to those who are afflicted with this infirmity. There was an application made for admission, by persons who had befriended a poor colored child that was blind,— but without effect, though the inhabitants of the town where he lived, petitioned the legislature in his favor. Those with whom the election rested decided against him. A letter from one of the poor boy's friends, (Benjamin Davenport,) to a member of the legislature says, " the reason assigned was because he had a colored skin. The Governor informed me that he had no objection to granting him a certificate; but the Trustees objected. He also informed me, that the Institution received nearly 3000 dollars last year from the unexpended appropriation to the deaf and dumb, making about 9000 dollars from the State last year. I understand the objection made by Dr. Howe, who seems to be the Principal of the Institution, is, if they should have pupils from the South, their parents or friends would not like to have them in the same school with colored children. I am not aware that the legislature intended any distinction of color, when they made the grant; nor do I believe they would countenance it." The boy, thus rejected, was remarkable for goodness of disposition and acuteness of mind. Dr. Howe is well known in America as a Philhellenist.

Another instance refers to the case of juvenile offenders, who were declared to be inadmissible at the house of reformation, on account of their complexion. But, perhaps, the strongest example of this vile feeling is to be seen in the conduct of Judge Story, while addressing a jury, who were trying a white man on a charge of murder. The victim of his savage ferocity was the steward or cook of a vessel he commanded. He had beaten and flogged him till he died. Three colored men of unexceptionable character deposed to the fact, of which they had been eye-witnesses. All suspicion of concert or collusion between the witnesses was precluded by the variation in its details of the evidence they gave. The defence was that the deceased had died from the effects of sickness, and not from the blows he had received. His wife, however, swore that he was in good health when he left her; that she had never heard of his having been ill; and that he had always had an excellent constitution. The prisoner was acquitted; the judge having told the jury that they must deduct from the weight of testimony, produced by the witnesses, the probable influence of their prejudices against a man of a different color from their own. No allusion whatever was made to a similar feeling on the other side; though it was just as likely to operate in favor of a white man as against him. Any one unacquainted with the state of the public mind and the character of the judge, would have supposed that the whites alone were the victims of an unreasonable prejudice.

Such an observation from the bench, in open court, in a trial for a brutal assault, accompanied with fatal effects and very suspicious circumstances, proclaims more clearly and more strikingly the diabolical spirit which pervades the nation, than a thousand anecdotes illustrative of what is practised by individuals in private life. Public opinion took part with the accused, and the judge congratulated him on an acquittal, by which his " character was fully vindicated."

When the examination of the public schools took place last year, the African schools, as they are called, were omitted in the list advertised, though it was particularly requested that a notice, relative to them, should be inserted at the same time in the papers. The pupils that attend them were not allowed to join in the procession, which greeted the President when he arrived in the city on his tour. The reason alleged was, that it would be offensive to a southerner if the colored children should turn out to receive him. A white man, who had the care of one of these schools, was convicted of having been in the habit of corrupting the morals of the young women under his care. He protested his innocence, and complained that all his predecessors had labored unjustly under the same imputation. The proofs against him were conclusive of his guilt, yet he was continued in his place under some pretence or other. His predecessors were probably as bad as himself. Few care for these children ; their virtues are a reproach to those who despise them. Why should they be punished or checked by the scorner, who encourage and promote those vices that give him an excuse for his contempt? He ought to thank them for helping him to keep the " niggers" down. A proper teacher is now appointed to the school in question.

During the preceding summer the spirit of insubordination had exhibited itself at Harvard University, with a degree of violence that called for strong measures of repression. One of the Freshman-class had insulted the Greek tutor, by telling him, when informed that it was expected he would translate whatever passage or word was proposed to him, that " he should pay no attention to the request." " I do not recognise your authority," was his expres-

sion. He refused to make any apology, and left
the college, with permission, and without censure
from the authorities. The junior class, though
urged by him not to interfere, espoused his cause
with great warmth, and proceeded, from one step to
another, in a course of outrage and annoyance, inconsistent with every principle of academical discipline. They broke the windows and furniture of
the offending teacher, assaulted both the officers of
the institution and the watch employed to protect
the property of the college; and interrupted at various times, by noises and brawlings, the religious
services of the place. This rebellious disposition
extended itself to the whole body of the under-
graduates; and the senior class issued a circular,
with no address, but with ample meaning. By this
document, they came forward as the vindicators of
their younger associates, and the accusers of the
president, who had threatened an appeal to the legal
tribunals of the country, if the riots were not dis-
continued. This resolution they characterised as
indiscreet, and incompatible with the relation in
which he stood of father to the pupils. After much
discussion on both sides, with the usual accompaniments of misrepresentation and disingenuousness
imputed and retorted, the whole Sophomore (or se-
cond-year) class, except three, were dismissed,—
re-admissible, however, after the ensuing commencement, on passing a fresh examination and producing

certificates of good conduct. Of the freshman-class several were dismissed for various periods, and for various offences. Indictments were found against three of the Sophomores for trespass, and another against one of them for an assault upon the college-watch at night. Seven of the senior class were dismissed for an indefinite time ; or, as the phrase is with us, rusticated *sine die.*

All these matters were laid before the Board of Overseers, who appointed a committee of inquiry, adopted the report it laid before them, and resolved, at a meeting held by them at the council chamber, Aug. 25th, 1834,—" 1st. That the students of Harvard University have no just or equitable claim to exemption from prosecution before the civil and criminal tribunals of the commonwealth for trespasses upon property or against persons, whether belonging to the University or otherwise. 2dly. That the proceedings of the President and Faculty of Harvard University, on the occasion of the recent riots and disturbances among the students at that seminary, meet with the entire approbation of the board. 3dly. That the circular published in the name of the senior class of Harvard University, relating to the recent riotous disturbances among the students at that seminary, is of a disorderly character, and entirely inconsistent with the station and duties of undergraduates at the University."

The committee, while it condemned the con-

duct of the students, employed language as little
appropriate to the rank of its members as to the
object they profess to have in view—of calming
and preventing the effervescence of juvenile irri-
tability. The following passage from the report will
shew how little the excited state of feeling had
cooled down among those who framed or adopted it.
" It is time that all the students of Harvard University should distinctly understand, that they have
no privilege of immunity for acts of violence and
outrage against persons or property, even though
belonging to the University. That if one portion of
them will brutalize themselves by deeds fit only for
the most debased of the human species, and if the
other portion of them, to screen them from detection
and punishment, will have neither eyes to see nor
ears to hear, nor a tongue to speak the truth, there
are tribunals in the country armed with powers not
only to repair the damages of property destroyed or
purloined, but to compel the delivery of testimony,
and to tear from their bosoms, upon the pains and
penalties of perjury, the guilty secret of crimes committed by their associates. That the exemption
from the grasp of these tribunals is an indulgence
always within the discretion of the government of
the University to withdraw ; and that, if they claim
from the president and instructors, who superintend
their education, the tenderness and forbearance of
parents towards their children, it must be upon the

just and equitable condition, that they shall fashion
their conduct towards those, their adopted parents,
by the rules of subordination and of submission enjoined by the laws of God and man upon the
dutiful child."

The circular of the senior class is composed in a
tone of defiance and accusation, that even the intemperate language it elicited from the authorities,
would not have justified. Some of the passages are
curious; as they illustrate, in a most striking manner, the deep-rooted alienation that exists between
the northern and southern sections of the Union.
" We understand," say these youthful malcontents,
" that the president has publicly denied ever having
declared to southerners that he did not wish any of
them in the college, or advised them to go somewhere
else; but, on investigation, we find that there are
many, who are willing to testify on oath, when it
shall be required, that he has used such language
towards them. Such observations may be forgotten
by those who make them; but they are not soon or
readily effaced from the memory of those to whom
they are addressed." The circular terminates with
these words :—" After a careful investigation of
facts, we are of opinion that the late disturbances in
the University have not been altogether 'without
cause or apology,' as stated in the president's circular; and, although we declare our decided disapprobation of all the depredations and outrages which

have been committed, yet we must say, they are not without provocation, and that the guilt lies by no means upon the students alone.

" Perhaps the circumstances which we have related, have been only the immediate occasion of the recent disturbances. The causes have been long in operation. Besides the local prejudices to which we have above alluded, the manners of President Quincy towards many of the students have not been such as to conciliate their esteem or affection. His defective memory, and the natural impetuosity of his character, often give him the appearance of acting in an arbitrary and capricious manner; and though his friends allow his sincerity and integrity, yet it cannot be wondered at, that many of the students, whom he has not made his friends, should entertain a different opinion. In relating these circumstances, we have endeavoured to be as impartial as possible, and have stated no fact, for the truth of which we have not obtained positive evidence."

One of the riotous students, having entered a plea of nolo contendere, was fined twenty dollars and costs on one indictment, and ten dollars with costs on another. Other punishments followed—to what amount or in how many cases I know not. Discipline was restored, and nothing occurred to prevent or disturb the " Commencement."

On the 8th I left Boston, with two friends, for Concord, in New Hampshire, and proceeded next day to Canaan, through Andover—upwards of 100 miles from the former city. Part of the way the driver of the stage had six horses in hand. He told me he sometimes drove eight in that way. As we came out of Boston, we passed the ruins of a Catholic convent, which had not long before been destroyed by a mob, excited by a spirit of religious intolerance against an innocent community of help-less women and children. They had been told that a young person was forcibly confined there; and, having been prepared for any kind of violence by some inflammatory sermons that had just been preach-ed from an orthodox pulpit, these advocates for summary conviction, and speedy punishment, as-sembled in full force and fury at the doors of the hated building, and set fire to it. The inmates, who were allowed some sort of warning, fled with the ut-most fear and precipitation, and escaped with the loss of all their property, but the little they had on them; having suffered much in their attempts to get away *. These outrages were but a continuance, in another form, of what had been enacted at New York, Philadelphia, and other places. The monster, which the public press had unmuzzled and unchained, was

---

* Some of the pupils were Protestants. One of them, when she first went to the convent, objected to the term " Superior." She acknowledged no superior, she said. Perhaps she thought that as " Governor " does not mean Superior, " Superior " could not mean Governess. " Subject " sounds harsh and insulting to American ears, though its correlative " government " is in constant use.

roaring for his prey; and those who had turned him
out of his den, now began to tremble for themselves.
Various schemes were devised to tame him; and a
municipal force was talked of against evils, which
were no longer to be tolerated because they were indiscriminate. The nation, it was said, was disgraced
by such proceedings; and the same men, who had
urged the populace to put down discussion by force,
now complained that religious liberty was endangered by the excesses they had themselves suggested
and sanctioned.

There were about sixty female children, besides
adults, in the Charleston convent when it was
attacked :—one of the latter in the last stage of con-
sumption, another subject to convulsion fits, and the
unconscious cause of the riot in a state of delirium,
brought on by the violence committed. When the
fire-engines arrived from the city, those who had the
charge of them refused to work them. All this was,
as the Committee of Inquiry reported, " perpetrated
in the presence of men vested with authority, and of
multitudes of citizens, while not one arm was lifted
in defence of helpless women and children, or in
vindication of the violated laws of God and man.
The spirit of violence, sacrilege, and plunder, reigned
triumphant. Crime alone seemed to confer courage,
while humanity, manhood, and patriotism, quailed or
stood irresolute and confounded in its presence." The
committee speak of the outrage as " an event of fearful

import, as well as the profoundest shame and humiliation."   " It has come upon us," they say, " like the
shock of an earthquake, and has disclosed a state of
society and of public sentiment, of which we believe
no man was before aware."   No wonder, indeed,
that the profoundest ignorance of the true state of
the country should prevail, when such sentiments as
the following could be addressed to the community
by those, who were expressly appointed to investigate the causes of this attack upon its tranquillity :—
sentiments, that pay homage to vulgar prejudice at
the very moment its bitter fruits are reprobated—
sentiments, that encourage religious intolerance,
while those, who utter them, would arrest the hand
it has put in motion.   " They lay aside "—I quote
the very words of the Committee,—" they lay aside
all questions of indemnifying the sufferers, as means
of aiding in the support of the Catholic faith.   Of their
individual feelings and opinions upon that subject,
their fellow-citizens can have no doubt; but they
look upon the obligations of justice as of higher import, and more deeply affecting our welfare as a
political community."   The first prisoner tried on a
capital indictment for this riot was acquitted.

There is a bitter feeling of animosity in many
parts of the Union against the Catholics.   The
Secretary of the Hartford County Education Society
said in his report in 1833: " Who that loves his
country or the true church of God, can be willing to

see Popery spread over the land?—a religion essentially at variance with all our civil and our religious institutions :—a religion, of which it has been truly said, that if it does not find a people vicious, it will soon make them so." " Beloved brethren," says Dr. Scudder to the pious young men of the Methodist, Baptist, &c., " you may live to see the day when the Popish Inquisition shall be transferred to America. You may live to see the day, when your Protestant brethren in the West will be obliged to lay down their lives by refusing to pay their supreme adorations to a piece of bread. You may live to see the day, when the blood-thirsty Roman Priests, who have sworn to do all they can to extirpate those out of their communion, plunge their daggers into their bosoms, and witness rivers of blood flowing down your streets. You may live to see the day, when another Papal monster, just made drunk with the blood of saints, and with the blood of the martyrs of Jesus, will go, at the head of a procession, to the Church of Saint Mark, to return thanks to Almighty God for such a horrible massacre," &c.

The above extracts are from a work printed and published at Boston in 1833. A passage in one of the notes may almost be supposed to have led to the Charleston outrage. " It is a subject which demands the most serious consideration of the judicial department of our nation, whether they should allow Roman Catholic priests to establish nunneries where the

' black veil' is taken. Such, in fact, are prisons in which females are kept locked up for ever. It is true they enter them voluntarily at first; but the question is, do they voluntarily remain there? It should be remembered that they are introduced into them at a tender age, &c. They have no hopes of escape. The bare mention of a wish to leave, might, in many instances, be followed with a deadly poisonous draught."

Allusions are made of a nature too indelicate to be quoted. The Catholics are not behind their opponents in illiberality, if we may judge from certain resolutions they lately passed at New Orleans, against a Presbyterian minister, for slandering them in an address he had delivered at Hartford, in Connecticut. After stating that his congregation had not succeeded in exculpating him from the charge, they resolved, that his residence among them was fraught with danger to the peace of the community;—that he be requested to leave the city;—and that, " notwithstanding the people of New Orleans would be pleased to enjoy the favorable opinion of their Northern brethren, yet they will never consent to sacrifice their own self-respect by adopting their opinions, and by becoming the dupes of a fanatical and aspiring priesthood."

A New Orleans paper calls the meeting on this occasion " one of the largest, decidedly, which ever took place" in that city.

Had it not been for the Catholic Bishop, the Irish at Boston and in the neighborhood would have retaliated on the Protestant churches, and the college at Cambridge, for the insult thus offered to their religion. It was said they had provided themselves with arms. The dislike which prevails almost universally against the Irish, does not originate entirely in religious differences. One of its most fruitful sources is the jealousy of the working-classes, who consider them intruders, and complain that they take the bread out of their mouths, by overstocking the labor-market. One man observed to me, that a law ought to be passed to send them back to Europe :— another said that such a law *had* passed. Sentiments of this kind met my ear wherever I went. Scarcely any one stood up in defence of a people whose faults would cease or be softened down by the removal of those insults which aggravate, if they have not produced, them.

We passed through Lowell,—the embryo-Manchester of the United States. The persons employed in the factories were well-dressed, and appeared to be in easy circumstances. A committee, appointed by the Friends of American Industry, to inquire into the state of the cotton manufactures, reported, in 1832, that " In many factories the proprietors have instituted savings' banks, to encourage the economy of the operatives, by enabling them to deposit such portions, however small, of their earnings, as they could spare; the proprietors allowing a moderate rate of interest, and being responsible for the safety of the capital. In one factory, which has made a return on this subject to the committee, where the wages amount to about 60,000 dollars per annum, the fund thus laid by has accumulated, in four years, to the sum of 26,400 dollars, or about eleven per cent. on the whole amount of wages paid." Two things recorded in this document are highly honorable to the national character. One is, that three months in the year are generally allowed, for the purposes of education, to the children employed; and, in the larger factories, schools are maintained at the expense of the establishment, for all persons connected with them. The other is, that many instances had occurred, within the personal knowledge of some of the committee, of young women applying what they had saved from their wages to pay off the mortgages upon their fathers' farms.

The Americans are trying to force manufactures; forgetting that their perfection too often proceeds from the low value of human labor, and is accompanied with a large mass of human misery. An exhibition of hot-house skill may gratify national pride; but national wealth would increase by the same industry, if left to itself, which, when employed in erecting pyramids, impoverishes the country it embellishes. The phrase " American system", like the words " patriotic" and " conservative", acts as a

charm on those whose sentiments are in perfect accordance with the presumed correctness of the idea
to be conveyed.

The exports of domestic produce from the United
States amounted, in 1833, to 70,642,030 dollars,—
having increased, beyond the preceding year's estimate, by the sum of 7,504,560 dollars. During the
same period, the corresponding augmentation of im-
ports was, in round numbers, eight millions on a
total of one hundred and nine millions,—thirty-four
of which were from articles free of duty. We are
punishing ourselves and each other by our short-
sighted policy. Had it not been for the tariff and
the corn-laws, each would have found, in a profitable
interchange of labor, that benefit which its detention
has afforded to neither. The queen issues a writ,
" Ne exeat regno"; and the bees are to make honey
out of the straw that covers them. " Protection"
has done for the Lowell manufacturer what it has
done for our farmer:—it has lowered profits by inviting capital. This is all very true in theory:—but
America is a new country, without any debt; and
England is an old country, with a very heavy one.
The one must have leading-strings, and the other
crutches!

The object my friends and myself had, in visiting Canaan, was to be present at a meeting of the
trustees of a school lately formed there. The Noyes
Seminary had obtained a charter of incorporation

from the legislature of New Hampshire; and the building being nearly completed, all that remained was, to settle the terms of admission, and provide for the appointment of a teacher, and the requisite control over the management and discipline of the institution.

A spirit of liberality unknown, or at least unheard of, in any other part of the Union, had inspired the townsmen of this sequestered spot with the noble resolution of opening the school they had founded with their donations and subscriptions, to the children of all whose means would enable them to enjoy its benefits, without distinction. No *cuticular* test was to be demanded as a qualification for entrance; —no disability was to be sought in impurity of blood:—exclusion or expulsion was to be based upon those considerations alone which would carry with them their own justification in the eyes of every liberal and impartial man.

While at Concord, a newspaper fell into our hands, containing an advertisement that menaced a determined opposition to the scheme. It was hardly, indeed, to be expected, that any plan so much in advance of the feeling that pervaded the whole country, should be suffered to go unmolested into operation. The resolutions, however, to which I refer, were passed at a meeting got up for the occasion, against the wishes of more than four-fifths of the voters in the town, if a fair judgment may be formed from the number of those who signed their names to the document. Just before we quitted the village, we were informed that not more than six opponents remained in the place :—thanks to the persuasive eloquence of my companions, who explained to an attentive audience, the day after our arrival, the principles and objects which the academy was to maintain and promote.

On our way to Canaan we passed through the district in which Daniel Webster was born and spent his youthful years. We heard many anecdotes of his kindness and attention to the friends and companions of his humbler fortunes ; his annual visits to whom were signalized by some mark of his sympathy for the distressed, and his recollection of old scenes and attachments. They, in their turn, are justly proud of a man, whose master-mind would do honor to any country.

Our approach and departure from this delightful spot were enlivened by the most picturesque scenery, that the greatest profusion and diversity of mountain eminences, with the finest contours and outlines, could produce, in addition to miniature lakes studded with verdant islets, and indenting their rocky shores with innumerable sinuosities. The people at Canaan were hospitable, intelligent, and disinterested ; simple in their habits, and frank in their manners. They seemed to love their native land with a rational affection, and to wish their attachment should recommend itself to the world by the efforts it led them to make for the adoption of a noble and benevolent policy to all its inhabitants.

The village, which is situated in the county of Grafton, and is likely to be connected with Boston by means of a rail-road, is admirably adapted to the purposes of this praiseworthy project. The climate is remarkably healthy; the water excellent; and the soil, though thin and rocky, well suited to pasturage. The vicinity abounds in fine views, such as the " Granite State" might be expected to present to the lovers of picturesque nature. Provisions are cheap; and the whole expense of education, including board and lodging, would not exceed 100 dollars for a pupil who should reside there the whole year. The scholars are to board with the inhabitants. There will be room for 100 boys. We had two public meetings; both opened and closed with prayer,—two ministers being present; one of them a trustee and a friend to the objects of the establishment; the other unconnected with it. The prayer, however, he offered up at the termination of the last meeting, breathed nothing but charity and goodwill, in language that promised a hearty co-operation or a generous neutrality. It was chiefly among the old people that hostility to the new school manifested itself; though some venerable revolutionists, who cheerfully bore testimony to the services of the colored soldiers during the war with the mother country, formed an exception. The younger part of the community, particularly the boys, were indignant at the narrow spirit of proscription, and were impatient to shew a better feeling, by entering their names as scholars. Taking all the circumstances of our reception into consideration, I had good reason to be pleased with what I had witnessed. I had seen in the West and in the East the same devotion to humanity—the same sacrifice of deep-rooted prejudice on the altar of justice; and I could not but foresee, in the alumni of Lane Seminary and of Noyes Academy an honorable rivalry in high thoughts and good deeds. Events have since occurred that have rendered this hope unavailing. The students of Lane Seminary, who had formed themselves into an abolition society, have dissolved their connexion with the institution, to the number of forty-one; and others, who were absent at the time, agreed in the " statement", though they were unable to affix their names to it. The Principal, during a visit he made to Boston last autumn, declared that he would, on his return, put a stop to the anti-slavery proceedings. The Executive Committee of the Seminary, four-fifths of whom are colonizationists, subsequently resolved that the society in question should be dissolved. No event could have happened more favorable to the cause of freedom, than the result of this threat. Every student whom it has driven from the establishment, will now form the nucleus of a new association, animated with all the zeal and energy that sympathy for persecution never fails to excite in great national controversies. The same feelings have struck their deep roots in the minds of the scholars at Amherst and Andover, in Massachusetts.

No man, who is attached to his country, whatever his opinions may be, can approve of such methods to stop and stifle inquiry as have been adopted at the Seminary. The Committee, whose report is dated August 24, 1834, stated (a very important admission) that the Colonization Society of Lane Seminary was instituted "merely with a view to counteract the peculiar sentiments of their opponents"— in other words to support slavery,—and recommended the following resolution:—"That rules should be adopted, prohibiting the organization in the seminary of any association or society of the students, without the approbation of the faculty,—prohibiting the calling or holding of meetings among the students, without the approbation of the faculty;— prohibiting students from delivering lectures or public addresses, public statements or communications to the students when assembled at meals, or on ordinary occasions, &c.; requiring the two rival societies to be abolished; and prohibiting any student from being absent from the seminary at any time in term time, without leave ; and providing for discouraging and discountenancing, by all suitable means, such discussions among the students as are calculated to divert their attention from their studies, excite party animosities, stir up evil passions among themselves, or in the community, or involve themselves with the political concerns of the country:—also providing for the dismissal of any student not complying with these regulations."

The board of Trustees acted upon these suggestions; and the students, finding that the promise made but a short time before by the Faculty, in a public declaration, to "protect and encourage free inquiry and thorough discussion," was thus violated, and that the executive committee could dismiss "any student when they think it necessary to do so," broke off all connexion with the institution. Matters seem rapidly approaching to that point of national determination, when no other alternative remains but the complete adoption of personal freedom or political slavery. Academical coercion and republican forms of government cannot long exist together. Monarchy may continue while freedom of associations is permitted, and, perhaps, because it is permitted, in its universities: but democracy cannot long survive when it has left them.

On the 11th our party separated, and one of my companions (Mr. Child) returned with me to Boston, which we reached by another route on the 14th.

CHAPTER XXXI.

Dr. Tuckerman.—Dr. Follen.—House of Industry.—Pauperism in Massachusetts.—House of Correction.—Juvenile Offenders. —Reformatory School of Mr. Welles.—War between Patricians and Plebeians.—" Thrice told tale" of Canterbury.— System of " Strikes."—Travelling Incognito.—Reception of George Thompson from England.—Progress of Abolition Doctrines.

Soon after my return I was introduced to Dr. Tuckerman, with whom I had a long and very interesting conversation on a subject to which he has devoted the best energies of an enlightened mind and a feeling heart. Every thing that he said relative to the method he had adopted of reclaiming the most vicious portion of the community, breathed the spirit of pure and consistent philanthropy. The domiciliary visits he had paid in pursuit of his benevolent object, had brought under his notice, he told me, many instances of docility and generosity among those who are too often supposed incapable of either.

He had succeeded in enlisting in this excellent work the professors of the most discordant sects, the peculiar tenets of which had proved no bar to a cheerful and effective co-operation. A great and marked improvement had resulted from their joint labors; and he had reason to anticipate a much higher standard of behavior from the extension of a system which teaches men self-respect by connecting it with the sense of religious responsibility in every action, whether of a social or of a personal nature.

The doctor was no " respecter of persons;" exhibiting the same solicitude for every child of Adam. I was anxious to hear, from a man of such experience in the calamities and infirmities of our nature, what impression had been left on his mind by an acquaintance with the despised and degraded class of the community. He replied to my inquiry, that he had met with many instances of exemplary virtue among them; and that there was no reason to suppose they were morally or intellectually below the level of the other race in similar circumstances. One example he detailed with great feeling. It was that of a poor woman who had nursed a sick neighbor for five months, during the absence of the invalid's husband. The patient was a most deplorable spectacle, being afflicted with dropsy in its most aggravated form. " I know not what would have become of me," said the poor sufferer, " if it had not been for the kindness of this excellent woman. She

has sat up with me three nights in succession; and
I fear that want of rest, and the fatigue she has to go
through on my account, will be too much for her."
The other expressed herself in the most modest and
unpretending terms, and appeared to think she was
merely discharging the common offices of kindness
to her afflicted friend. " It was a sight," added
the amiable philanthropist, " that might well have
stopped a ministering angel on his errand of mercy—
to look at and admire."

This reverend Doctor was not contented with professing an exemption from the vulgar prejudices of
his age and nation. No distinction was made at
his servants' table; nor were those ever divided in
his house, whom he had taught, by his example, to
live, as they were to die, in Christian love and affection.

The Doctor very politely offered me a seat in his
gig the next day, for the purpose of viewing the
public establishments for paupers and juvenile offenders.

The intervening evening I passed, as I can hope
to pass few in future, with professor Follen, of Cambridge, and his lady. The professor, who had been
driven across the Atlantic, by the enemies of political liberty in his own country, had not, like too
many exiles from Europe, attempted to conciliate
the friends of personal slavery in the land of his
adoption, by open advocacy or servile indifference.

He had " chosen the better part," after mature deliberation; and had come out with a manly courage,
tempered by mildness, and sustained by principles
that placed him above the influence or imputation of worldly and interested motives, as an abolitionist. His " Address to the people of the United
States " on the subject, is a master-piece of sound
logic, and literary composition. His zeal and good
sense were amply and ably seconded by his lady;
and if a pure love of freedom, a sincere conviction
that the happiness of every one is the happiness of
all, and a heartfelt sympathy with the injured and
the oppressed, could have disarmed animosity, it
might have been expected, that the enemies of the
cause would have spared the advocate, and that Dr.
Follen would have escaped the obloquy and insult
that have been heaped upon him. But perhaps the
injustice done to the man is the strongest testimony
in favor of his reasoning. Scurrilous paragraphs
in the public prints, and threats of vengeance, are
the natural weapons of those who dare not deny
facts, and cannot answer arguments. What may we
not hope to see on the side of emancipation, when
persons most distinguished for scientific attainments
and social refinements, are in its ranks,—prepared to
make every sacrifice in the performance of a duty
which colder hearts and less logical heads, consider
superfluous or premature ? Such minds are " enthu-
siastic" to those only who make the imputed " fanatic-

ism" of others a cloak for their own apathy. From Mrs.
Follen I had still further proof of the little value to
be placed on the received estimate of the tawney
man's real character. Colonel May, who has had
frequent opportunities of observation, assured her
that he had never known more than two confirmed
cases in Boston of drunkenness among the blacks.
This testimony is the less to be suspected, because it
comes from one who is not an abolitionist.

The next day, Dr. Tuckerman took me with him
to the house of industry; which, with the buildings
appropriated to the reception of young offenders,
stands on the other side of the water, and at the distance of two or three miles from the city, in a very
beautiful situation, combining the advantages of sa-
lubrious air and charming views. Those paupers
who do not receive relief at their own houses, (and
it is rarely given there, except from peculiar considerations,) are sent to this establishment; where they
are, if able, set to work, on the land which adjoins
it, or in the house: and the produce of their labor,
beyond what is wanted for domestic use, is sold.
The institution appeared to be well conducted, with
the exception of the department assigned to the insane; the treatment of whose complaint interferes
with the arrangements of the house, while it is itself
impeded by the vicinity of the paupers. It adjoins
the apartment in which the colored people, with
the usual disregard of their feelings, are lodged

apart, and must, from the noise and confusion which prevail, be the source of great annoyance to them, particularly to the sick. Separated by a thin boarding from one room we visited, was an idiotic old woman, whose shrill and monotonous cry, " give me my dinner—I want my dinner," was inexpressibly painful and offensive. Though not so badly managed as in the alms-house at New York, the lunatics are far from being in a satisfactory condition. The patients are from time to time, removed to Worcester Asylum, where they are cured in a large proportion of cases, in the early stages of the disorder. In the infant school here, the stain of color is visible among the pupils. " The common class shun their society." In the infirmary, where these poor creatures were, I remarked, as I did in almost every place of the kind, strong indications of assiduous attention to the helpless and infirm. A woman was brushing away the flies from a child who was sick in bed. Upon inquiry, I was told there were not many of this class paupers. One of them, an old man, ninety-seven years of age, had served in the American navy, during the whole of the revolutionary war. He had no pension; and he could find no Greenwich Hospital * in the Sailor's Snug Harbor.

The children were shortly to be removed into a separate building, where more attention can be paid

* Every one who has seen this place, knows that there are plenty of colored pensioners among its inmates.

to their education. Here, as at other places, they
are (nine in ten) affected, soon after their first
entrance, with sore eyes. The remedies applied,
usually remove the complaint in a week or ten days.
They are bound out at a proper age, as apprentices,
with a good prospect of doing well; as the demand
for them is greater than can be supplied from the
establishment. There are about fifty acres of land
attached to the house, the inmates of which amounted
to 528;—120 men, 103 women, and three children,
being permanently on the establishment, from their
age and infirmities. The number of native poor has
diminished, while that of foreign poor has increased.
Out of 1273 adults and young admitted at different
times, 705 were foreigners, and thirty-nine of unknown origin; while 529 only were Americans. In
the last three months there had been twenty-six
from Boston, forty-four from other States, and 140
of foreign " growth." Of 132 children in the house,
there were but twenty-five whose parents were American. The emigrants were chiefly of recent arrival,
from New York and the British provinces.

  The close connexion between pauperism and intemperance has long been seen here. A recent change in
the law had poured in from the country, where they
were no longer entitled to relief, a large influx of
casual poor, who look to Boston as a place of refuge. Many, too, are sent to the city, in order to
get rid of a burthen. The most vicious and intract-

able class are composed of occasional paupers—a
floating mass of fraud and filth. If not discharged,
they generally get tired of the confinement, and
elope with what property they can lay their hands
on. It is not long before they contrive to be re-ad-
mitted. There were 350 the preceding year, of this
description. They average thirty-four at one time
in the house, and usually remain about six weeks.
The medium term of their age is thirty-four or
thirty-five—shewing pretty plainly that they are not
all disabled or infirm. The facility with which their
wants are supplied, is a direct premium upon idleness and begging.   Indiscriminate alms-giving is
found to have the same effect. It is much to be
feared that the feeling of disgrace attached to those
who are pensioners on the public charity, has less
influence on the general mass of society than it had.
The relatives of the paupers, during the visits they
make to the house, are too apt to contrast its comforts and good fare with the hardships they sometimes have to encounter at home.   The superintendant was fully aware of the frauds practised by many
of the Irish, who conceal, either about their persons,
or with a friend, whatever property they have been
able to save, and remain in the Boston "asylum"
till they can obtain employment.   Their number increases with the fund for their maintenance; and
the difficulty of avoiding to encourage the disease,
by the means used for its relief, is sensibly felt by

the guardians of the poor. Of those last year in the house, 159 had been admitted for the second time; seventy-six for the third, thirty-two for the fourth, twenty-seven for the fifth, twelve for the sixth, &c.

According to a report, laid before the House of Representatives in Massachusetts, by the Commissioners it had appointed, in February, 1832, to inquire into the state of pauperism in that commonwealth, it appears that one in twenty-one and a half was receiving relief; the number being 12,331 out of 264,327, the whole population of sixty-eight towns, or districts. Of these, 5927 were States' poor, that is, persons supported not by the parishes or towns, but out of the public fund, in accordance with the existing law and practice. The amount of their allowance had increased from 14,000 dollars in 1792, to 72,000 in 1820. Many of these consisted of " wandering or travelling poor," who, speculating on the provision made by the State for casual poor, came into it from other States, and roamed from place to place, during the summer; claiming what they conceived a right, and sheltering themselves in the alms-houses or other asylums in the winter months. A direct encouragement was thus given to pauperism and fraud, as idleness was fed by legal enactment, and each town endeavored to throw off the burthen from its own shoulders upon those of its neighbors. There were three modes of providing for the poor:—in poor-houses, by out-door allowances, and on farms, where land could be obtained for their employment. When they were boarded out by the overseers in private families, the expense was much greater than when they were under the care of a contractor, by whom they were set to work.

In one town, the annual cost, which had been from 1000 to 1200 dollars, was reduced to an average, during three years, of 535. In another, the average cost, which for twelve years had been, while they were boarded out, 1600 dollars a-year, was reduced to 1050, when they were maintained under the same roof by a contractor. A third case, that of Sheffield, was more remarkable, the reduction having been from 1967 dollars to 665. Out of forty-nine, who had enjoyed their share of the former sum, no more than seventeen were willing to receive relief at the alms-house; where alone, except they were ill, it was to be had; and two of the States' poor immediately removed to an adjoining town, where they might receive their allowance without restraint or confinement. This diminution, in the expenditure for the poor, was effected in the course of four years; at the end of which time there were but eight inmates of the alms-house.

The result of employing the poor on farms, appropriated to that object, was highly satisfactory. By this expedient, the average expense at Salem was, for ten years, one half of what it had been, during the same period, when the poor had no work; while the establishment got rid of fifty of its inmates, and was more easily conducted. The expenditure at Waltham and Littleton, which had been 675 and 800 dollars respectively, was brought down, partly by the farm, and partly by interdicting the use of spirituous liquors, to 239 dollars four cents, and 244 dollars, thirty-eight cents. By means of the farm, Marlborough, instead of paying 1550 dollars per annum, was charged but 310 dollars seventy-eight cents for its poor.

Many instances of a similar kind, were cited by the committee.—In one case, the profits of the pauper-farm exceeded the outlay by the sum of 228 dollars seventy-five cents.

By statistical tables annexed to this valuable document, it is shown that the effects of intemperance on the comforts and character of the laboring classes are most deplorable; three fourths, and even nine tenths, of the mendicancy having arisen from drinking.

In pursuance of the recommendations contained in the above report, measures were taken for the gradual, but complete, repeal of the law, which provided for the support of the casual poor out of the funds of the commonwealth;—districts are to be formed with corporate privileges, under the care of a Board of Directors, with the view of providing for the poor by setting them, if able, to work; and each town to have, upon proper application, a share, in proportion to its population, of the fund (300,000 dollars were recommended) to be raised for the purpose.

Having left the house of industry, we crossed over to the house of correction, which, with that of reformation, occupies a building close by. The master was out; but one of the prisoners took me round the institution; Dr. Tuckerman being indisposed. The person, who thus acted as my guide, had been committed for intemperance; his habits of inebriety being so confirmed, as to deprive him of all power to resist temptation, or control his besetting propensity. He acted as clerk, and was exempted from wearing the prison dress, on account of the excellence of his general character, which was unexceptionable in all respects, but that of the unfortunate infirmity to which I have alluded, and which rendered him, when under its influence, perfectly furious and ungovernable. There were in the house, at the time, 174 men and 62 women,—among both of whom was a large proportion of foreigners,—chiefly Irish,—considerably more than of colored persons, in proportion to the relative amount of their numbers in the community. There were but six men and four or five women of the latter. The sexes are placed in different parts of the building. The sleeping cells for both are constructed upon the Singsing plan; and the meals are taken there in a similar manner.   On each side of the block of building which contains them, and which has an ample and well-aired passage on all sides, are five tiers, each containing eighteen cells, the opposite cells corresponding to each other, and so built as to prevent any correspondence or communication between the male inmates of the one and the women in the other.   There is a watch going his round during the night.

Various kinds of works, suited to the difference of age and of sex, are carried on here.   The prisoners are sent hither for minor offences, the term of their detention varying from twenty days to a year or upwards.   Adjoining the cells, I observed a placard, containing the names of their occupants.—I took the opportunity of asking my guide, who informed me for what purpose it was stuck up, and who was not aware that I was acquainted with the circumstances of his case, whether this public exposure had not a bad effect on the minds of many, who thus became known both to visitors and to fellow-prisoners.   His reply was, that he had no doubt it tended greatly to diminish the chance of recovering self-respect, and retarded the progress of self-improvement.   The greatest villain is still a man; and the less there is of humanity left in any one, the greater ought to be our solicitude for its preservation.

Having finished what was necessarily a very cursory inspection of the institution, from the wish I felt not to keep my benevolent companion waiting in the parlor, I proceeded with him to visit the adjoining establishment for juvenile offenders. The mistress of the female department, who received us at the door, seemed, as every one we had met before had been, delighted to see the Doctor. There were sixty-four boys and eighteen girls; the latter of whom do all the work of the house. As they were much straitened for room, the system of labor for the boys was imperfect; proper arrangements, however, were to be made, when a new building, which was intended for them, would admit of it. In the mean time sufficient occupation was given them to employ their time properly. The legislature had granted 20,000 dollars towards the erection of the new establishment. Not much to the credit, however, of the proper authorities, a resolution had been made against admitting any juvenile offender, who might happen to have a drop of the prohibited and proscribed blood in his veins :—so that those, who are said to stand most in need of reformation, are excluded from its benefits, by the very persons who complain that they are incorrigible. The average cost of the children, whose age is from nine to eighteen, is twelve cents per diem.

They are sent hither by the police and municipal courts, and are bound out as apprentices at the proper age. Parents, when domestic discipline is found an inefficient instrument of correction or coercion, avail themselves of this institution to reform their children—having obtained the requisite conviction. A vigilant eye is kept upon them, after they have been discharged; and three out of four are found to conduct themselves well. More than half are foreigners. The institution resembles the houses of refuge at New York and Philadelphia, as far as the limited number of its inmates, the confined nature of the building, and the temporary system of economy, which characterises its state of transition, will admit of.

Conversing afterwards with Dr. Tuckerman upon the subject of philanthropic projects, he told me that any suggestion for the improvement of society that might require pecuniary aid, was always promptly seconded by the wealthy class of Boston; and that probably no place existed where there was a greater amount of generous sympathy with the ignorant and unfortunate, or a more anxious desire to co-operate, with purse or person, in affording instruction to the one and relief to the other. Would that there were no exception or qualification to be made to this eulogy! There are few cities of equal population where there is less crime and vice than in Boston.

A large part of the following day I spent at the reformatory school of the Rev. Mr. Welles, whose

house is not far from the establishment I have just
described. He had formerly the charge of one of
them, and had been displaced from motives that are
too apt, in his country, to influence those who have
the appointment to public offices. Many found
fault with his system, because they could not understand it: others could not understand it, because
they had found fault with it. To be successful in a
new course of action is considered an imputation on
the old; and many mistake the hatred of innova-
tion for an attachment to what is established. Whatever were the causes in operation, the superintendant
was removed from his situation, and sought a more
independent field of usefulness in a private establishment; where his plans would not be condemned
till they had failed, nor thwarted before their completion.

Mr. Welles, while explaining the principles that
had guided him, struck me as a man remarkably
clear-headed in his views, and practical in his proceedings. He seemed to have elaborated from his
own mind those general rules, which are usually obtained by a long and tedious induction from the experience of others; and to have found in his own
heart that knowledge of human nature which most
men acquire from viewing the actions of those
around them. He worked in a narrow circle; but
its proportions were perfect. I was introduced,
after a preliminary conversation, to his pupils, who

were assembled for the exercises of the day in the school-room.   There were twenty-eight present. The business of the morning commenced with an inquiry into the conduct of the boys during the preceding day,—an usage which is observed every night, but which had been deferred in consequence of the master's absence.   The second assistant, a pupil himself—for at the time there was no under-master,—accused one of the boys of having been angry in a dispute with another.   When interrogated with great mildness and affection by the master, and reminded of his duty to God, who requires " truth in the inward parts," he replied, that he did not think he was angry.   Others, who had witnessed the transaction, thought he had been so.   He owned he had not felt pleased with his opponent.   When asked for a definition of the word " anger," he was confused, and conscious of having prevaricated. Mr. Welles explained its meaning to him.   All present were very attentive.   An appeal was made to them ; and the evidence adduced against him was confirmed by the general sentiment.   It was the Jacotot system applied to morals.   The defence of the accused was fairly submitted to the consciences of the auditors ; as the answers of one under a scientific or literary examination would have been tried by their understandings ; and a similar benefit to each individual was derived from the discussion elicited.   The poor boy was overpowered by his

sense of guilt. He wept aloud. Nothing like ex-
ultation or contempt was exhibited by any one. He
was then reminded of the forgiveness that had followed a former fault, because it was frankly acknowledged; and as he was already suspended from his
grade, as a punishment for previous misconduct, he
was told that he must continue so. As the trial advanced, the number and strength of the proofs
against him increased; while the generous feelings
of the accusers were called forth in favor of a fallen
brother. The scene was highly interesting, as the
breach of truth involved in his denial became the
subject of animadversion. A lie was shewn to be
more culpable and degrading than anger. Some
admirable observations on the tendency and results
of falsehood to the individual addicted to it and to
society, were made. The nature of lying was asked
of all present, and the answers evinced their thorough acquaintance with the subject; as they agreed
that the criminality depended upon the impression
left, and not on the language employed. The convicted party was then condemned to be suspended
from all the *bon* grades, and to be placed in the lowest, if proved to have been guilty of intentional deception. When this case was disposed of, one of
the monitors accused some of the boys of infringing
the discipline of the place. Upon investigation,
however, it came out that some mistake had been
made.

The master dismissed the case, observing that he had expressed himself imperfectly; it being a principle strictly acted up to, that no punishment is to be inflicted for acts not known to be unlawful. As it is therefore presumed that what is not expressly prohibited is permitted, (except in cases which manifestly do not, from their nature, come within the rule,) some of the pupils, who had been wading in the water, were declared not to be wrong-doers; the restriction which appeared to apply to them being confined to bathing. One boy said he had gone in merely to wash his feet. He was admonished to be careful that he did not deceive himself, and to consider well before he persisted in the explanation. Another, who had been before degraded, was told that his father had been to see him; but when he found what situation his son was placed in, he had left the house without seeing him. This information was conveyed to the offender in such a spirit of kindness and friendship as not to humiliate him in the eyes of the rest, but to urge upon him the propriety of attending more strictly to his duties. He then took his place in tears with his face to the wall. The boy who had been dabbling in the water was again asked why he had done so. He had been playing, he said, with bare feet, and wanted to wash them. He was advised to examine his own heart, and to be sure that he was correct in his assertion. As the case was not clear, no further notice was taken of it.

A long and intricate investigation then followed, and terminated in the conviction of two boys, who were condemned to degradation, and addressed on the offence they had committed. The most considerate and gentle language was used on the occasion; and the regret which was felt for the necessity of applying correction was as perceptible as the remorse it gave rise to. The poor fellows sobbed aloud; and the sympathies of the whole audience were excited to a degree that was most affecting and impressive. After this the names were called over, and responses given successively of good, or bad, or indifferent conduct—each being marked in a book kept for the purpose, according to the statement given, which is voluntary and open to the objections of any one. The places in the grades were then awarded. Wherever reproof was called for, it was always accompanied, under much that was vexatious and painful, with singular forbearance and mildness. It was now one o'clock in the day; and, as it was too late for the usual exercises, the school was dismissed to play.

Of the *bon* grades the lowest consists of those who have shewn a positive inclination to do well. The second, where the habit of doing well has become regular. The third, where it has become constant and undeviating. The *mal* grades correspond as to scale and the character of the occupants. For three good marks a counter or franc is given; and these pass as currency, to be withdrawn or augmented, according to an estimate made every Saturday of the week's progress. There must be three left for each pupil, to provide against contingencies. The balance of the account determines the classification. The small punishments are made up of these fines or forfeitures. Certain indulgencies—such as permission to go out—are purchased by them; the reasonableness of the permission being thus fairly tested by these evidences of good conduct. Every one's moral wealth is thus equitably measured, and its value paid on demand. The different grades are kept separate, as far as is practicable, in occupations and amusements. It should be observed that the prohibitions to do wrong, and the privilege to do what is proper, are alike for all—master, monitors, and scholars. The exceptions are where demerit requires an abridgement of natural right. They take their meals together; and when the arrangements are completed, the whole establishment will sleep in the same room with the master. There were then but thirteen thus immediately under his vigilant eye. Seven or eight were waiting for admission.

So confident is the manager of reforming the most depraved and abandoned youth, that he is willing to give bond in any reasonable sum for the complete restoration to good conduct of any lad under sixteen or seventeen years of age, however hopeless his case may seem to be. When first admitted, the pupil is soothed and softened by the most open and parental reception. What has past, he is told, will not be remembered or recalled to his attention. He is exhorted to a life of virtue, and made acquainted with the kind of behavior that will be expected from him. He is not allowed to converse with the others on his first arrival; nor are they to question him on any subject whatever. The average duration of this silence is two days. During the first period of his residence, a pupil must not do any thing without obtaining permission from the proper authorities. Hence he is enabled to observe what is passing, and obtain a knowledge of the customs and rules of the place. He is not embarrassed by inquisitive or impertinent questions; and is spared the difficulty that a novice feels, in applying general instructions, which often appear unintelligible and contradictory. It is found, that what is required to be done is always done ultimately, whatever be the struggle at first against compliance. The most refractory seldom hold out more than twenty-four hours against what their own experience and the testimony of others concur in shewing to be for their advantage. There is no instance of a failure on this head. Nothing but reading, writing, arithmetic, &c., the common course of an elementary education, is taught here. The mode of instruction is by questions,—oral, not from books. The monitors see that the question is clearly worded and comprehended by the pupils. The answer results from the efforts of their own minds.   As little as possible is imparted by the master.   An appeal to the whole class is made in case of an erroneous, or no reply.   The mind is thus led to the attainment of truth by the exercise of its own powers; and all are successively teachers as well as learners.   The best parts of Jacotot's system of self-instruction, as well as much of what is to be found at Hazlewood School, near Birmingham, are put in practice here; though Mr. Welles never heard the name either of Mr. Hill or of the Louvain schoolmaster.

It was suggested by some foreigners who had visited the school a year or two before, that the presence of the master would be necessary to insure its success in another country:—an opinion of which Mr. Welles would be the last to admit the justness, while he sees the same materials existing everywhere, as well for the correction as for the curse of immorality.

After dinner I was taken to hear the exercises of the school; and, as the subject of study was natural history, I was requested to put a few questions to the pupils.   They were accordingly asked whether the elephant, when described as exhibiting more sagacity than other animals, was possessed of faculties more adapted to the purposes of its existence than theirs?   The answer was, that he was not.   A similar reply was given to the question, whether one species of animals was naturally more cruel than another; and a proper distinction was drawn between blind in-

stinct and responsible reason.   It was agreed on all
hands, that we had no more right to kill a tiger than
a dove, on account of its ferocity alone ; and that the
whole brute creation had a claim upon our kindness
and forbearance, where our personal safety or comfort was not concerned.   I regret that I did not push
my inquiries further, and direct their attention to the
various forms and tints which distinguish the numerous tribes of human beings ;—diversities adapted to
their moral and physical condition,—all alike the
work of an omnipotent hand,—and all equally entitled to our admiration and respect.

I was highly delighted, and, I hope, instructed, by
all that I saw; and regretted that the lateness of the
hour (it was past four o'clock, and I had arrived at
ten,) compelled me to take my leave of an establishment, the principles of which, if universally put in
practice, would do more to advance the well-being
and happiness of man, than all the discourses of all
the learned doctors, who seem to value learning as
misers value wealth,—not for its employment, but its
amount.   There is nothing exclusive or qualified in
the mind of Mr. Welles.   His efforts have been directed to the improvement of the human mind; and
his benevolence would be enlarged by those very
circumstances which would limit that of inferior
men.   Prejudices which would prompt many to
            " Shut the gates of mercy on mankind,"
would with him be an additional motive to open

them. To sacrifice the better feelings of his conscience and his conviction to others, would be to
frustrate his own designs,—to make virtue ancillary
to wickedness,—and to encourage, in the minds of
his pupils, that attachment to false and factitious associations which he has rooted out of his own.

It has been observed at Boston, that the son of a
wealthy man rarely succeeds in commerce. This is
the case in most places. A remark I heard connected with this subject, proves, if correct, that riches
may injure the family of the possessor as much by
giving prudence to others, as by taking it from himself. Few lawyers at Boston, whose fathers have
large fortunes, have much practice,—from an apprehension very generally felt, that the chance of professional skill decreases with the necessity for its acquirement; and, perhaps, because most people feel a
wish to befriend those who stand more in need of their
assistance than others. Many, if not most, of the merchants who are settled in the Southern cities, are from
the East,—to which they generally return to enjoy the
fruits of their industry, and to bequeath them to their
sons, who not unfrequently, by their extravagance,
descend to that rank from which their fathers had
risen, and leave their children to pursue the same
upward course, and their grand-children the same
decline which have marked the lives of their parents
and their own:—thus connecting the alternations of
good and bad fortune by a link which may be seen

in an almost regular recurrence of the same process under the same circumstances. So much, indeed, is this the case, that the names of those families who were formerly most distinguished for their wealth and their influence, may now be seen over the door-ways of the petty shop-keepers in the lowest parts of the city; while those they have displaced will be found at the " West-end".

In spite of these facts, which are open to the observation of all, however highly colored the picture I have drawn may seem, and which tend to reconcile society to the disparities which .unavoidably attend it, the aristocratical feeling prevails in the United States much more extensively than is generally believed in Europe; and symptoms of a retaliatory spirit are not wanting. " I have inquired," (says a writer in the Annals of Education, for June 1833,) " of intelligent gentlemen who are familiar with some of our most respectable manufacturing establishments in this country, whether some plan could not be devised—perhaps familiar lectures—for giving laborers of all ages such daily instruction on practical subjects, as would be adapted to their means and capacities, and at the same time insure their interest. The reply has always been in the negative, that they are a class of people who could never be brought to desire improvement, or to attend to instruction, even for amusement:—that the only way to get along with such ignorant people, was to keep them from mischief, by keeping them constantly employed." The feeling that dictated these sentiments is openly and freely met by the indignation of the operatives. In " an address to the working men of New England," published by their request, at Boston, in 1832, as it was delivered in various sections and towns of the Union, by Seth Luther, is the following passage : " We observed, that it is becoming fashionable in our country to cry out about ' national glory,' ' national wealth,' ' march of improvement,' ' march of intellect.' We have pointed out to you the occasion why the monopolists of Europe raise this cry ; and you will, ere long, probably discover the same design in our own country —to wit, to prevent the ' common people '—the ' lower orders ' — by which our ' higher orders ' mean farmers, mechanics, and laborers, from thinking, reasoning, and watching the movements of these same ' higher orders.' " Again :—" The owners of mills oppose all reduction in the hours of labor, for the purposes of mental culture. Not that they care about hours of labor in cities ; but they fear the contagion will reach their *slave mills.* Hence, they go into the shop of the carpenter and others, who carry on business, and actually forbid them to employ what they sneeringly call ' ten-hour-men '— telling the employers, ' you shall not have our work, unless you do as we say.' We have appealed to their sense of justice, their sense of humanity, their love of country, to consider the evils they are bringing on the poor through ignorance. What has been the reply? One says, 'if a man offers to work for me ten hours, I will kick him off my premises:'—another says: ' O ! they can't stand it more than a day or two ; and they will soon come back to *beg* to go to work.' "

The speech abounds in charges and insinuations of the same kind. In an appendix, the writer says: " We insist that, if congress have power to protect the *owners* against foreign-competition, in the shape of goods, they have the same right to protect the *operative* from foreign competition in the shape of importation of foreign mechanics and laborers, to cut down wages of our own citizens. We call upon manufacturers to do justice to the operative, and warn them to remember that working men, the farmer, mechanic, and laborer, are the majority, and are determined to be gulled no longer by the specious and deceptive cry of ' American industry,' while they are ground down into the dust by importation of foreign machinery, foreign workmen, and foreign work, and deprived of improvement for themselves, and an opportunity to educate their children, merely to enable the rich to take care of themselves—while the poor must work for such prices as manufacturers see fit to give, or starve, as a reward for votes given for their oppressors."

The Jackson party have managed to " suck no small advantage" out of these prejudices. They are supported by the " operatives," because they are hostile to foreigners, and foreign capital; and they are supported by foreigners, because Jackson is supposed to be an Irishman.

A trip to the United States, is often recommended as a cure for morbid attachment to political equality. It would perhaps be a better remedy for a similar predilection in favor of social disparities. It is not every one that can reason: but all can feel the force of the ludicrous. Among the many odd questions that are put to Englishmen about the customs of the old country, is one that shews how much the conception of external finery enters into the abstract idea of rank entertained by those, who have no other mode of distinction. " Do not your noblemen wear a great deal of gold about their persons?"—seems to us a very silly question:—yet it is pregnant with meaning, and proves that the conditions on which respect is to be obtained, are as little understood under a republic, as under a monarchy; and that the imagination is equally inclined to confound the means with the end in both hemispheres. The judgment is misled, in one case by the eye, and in

the other by the ear. We listen to the title; while
the Americans look to the metal.

I was once asked, by an intelligent person, whether men of rank in England associated with com-
moners; and another, who had evidently received a
good education, assured the company, at an hotel
where I was, that a peer of Great Britain would, if
he by chance invited an American to dinner, place
him at the bottom of the table—to shew his hatred of republican principles. It was in vain that
I tried to point out the improbability of a distinction which would necessarily imply the relative superiority of the very person it was intended to depress. He had the best authority for what he said;
and his auditors, who were accustomed to elevate
themselves by mortifying their own countrymen,
would readily believe what they thought I had an
interest in denying. His informant had probably,
as an English lady afterwards observed to me, mistaken the top of the table for the bottom, and ima-
gined he was "humbled" below his deserts, while
he was "exalted" above them. It is somewhat
difficult to make a transatlantic republican comprehend that social equality is encouraged, while it is
checked, by political inequality; and that rank is
respected the more because it is not insisted upon.
Englishmen sometimes take advantage of this imperfect idea of our customs to impress on the minds
of those who entertain it, a sense of their great im-

portance. A lady, speaking to me of one of my countrymen, whom she had met at Philadelphia, added that he was highly connected, and a frequenter of the very best society at home. " He was a fellow-commoner," she said, " at the same college with the late king." I told her it was an honor easily acquired to be a fellow-commoner at any college— though he might perhaps claim the merit of discovery, if he could point out one where the Prince of Wales had been a student. " That might be," she replied ; but he had told her so himself—he certainly had been fellow-commoner at the same college with the heir to the throne of the United Kingdom. It is not unlikely that his Majesty had dined, when a young man, in hall at one of our colleges, where this consequential gentleman had purchased the privilege of sitting at the Fellows' table.

The aristocratic feeling is carried further in Philadelphia than in London ; or rather, what is thought in the one to be indicative of high standing in society is more insisted on than what is known in the other to be often assumed by pretenders. If an English gentleman were to be reproved by a friend for stopping in Regent Street to speak to one whose dress denoted poverty, he would consider it an impertinent interference, and a mark both of a vulgar mind and of a want of good-breeding, to impute to him such an equivocal station in society that freedom of action could not be indulged without the risk of

" losing caste." It was hinted to me by a very sensible woman, that my report of American manners and customs would be discredited or undervalued by her countrymen, when it was known that I had travelled with stage-drivers and conversed freely with working people.

I left Boston on the 19th of September for Brooklyn, for the purpose of visiting Canterbury again, on my way back to New York. I had heard that the school was given up; the pupils having been so much alarmed by an attack upon the house during the night, that they would no longer remain exposed to the repetition of outrages by which their comfort was destroyed and their lives endangered.

On my arrival at Canterbury, I was introduced by Mrs. Phileo (late Miss Crandall) to her husband, from whom I received an account of what had passed.

On the 9th of September, about midnight, five separate windows in the house were simultaneously broken, and the frames forced in. No noise preceded or followed the outrage. Mr. Phileo and Mr. Burleigh immediately went out, but could neither see nor hear any one. No alarm was raised in the village; and no one came out to inquire into the cause. There were two windows broken in one sitting room—one in another at the opposite side of the house, and in a chamber on the ground floor, where two of the pupils slept, two windows were completely destroyed, the glass having been thrown upon one of the beds. It was fortunate that the inmates were not injured, as the wood-work was in such a state when I saw it, that it had yielded to the blow, and remained suspended over that part of the bed where the girl's neck must have lain. Crowbars or thick poles must have been employed by powerful men to have produced such destruction. Mr. Phileo, who had previously (Aug. 12) drawn up an address to the select men of the town, offering to quit the village, if the property could be disposed of without loss, and the law of exclusion be repealed, called with another person (Mr. Hinckley, of Plainfield) upon Mr. Judson, the town-clerk, to state what had passed. Mr. Judson opened the door, and was introduced to Mr. Phileo by his companion. The ceremony of shaking hands having been performed, and no invitation given to walk in, the following conversation, as far as my informant could remember the words, took place. Mr. Phileo : —" I should be happy, Sir, to see you for a few moments." Mr. Judson :—" I do not want to see *you*, Sir, any more than I now see you." " I have business with you."—" I have no business with *you*." " I have with you, Sir."—" I will do no business with you, Sir. Your conduct has been such lately, that I have no confidence in you." He then shut the door, saying, " good night."

As soon as the pupils were able to quit the village, they returned to their parents, leaving but a few in the house, who were waiting for instructions from home. Mr. Phileo had two men for several nights to watch the house. Not one of the authorities of the town had been to inquire into the matter, and none of the neighbors had called to offer assistance, or express sympathy with the sufferers. No reward, except by Mr. Phileo himself, had been offered for the detection of the offenders. Exclusive of the bills owing by the scholars, there was a debt of 1,300 dollars on the house. He had been sued for part of it. The school was in a prosperous state when it was thus suddenly dispersed. There were twenty pupils, and every prospect of increasing the number to thirty, when the profit would have been sufficient to cover the expenses and pay off the incumbrances. Several applications had recently been made for admittance. Two young women had come from the Havaña in Cuba to New York, with the intention of proceeding to Canterbury; but returned home as soon as they heard what had taken place. Two more were coming from Hartford, as many from the East, and another from Worcester; while letters had been received from other quarters requesting information about the establishment. One arrived from Boston just after it was broken up. The intention of this much injured and meritorious woman was to quit the scene of her heroism as soon as her debts were liquidated, and leave the actors to torment one another and prepare for the contempt of the world.

Mrs. Phileo talked to me of going to England— an asylum from persecution that more than one American told me would, ere long, be sought by his countrymen. It was Connecticut that Hampden looked to when about to quit his native land, op- pressed by regal tyranny,—it is Connecticut that his disciple would now fly from—the victim of a perse- cution infinitely more galling and cruel. " One refuge seemed to remain," says the American Quar- terly Review, " an asylum from the measures of tyranny seemed to be open in the wilds of America. The Star-chamber and the High Commission Court, two of the vilest institutions that had been ever used," (Dagget and Judson had not yet appeared,) " for the purposes of persecution, had already driven great numbers of the Puritans to New England. Say- brook, at the mouth of the Connecticut, so called from its first proprietors, Lords Say and Brooke, who had from their boyhood lived together as brothers, and whose ties of affection had been cemented by a con- stant agreement in public life, was now selected as the place where they might found a patriarchal com- munity."

I called, as a friend of Mrs. Phileo, on Mr. Judson, with the view of inquiring whether any measures had been, or would be adopted by the town authorities to discover the perpetrators of this disgraceful outrage. He was not, however, at home, and I proceeded to the residence of one of the select men, as I was anxious to hear both sides of the question,—but I was not more fortunate there. My third visit was successful, as Mr. Bacon, another select man, was within. He received me very civilly. I was accompanied by Mr. Parish, a very worthy and sensible old man from Brooklyn. Mr. Bacon told me that no proceedings had been instituted for the detection and prosecution of the offenders, and he had no reason to suppose that there would be any. The matter had not been brought officially before the authorities. I reminded him of Mr. Phileo's application to the only magistrate of the place. I asked him whether the school had given any ground of complaint by misconduct. He replied, not the least, but the inhabitants had been justly indignant with the mistress for introducing a class of people whom they did not wish to see among them;—that remonstrances had been made without effect,—that no notice of her intention had been given to them; and that even her father had not been consulted. I remarked, in reply, that every one in a free country had a right to act as he pleased, providing he did not injure the property or persons of others, whose wishes ought not to influence or determine him in the pursuit of what he might consider the performance of a duty or the gratification of a harmless whim; and that a parent cannot exact implicit obedience from a child who is old enough to judge for himself.

He then said she had acted contrary to the law of the State; and I recalled to his recollection what he seemed to have forgotten, or thought I did not know, that the law to which he had alluded was passed after, and in consequence of the establishment of her school; and that it was hardly fair to expect she would bow to the authority of an enactment, while she was taking the only steps in her power to prove its unconstitutionality. We then took our leave of Mr. Bacon, and returned to Brooklyn.

The following Monday I went to Hartford, where a cause had lately been tried of great importance to the working classes. A suit had been brought by a manufacturing company against some men for conspiring together to raise wages by effecting a strike, and to hinder others from engaging in the employment of the plaintiffs. After a week's hard fighting, the verdict was in favor of the defendants, as the other party could not make out such a case of direct injury as would entitle them to damages. The spirit of combinations by which the whole Union has been for a long time agitated, is likely to be considerably influenced by this decision; since it places the courts of justice in a position of strict impartiality between the contending parties.

It was a novel case, and the lawyers were puzzled to find any analogies to take the place of precedents.

The plaintiffs had appealed to a higher court. In the mean time the operatives, it is to be hoped, will discover that strikes are more injurious to them than to their masters. What with the fall of wages, which the derangement of commerce through its various channels from the producer to the consumer occasions, the loss of labor during the continuance of the " turn out," the introduction of rivals, and the cost of maintaining a greedy and ambitious executive, it is generally found that the termination of a strike finds the workman in a worse situation than he was at its commencement.

It is lamentable to see the great body of the mechanics united in the pursuit of an unattainable object, calling out for a maximum of rent, and a minimum of wages, accusing the rich of oppressing the poor, and bankers of growing wealthy by preying on the community, insisting upon a metallic currency to the exclusion of paper, deprecating the introduction of every thing foreign, and waging war against invention;—while designing demagogues are climbing on their shoulders to office, flattering them in their illusions, and cajoling them out of their rights. The system of combination is not confined to sex or country. The "young ladies" of Lowell have declared they will no longer submit to the tyranny of the cotton-lord; and the operatives of Canada are making common cause with their brethren on the other side of the lakes. The country has long been

distracted with these disputes. In 1828, the jour-
neymen cotton-weavers of New York struck for
wages, and several of them cut the webs out of the
looms of an establishment, the owner of which refused to comply with their demands, his own workmen having declined joining them. Another set of
men, employed on the river, carried their resistance
so far, as to attack a packet ship (the Sully) with
the view of persuading or compelling her men to
desist from their work. The captain was severely
injured by them. Two or three other vessels were
treated in a similar manner; and it was not till the
police had been called in that the riot was quelled.
This violence has yielded to a more regular organization and a quieter mode of proceeding,—more per-
nicious, perhaps, to society, as the combination continues longer, and is mixed up with political ran-
cour.

A work, which excited the public mind in England very strongly some years ago, " The Claims of
Labor against Capital," was republished in America,
and appears, in conjunction with others of a worse
tendency, to have had a bad effect upon society by
loosening the ties that bind its members together.
Some of the doctrines, however, inculcated by the
writers of these publications, were of such a revolting
and preposterous nature, (such as community of women and equal division of property,) as to carry
their own remedy and refutation with them. The

good sense of the country preserved it from applying a real and a permanent poison as a cure for
imaginary and partial disorders.   The " Fanny
Wright's men " have dwindled down to a small sect,
who have neither mind to reflect nor conscience to
feel.   The foundress has followed the example of
Mary Wolstonecraft, and is now performing the duties of married life in France ; while the colony she
planted in the West, by pursuing an opposite course,
has disgusted every man who has any regard for the
decencies and duties of life.

When I left Hartford there were three places
taken by the stage, they were marked in the way-
bill, (1) a lady, (2) a lady, (3) a colored man.   I was
rather surprised to see the latter " booked."   I asked
why the names had been omitted.   I was told it was
to secure the first two against annoyance ; and to
show those, who applied for places, what sort of a
fellow-traveller they were to have in the third ; that
they might take what steps they thought fit on such
an occasion.   I thought I had seen most of the
" whims and oddities " of the country ;—but here
was one more amusing than any I had yet met with.
Concealment of names employed at the same time
to shelter one party from insult and expose another
to it !—a general description, serving as a protection
and an opprobrium to persons who are in close
contact, and people travelling incognito in the same

vehicle, because they are respected, and because they are despised !

While I was at New York, I was introduced to an Englishman, (Mr. George Thompson,) who had just arrived with the intention of lecturing upon the subject of slavery, in connexion with the prejudice against color. He was sent out by an anti-slavery association in Scotland; as the Americans send out missionaries to Burmah or Africa; and the reception he met with, like the cannibal propensities of savages, proved the necessity of a remedy by the violence of the diseased against the physician. Threats had long been uttered through the press against him. While boarding at one of the most respectable houses in the city, he was informed by the landlord, with expressions of regret that he was compelled to communicate the illiberal sentiments of his countrymen, that he must forthwith look out for some other establishment; as his guests had all signified to him, in a body, their determination to remain no longer under the same roof with the English agitator. The papers took good care to let the public know what had passed; adding, with a few embellishments, a hint, that they trusted no one would take him in, except upon the condition that he would not address a public audience on the subject of slavery:—a higher tribute of respect to the man than to their own cause. I heard several men

conversing upon the matter, and applauding what
had been done. Free discussion is not allowed
whether to strangers or to citizens. The most enlightened and liberal people in the world are afraid of
having the merits of their political and social system
submitted to an open investigation. The same persons who call on you to admire, forbid you to condemn. Write against freedom, and your work will
be received with the highest honors*; speak in favor of it, and you run the risk of being tarred and
feathered. You may praise America from your
hatred of tyranny; but you must not censure her
from your hatred to tyrants. If you chance to hint
that the cap of liberty, which you see glittering at
the top of a long pole, is placed so high that every
fifth man cannot reach it, and is so shrunk by exposure to a bad air that the other four cannot wear
it, you will soon wish yourself back in a free country.

The new mission of philanthropy has been eminently successful. Such has been the persuasive
eloquence, with which its objects have been ad-
vocated, that, after sixteen public addresses delivered in the course of a fortnight, urgent applications had been received in February from upwards

---

* The Bill, passed by the British Legislature, for the Abolition of Slavery, is now, with marginal notes by the Committee
of the West Indian Planters, in the library of the Athenæum
at Philadelphia.

of 100 different places for immediate lectures. The cause is, indeed, making the most extraordinary progress; the prejudice which seemed to be the chief obstacle, having become its auxiliary,—for all, who are converted, feel that they owe reparation for the injustice they have committed. An anti-Slavery Society has been formed in Kentucky, under more favorable auspices than any that ever attended similar associations in the South.

Two ministers of the Baptist persuasion (Dr. Cox and Mr. Hoby) have just embarked from this country for Richmond in Virginia, on a spiritual mission to their brethren in the United States. They have made up their minds to bear reproach, and persecution, and death itself, in the performance of what they consider a sacred duty. They will remonstrate with the teachers of religion on the neglect of its high duties in their congregations and in themselves: and they are sustained by those principles which can alone ensure success to human efforts, or afford consolation under their failure.

The tie which supports slavery, by binding together the churches of the South with those of the North, will now present the best point of attack upon it. There were, in 1833, 752 Presbyterian churches, with 51,599 communicants in the slave States. The Baptists had 3007 churches, with 215,513 communicants; while the Methodists were still more numerous. There was not one society of orthodox Congregationalists in that section of the Union. We can readily believe that the Pilgrims never passed the Potomac; for their doctrines are not to be found on the other side. There are more abolitionists among the latter than among other religionists. Their independence of ecclesiastical jurisdiction and of sectarian connexion, will explain the reason, while it explains also, why they never gained footing among the planters. They might have proved troublesome, and they could not have exercised any influence in the North.

CHAPTER XXXII.

Plunder and Murder of the Blacks at Philadelphia.—Their Forbearance and Resignation.—How to prevent Riots.—Advice to the Victims.—Results to be seen at Columbia.—John Randolph's Last Moments.—His Will disputed.

On the 26th, I went to Philadelphia, where I made inquiries into the causes of those riots, that had taken place in the city during my absence. They were similar, in their origin and objects, to what had previously occurred at New York; and were clearly the result of a preconcerted organized plan—the end aimed at, being the expulsion of the blacks; and the plot embracing many, whose rank in society would secure concealment, while it gave facilities to the conspiracy.

I will give the facts, as far as I was enabled to ascertain them, in the exact order in which they occurred. On the 14th of July, the " Pennsylvania Enquirer and Courier," speaking of the New York riots, made use of the following words: " With regard to Philadelphia, we have not the slightest apprehension; for no public journalist in this city would, under existing circumstances, give place to a call for a meeting of abolitionists : and we feel assured that the proper authorities will be fully sustained by the community in preventing, by force if necessary, the circulation of any hand-bills having reference to an abolition meeting."

On the 29th, the same paper had the following paragraph. " We perceive that the ' Journal of Commerce' has charged the ' Courier and Enquirer ' and ' Commercial Advertiser ' * with provoking the riots. This charge is in a certain sense true ; but we, nevertheless, rather approve than disapprove of the course pursued by those journals, when we consider the circumstances. The papers, alluded to, observing the movements of the fanatics, saw that unless they were indignantly checked by the people, —unless some strong and decided demonstration of public feeling was made against them, the people of the South would take the alarm, and a disruption of the Union be the result. Hence it became the object—the commendable object—of the presses alluded to, to obtain a decided expression of sentiment ; and, in order to obtain it, they perhaps went too far, appealed too warmly to public opinion and feelings. At all events they accomplished their object. A popular demonstration upon the subject

* These are all New York papers.

of amalgamation was given—a demonstration that the fanatics are not likely soon to forget; and, though our contemporaries in New York cannot but regret the excesses committed by the mob,—cannot but deprecate the recurrence of any similar scenes, and more the necessity for them, still they must feel conscious of having discharged a duty—of having stepped between a band of wild and erring enthusiasts, who were rapidly urging on a civil revolution, or a dissolution of this beautiful Union." After these hints followed a direct appeal to the ferocious passions of the populace; and the next day the rabble, who had thus been tutored and prepared, rushed upon their prey with the savage delight of well-trained blood-hounds, and the hope of plenary indulgence and perfect impunity.

The riots took place on the 12th of August; on the 11th the following communication appeared in the "Commercial Herald:" "Among the evils to which our good citizens are subjected, there is none more universally complained of, than the conduct of the black porters who infest our markets*; it being

---

* Forty years ago a colored man appeared, for the first time, as a carman at Philadelphia. Great jealousy was excited among that class of men; and every expedient was tried to get rid of a competitor whose success would draw others into the business. Threats and insults were followed by a report that he had been detected in stealing. The Quakers came forward to support him. They inquired into the grounds of the charge,

the business of these colored gentlemen, for the most part, to market for the public-houses. Is there no way, Mr. Editor, in which the persons of our citizens can be protected from their assaults? Is there no way in which the rudeness and violence of these ruffians can be prevented? If not, it is high time for the ladies at least to retire, and give up the privilege of marketing to those with whom might is right?"

It is evident from this diabolical calumny, that the attack, which followed next day, was preconcerted. The colored porters are remarkable every where for their civility. It would be easy to magnify any accident, that might happen from a man carrying a heavy load through a crowded market, into an intentional insult; and thousands would be ready to give credit and circulation to the complaint. All doubt upon the subject will be removed by reference to what occurred on the night of the ninth. One of Mr. Forten's sons, a boy about fifteen years of age,

and published its refutation. Their patronage maintained him in his situation, and encouraged others to follow his example. There are now plenty of them thus employed. At New York, a license cannot be obtained for them; and a black carman in that city is as rare as a black swan. This little anecdote ought to call up a blush on the cheek of many a " Friend." It tells him, in language as plain as his garb, that he might have protected these unfortunate men from rapine and murder, if he had acted in conformity to the practice of his forefathers, and his own professions.

who had been sent out on an errand, was attacked, on his return, about nine o'clock, by a gang of fifty or sixty young men in blue jackets and trowsers, and low-crowned straw hats. They were armed with cudgels, which they made use of to strike him as he lay stunned by a blow he had received from one of them. Their eagerness to get at him enabled him to escape; as their sticks crossed one another in the confusion, and he ran off. A neighbor—a white man,—followed the gang, out of regard for the lad's father, and was present when they were dismissed in an adjoining street by their leader. They were thanked for their services, and informed that they were to meet on the same spot, and at the same time on the 11th, the next day being Sunday. " We will then," he exclaimed, " attack the niggers." On the Monday, Mr. Forten communicated what had passed to the mayor, who sent a police force to the place of rendezvous, and took seven of the gang into custody:— one of whom had unguardedly displayed a bludgeon, vowing vengeance against the blacks. The rest made their escape. The culprits were bound over to keep the peace in recognizances of 300 dollars each. The city was thus prepared against the me- ditated assault; and the outrages were confined to the districts out of the mayor's jurisdiction. Having, however, obtained authority from the sheriff, the chief officer of the city proceeded to the scene of action with constables, rushed into the mob with great courage, and dispersed the rioters, having taken several prisoners. Mr. Forten's life was threatened; and both the mayor and the sheriff, by whom he is most deservedly respected, promised to protect him. His house was guarded by a horse patrol, who continued in their rounds to pass it at short intervals; and the *posse comitatus*, amounting to 5000 men, well armed, were called out, as the municipal authorities were determined to put down the disturbances at once in their district, by shooting the offenders, should they persevere in their nefarious proceedings. Had not these energetic measures been timely taken, the whole city might have been a prey to thieves and vagabonds.

An Irishman, of the name of Hogan, behaved most nobly on this occasion. Having heard that Mr. Forten's house was likely to be attacked, he offered his services to defend it. " Whoever," said he, " would enter at this door, to injure you or your family, my friend, must pass over my dead body." These facts I had from Mr. Forten himself. Another person,—a benevolent Quaker,—whom the blacks, as one of them told me, almost adore for his kindness to them, related to me what he had himself witnessed. He went among the mob, and listened to their menaces, and imprecations against the colored people. The leader, with whom he entered into conversation, (he had not his Quaker dress on,) producing a long knife he had concealed in his bosom, swore he would bury it in the heart's blood of the first black he could get at. The objects of their blind fury, determined to defend themselves with what weapons they could find, had taken refuge, to the number of fifty or sixty, in a building that belongs to them, and is known by the name of Benezet Hall. The staff-officers of the besieging army lay concealed in an alley close by, where they consulted together, and issued their orders, or encouraged the troop to " march forward;"—shouts, that had but little effect, as the party to whom they were addressed moved to and fro in one mass, propelled by those behind, and receding as their fears increased with their proximity to the enemy. The " friend " alluded to succeeded at last in persuading the besieged to re-enter the house, from which they had sallied out; and, with the assistance of a constable, they made their escape by a back-way. The mayor was present, and harangued both sides, exhorting the besieged to remain passive, and not to exhibit any marks of opposition to the other, on pain of forfeiting the chance they had of his protection. This communication was loudly cheered by the rioters:—one of whom called out, " D——n that nigger—see how he insults us!—he is smoking a cigar." My informant, who had marked one of the leaders, delivered him over to a constable ; and they proceeded with him to a magistrate. But the latter declined acting. Other cases occurred, where both magistrates and constables shrunk from their duty. Three constables declared before two magistrates, after the Quaker had retired, that they would not protect his house, if it were attacked or set on fire. The authority of the law, in fact, was gone ; and the peace of the community was at the mercy of a ferocious rabble.

When subscriptions were solicited, after a temporary calm had taken place, to repair the damages done by this frightful whirlwind, some of the citizens refused to give any thing for such an object; observing, that they should have no objection to contribute something, if a fund were raised to send the blacks out of the country—thus openly avowing a participation in that brutal antipathy, which had occasioned the loss both of property and of life. Two at least were killed. One of them was so severely beaten, that he was found at the back of his house covered with blood—he was taken insensible to the hospital, where he soon after expired. The other was drowned in attempting to cross the river with his child. He was seized with cramp or with fear, and had but just time to deliver the infant into the hands of his wife, who was standing on the bank, when he sank beneath the water, and yielded to a death less cruel than the destiny which awaits so many of his race. The blood of the former victim I saw on the ground where he fell. Near the spot stood a tub, into which a woman put her infant children, while she concealed herself behind it from her pursuers, who were hunting for her in the yard. She declared afterwards that the tub, on which she kept her eyes fixed, moved convulsively, as the babes within trembled with fear. Not a cry or a sound issued from it. She had cautioned them to be quiet; and they lay silent as their mangled neighbor.

The furniture of one of the houses I visited was broken to pieces. Chairs, looking-glasses, tables—nothing was spared. The owner escaped almost by miracle, leaving his wife and child up stairs.

The rioters were under the command of a leader, and were searching for plunder; as the master of the house was known to have money upon the premises. He had just built a house, and one reason for attacking it was, that he had employed colored men. Another house I saw, had every thing—windows, staircase, bedsteads, doors—demolished. The proprietor concealed himself in the chimney. His wife was beaten. They had thirty dollars stolen from them. It was a good substantial house.

The mob consisted chiefly of young men—many of them tradesmen. One of the sufferers, a man of wealth and great respectability, was told afterwards by a white, that he would not have been molested, if he had not, by refusing to go to Liberia, prevented others from leaving the country.

I was astonished to meet with so much patience and resignation, under such a series of injuries—

equally unexpected and undeserved. Several of these kind-hearted creatures observed to me, that what had happened was designed by the Almighty for their good; as it had brought out friends whom they had never seen before. It appeared, from all I could learn, during two or three visits I paid to the sufferers, that the Irish laborers were actively employed in this vile conspiracy against a people of whom they were jealous, because they were more industrious, orderly, and obliging than themselves. They were but instruments, however, in the hands of a higher power. An elderly woman, who possessed considerable acuteness and observation, gave me a very clear account of what passed in her own dwelling, where I saw her. The door and the windows were forced in; and she hid herself in a closet, whence she heard and saw all that took place. Some money, that she had left on the chimney-piece, was the first thing seized. The furniture was then destroyed; while several men in black masks, and disguised with shabby coats and aprons, searched about the room to see if any one lay there concealed. She recognised one man's voice, reproving a lad with an oath, for saying they had done enough. This man she washed for. The next day he told her he should not employ her any longer. She laid her complaint before the mayor; and the party accused was bound over to appear at the proper time. While in court, she saw a well dressed man step up to the mayor, and whisper something in his ear. The colored people were immediately ordered out of court. This distinction, before the very seat of justice, however disgraceful to the country, had an object beyond the degradation it implied. The parties, most interested in investigating the truth, were to be excluded; because they had been eye-witnesses of the transaction, or were most competent to understand its details. This woman was remarkably shrewd, and equally quick in seeing the drift of a question, and giving point to the answer. One remark she made with regard to something that had recently occurred, more than once, to herself and other women, confirmed the view that Solon took of human nature, when he omitted parricide in his penal code, ne non tam prohibere quam admonere videretur. The same may be said of the discussions upon the subject of amalgamation.

Another woman, on opening her door when summoned by the rioters, saw, in the first person who entered, a tradesman to whom she was well known. He made some excuse and retired, calling off the " pack". On the following day her windows were repaired; and her neighbors, to whom she had related the events of the preceding night, missed her,— and she had not returned when I was there. She would most likely make her appearance again, when her evidence could be no longer useful. These persecuted, inoffensive people were driven from their dwellings into the fields and lanes, where many passed the night in a state of destitution and apprehension. The municipal authorities refused to admit them into the almshouse, though application was made for the purpose by a respectable man, a physician, from whom I had the information, and though the establishment was untenanted. The mayor, when requested to grant them the place for an asylum, declared that, as an individual, he had no objection to assist them; but that, as chief magistrate, he was afraid to let them in, lest the building should be torn down. He recommended that they should be got in clandestinely. About a dozen procured a retreat there, through the exertions and upon the responsibility of the person to whom I allude. He himself assisted them in his own house to the utmost of his power. Having observed to him how much I had been shocked at the brutality I had witnessed and heard of against the blacks,—" You have not", said he, " seen one-tenth of the horrors that are constantly practised here. I myself have frequently men brought to me with bruises and broken heads, inflicted for no other reason than that they have not made way in time for the white lords of the creation. There," he added, pointing to a little girl who was in the room, " that poor child was sweeping the pavement in front of the house a few days back, when a ruffian struck her a violent blow on the head, and she fell into the street, where her mistress found her in a state of stupor, unable to move, and afraid to cry for help." After this assault the poor creature was afraid to venture out by night,—though she said, that if her master wanted any thing, she would go for it. She was a very good girl; extremely diligent and trustworthy. There was a little colored boy in the house, remarkable for his sensitive feelings. If any thing was said to him that implied inattention on his part, he would shed tears, and redouble his exertions to please his benevolent protectors.

Every one bore testimony to the good conduct and forbearance of the blacks under these severe trials. The Pennsylvania " Enquirer and Courier", a strong anti-abolition paper, expressed itself in the following manner :—" The scene of action lay within the district of Moyamensing ; and the magistrates there declined any interference, on the ground, as they alleged, of their exertions in quelling the riot on the preceding night having met with the disapprobation of the inhabitants of the district. This appears to be a very singular reason for not attempting to quell a disturbance, more disgraceful than any that our citizens have ever witnessed ; but, as we received it from one of the magistrates himself, we are bound to give it to our readers, as the only reason we can give them why the disturbance was not immediately suppressed.

" From the same source, as well as through other channels, we are assured that, notwithstanding the fearful height which the riot reached, and the great

destruction of property that followed, the whole affair
might have been effectually suppressed by the exertions of twenty or thirty resolute and determined
men. This, however, was not done; and the dwellings of unoffending blacks, against whom not a shadow of offence was even alleged, were shamefully
abused,—the inmates compelled to flee for safety,
and their furniture broken up and scattered about the
streets."

I was assured by a person of the strictest veracity,
who had conversed with many of the inhabitants of
the district after the riots had ceased, that an extraordinary degree of apathy and indifference prevailed
among them with regard to the injury inflicted upon
the sufferers, the punishment of the offenders, and
the reparation to be made for the damage done. The
proprietors of the houses in that quarter seemed
anxious to get rid of a population, the presence of
which they considered prejudicial to their interests,
by preventing the introduction of a more wealthy
class of people.

A committee was appointed by the inhabitants of
Philadelphia, to inquire into the causes and consequences of these riots. I have extracted a few passages from their elaborate report, as I think they
evince a degree of pusillanimous partiality irreconcileable with the duties they had undertaken to perform. " They came"—such are the words they use
—" to a determination to avoid, so far as a faithful

discharge of duty would permit, the vexing and dis-
tracting questions and opinions which influence the
minds of a large portion of our citizens in relation to
recent events." This, one would have thought,
amply sufficient for the purpose;—but, no,—they
must add—" The committee are sensible of the importance attached to the opinions and questions to
which they allude, and of their probable momentous
and extensive influence on the peace and welfare not
only of this district but of the whole United States."

" Among the causes which originated the late
riots, are two, which have had such extensive influence, that the committee feel they would be subject to censure, if they did not notice them. An
opinion prevails, especially among white laborers,
that certain portions of our community prefer to
employ colored people, whenever they can be had,
to the employing of white people; and that, in consequence of this preference, many whites, who are
able and willing to work, are left without employment, while colored people are provided with work,
and enabled comfortably to maintain their families;
and thus many white laborers, anxious for employment, are kept idle and indigent. Whoever mixed
in the crowds and groups, at the late riots, must so
often have heard those complaints, as to convince
them, that the feelings from which they sprang, sti-
mulated many of the most active among the rioters.
It is neither the duty nor the intention of the Com-

mittee to lay down rules for the public, or the government of individuals, but they deem it within the obligations imposed upon them, to make the statements they have made, and leave the matter for correction to the consideration and action of individuals." Whether the hated competition, or the unreasonable jealousy, be " the matter for correction," we are not informed. I may just observe, that the same people cannot well be a burthen to the rich by their idleness, and a nuisance to the poor by their industry. " The other cause, to which the Committee would refer, is the conduct of certain portions of the colored people, when any of their members are arrested as fugitives from justice," (meaning the justice of the slave owner). " It has too often happened, that, when such cases have been under the consideration of the judicial authorities of the country, the colored people have not relied on the wisdom and justice of the judiciary; on the exercise of the best talents at the bar, or on the active and untiring exertions of benevolent citizens, who promptly interest themselves in their behalf; but they have crowded the court-houses and the avenues to them, to the exclusion of almost all other persons: they have forcibly attempted the rescue of prisoners, and compelled the officers of justice to lodge them for safety in other prisons than those to which they had been judicially committed. Scenes like these have given birth to unfriendly feelings for those who have thus openly assailed the officers of justice."

This spirit of contumacy in a race remarkable (according to Dr. Channing) for want of sympathy with one another, must certainly seem unaccountable as well as vexatious. The American, who assisted Lafayette to escape from the prison at Olmutz, and the Englishmen, who performed the same friendly office for Lavalette, have been held up to the admiration of mankind.—But then the objects of *their* sympathy were the victims of political slavery, and had *only* conspired against the government of their country. Though " it is neither the duty nor the intention of this Committee to lay down rules for the government of individuals," yet they are kind enough to make an exception in favor of those who stand most in need of their paternal solicitude. " As the peace of every community," they are pleased to say, " however large and peaceably disposed, may be endangered and broken by the machinations of a few designing or turbulent persons, it is deemed a portion of the duty of this Committee, to make such suggestions as, in their opinions, may tend to avert so dreaded an event, as an irruption upon the quiet of any portion of our population. Nothing will tend to win the good opinion, and secure the good offices of the community more than a respectful and orderly deportment. It would do much good if those of the colored population, whose age and character entitled them to have influence, would take the trouble to exercise it, and impress upon their younger brethren the necessity, as well as the propriety, of behaving themselves inoffensively and with civility at all times and upon all occasions; taking care, as they pass along the streets, or assemble together, not to be obtrusive, thus giving birth to angry feelings, and fostering prejudices and evil dispositions."

The horrid murder, of which I have spoken, is thus alluded to in this singular document. " The case of Stephen James is entitled to *some considera-tion.* He was an honest, industrious, colored man, a kind husband and a good father. He had retired to rest on the night of the 14th of August, but was aroused by the clamor of the mob. The cries which met his ears soon informed him that he was in danger, and he fled for safety. He was, however, overtaken, and wounded in many places, even unto death. He never spoke, after he was found wounded in the yard. The Committee do not believe, that among all the persons who made up the mob assembled on this occasion, there was one wicked enough to contemplate taking the life of an inoffensive and unoffending aged man.—Yet in truth they did this accursed thing. These facts are stated to induce men to reflect upon the desperate deeds, which mobs, without desperate intentions, may commit."

While complaints were thus made, in a free State, that the free blacks were too industrious to please the lower classes, they were accused in a slave-State of being too respectable to please the higher. " The Grand Jurors of the State of Missouri, empannelled for the county of Saint Louis," recommended, a few days before, that the law against the introduction of such persons having proved " entirely inadequate in its provisions to accomplish the object of this constitutional provision," the evil should be met " by the strongest legislative enactments with the utmost certainty and despatch." " Let not individuals of this class," they imploringly pray, " come to the State and remain for years, drawing around themselves families and property, and forming connexions, until the sympathies of the people would make them exceptions to the general enforcement of the law."

Not long after this, Dr. Parrish, one of the most amiable and respected of men, was mobbed at Columbia in Pennsylvania, and his personal safety threatened, for trying to undeceive the public mind with respect to the condition of the colored citizens of Philadelphia. They had been most grossly libelled by an advocate of the Colonization Society; and the Doctor had sent home for official documents, to disprove the charge against them. A gang of young men, who came to the house where he was staying, with the intention to assault or insult him, were awed into forbearance by his mild firmness—but he judged it prudent not to address the people on the subject.

Some dreadful riots, accompanied with destruction of property, broke out at the same place in October, owing, it was said, to the marriage of a white woman with a black man. The complexion, however, of the latter was so little to be distinguished from that of his wife, that he was taken for a white in Maryland, where he was travelling with a black, whom he saved from incarceration by declaring that he knew him to be a free man. This evidence was acknowledged by the authorities to be satisfactory, and his companion was released by the intervention of one who was not recognised, even in a slave-State, as subject to the same suspicion and disqualification. This account I received from a person who was well acquainted with him, and had himself been driven out of Columbia by a set of ruffians, who had got possession of all the offices in the district, and were striving to exclude the colored people from every employment. It is to this feeling that the disturbances are to be traced. At a meeting of the working men of Columbia, August 23, resolutions were passed against the blacks. The preamble, as it was published, contained the following sentiments.—" The practice of others in employing the negroes to do that labor, which was formerly done entirely by whites, we

consider deserving our severest animadversions."—
" Must the poor honest citizens, that so long have
maintained their families by their labor, fly from
their native place, that a band of disorderly negroes
may revel with the money that ought to support the
white man and his family, &c. ? " " As the negroes
now pursue occupations once the sole province of the
whites, may we not in course of time expect to see
them engaged in every branch of mechanical business ? and their known disposition to work for any
price may well excite our fears, that mechanics at
no distant period will scarcely be able to procure a
mere subsistence." It is very singular that whites
are imported into Jamaica, because the blacks ask
too much for their labor, and are exported from
Pennsylvania, because they ask too little.

After this bill of grievances, it was naturally
enough resolved by these ill-used men, that—(I use
their own words)—" we will not purchase any
article (that can be procured elsewhere) or give our
vote for any office whatever, to any one who employs
negroes to do that species of labor white men have
been accustomed to perform." " Resolved that the
Colonization Society ought to be supported by all the
citizens favorable to the removal of the blacks from
this country." On the 26th of the same month, the
citizens met and passed *their* resolutions—James
Given, Esq. in the chair. One of them was to this
effect: " That a committee be appointed whose

duty it shall be to communicate with that portion of
those colored persons who hold property in this
borough, and ascertain, if possible, if they would be
willing to dispose of the same at a fair valuation;
and it shall be the duty of the said committee, to
advise the colored persons in said borough to
refuse receiving any colored persons from other
places as residents among them."

It is to be presumed, that the committee, appointed
for these praiseworthy purposes, were unsuccessful
in obtaining what they counted on, their "fair
valuation"; ejectment being soon after substituted
for "purchase," and the owners compelled to move
without any valuation at all. One of the sufferers,
writing to a friend in Philadelphia, says: "We had
another severe riot in this place last night, which
causes our minds to be very uneasy. The rioters began
their work of destruction between 11 and 12 o'clock,
and continued till about 2 o'clock, when we were
alarmed by the cry of ' fire! ' On looking, we beheld
Mr. Cooper's (carpenter) shop enveloped in flames
from top to bottom. It was entirely destroyed, together
with all his tools, and a large quantity of lumber of all
kinds dressed out for a large building now going up
in this place, together with Mr. Eddy's stable adjoining. It is supposed to have been set on fire
by some incendiaries. Four houses were nearly
destroyed by the rioters. One of the inmates,
named James Smith, was nearly beaten to death.

The rioters entered their houses and destroyed every bit of furniture that they could find—even the stoves were broken in pieces, and the flour was thrown out into the street. I feel no disposition of abandoning my house, until I have disposed of my personal property, unless they will persist a good deal further." Not one angry expression, nor even a complaint occurs in this letter. It is dated, October 3d, 1834, and is now in my possession. The report of the Philadelphia Committee, before quoted, appeared on the 17th of September. How far it was calculated to protect the black man, may be seen in the proceedings against him at Columbia.

Dr. Parrish, of whom I have just spoken, was present at the last moments of John Randolph. This eccentric Virginian had emancipated his slaves by will in 1822, and had ten years afterwards appointed a different disposition, and ordered them to be sold. On his death bed he made a most solemn declaration, in accordance with his first intention; and, as the latter bequest was accompanied by circumstances that indicated the presence of temporary insanity, a strong hope is entertained, that the last wish he expressed may be carried into effect. The matter is now in course of litigation; and Judge Leigh, of Virginia, who is one of the executors of the last testament, by which he is to receive a legacy of 10,000 dollars, in addition to one of 5000 to his son, has, it is said, very honorably renounced his claim,

from a conviction that it is inequitable if not illegal.
Dr. Parrish attended both as physician and as witness,
when the nuncupative will was announced. John,
or Johnny—the favorite slave of the dying man, remained in the chamber the whole time; having locked the door at his master's desire, and put the key in
his pocket. This was done to insure the presence of
a white man ; that the benefit intended for the slaves
might not by any possibility be defeated for want of
legal proof. The scene, as it was related to me by
the Doctor, must have been singularly interesting.
It took place in an hotel at Philadelphia. The invalid, who, as is well known, was remarkably tall
and thin, being upwards of six feet in height, and
but fourteen inches across the shoulders, raised himself up from the bed on which he was reclining, and
desired his man to draw a blanket in the Indian
fashion over him, so as to cover the whole of his
person but the face, and to place his hat—a very
shabby worn out habiliment—upon his head. He
then requested that a silver button, worn by his father, should be fixed on his shirt, and John cut a
hole in the linen for that purpose. When these
ceremonies, by which it would seem he wished to
denote his Indian blood on the mother's side, and his
patrician descent on the father's, were completed,
three other witnesses were called in, and he declared
his intention to emancipate all his slaves, dwelling
with great emphasis on that part of his will which

provided for their comfortable support. The negro stood by absorbed in grief. The other witnesses were the landlord of the house, and two young men whom Dr. Parrish had invited, with the view of being prepared, not only to produce a sufficient amount of testimony, but to obviate any objections that might be made to his religious principles, which might perhaps be thought to bias the mind of a Quaker, while giving his evidence in favor of the slaves.

Every witness was distinctly asked, in succession, if he fully comprehended what he had heard. The Doctor then retired with the landlord, and, on his return about an hour after, he found several of the testator's friends in the room. His patient had, however, become incapable of utterance, and shortly after, John Randolph, of Roanoke, was no more.

I have omitted to state that the dying man exclaimed, in the presence of his physician and his slave—" Remorse! Remorse! You do not know what remorse is, Doctor. Shew me the word in a book!—look for it in a dictionary!"—It could not be found in a printed form.—" Write it down then." The Doctor wrote it down on a card. " Write it on the other side too:—and let Johnny make a mark under it with a pencil." The card is now in possession of the physician, with the pencil marks upon it.

" John Randolph, of Roanoke, had about 400

slaves. Their value was estimated at 100,000 dollars.
He gave them clothing enough at Christmas to last
them the whole year—as coats, hats, bedding, blan-
kets, &c., and all who took care of what they received were well dressed men. He sent food from
his own kitchen to all the unmarried ones, and plenty
of provisions to be cooked by those who had families in their own cabins. He had five or six nurses,
whose business it was to attend to the sick. And
his overseer had special directions never to inflict a
blow. He punished them as we punish children—
by withholding some favor, as sugar from the
children, and meat from the men. Whenever he
rode over the plantations, the field-servants took off
their hats and he touched his. He always had
some witty remark to amuse them in their labor, and
conciliate their love. His body-servant had the
keys of the house, and often carried his master's
purse; and, though he was by no means uncom-
monly kind, yet they all loved him when alive, and
lamented his death."

The above statement is made by a correspondent
of the Salem Register, who strives hard to shew that
slavery is *not* a " bitter draught." Yet what was
the most urgent wish of this man's heart in his
dying moments? What was his last act of benevolence to these grateful creatures, when about to quit
them for ever, and appear before the great Father
and Judge of all?—A grant of freedom, with all the

forms and precautions that his sense of duty and his knowledge of the world could suggest!

His will, which is dated Jan. 1, 1832, bears internal evidence that the testator (a man remarkable in general for his acuteness) was at the time in a state of mental aberration. " I do hereby appoint," he says, " my friend William Leigh, of Halifax, and my brother, Henry Saint George Tucker, President of the Court of Appeals, executors of this my last will and testament; requiring them to sell all the slaves, and other personal or perishable property, and vest the proceeds in Bank Stock of the Bank of the United States, and, in default of there being such bank, (which may God grant for the safety of our liberties,) in the English three per cent. Consols; and, in case of there being no such stocks, (which also may God grant for the salvation of Old England,) then in the United States three per cent. Stock; or, in default of such stock, in mortgages or land in England."

Now, whether a man's attachment be greater to one country than to another, he can hardly be said to be of sound mind, if he wishes the property he leaves behind him to aid in injuring the welfare of either or of both—while his legatees are to profit at the expense of a whole nation—perhaps their own, or share in its downfal.

Objections to the last will have been taken on the part of the slaves, who are allowed to sue in formâ pauperum—and commissions have been issued by the general court of Virginia at Richmond, to take depositions in Philadelphia and London on the matters in issue.

I must now reverse the picture, and pass from the benevolence of the departed, to an opposite disposition in the living, slave-holder. A planter's wife, who had the character of a pious Christian, upon hearing that I had said, in the warmth of discussion, that I should have no objection to my daughter's marrying a colored man, if no one could find any other objection than his complexion, declared, with great indignation, that she would not admit a man of such abominable sentiments to her presence. Yet the chief, if not the only, society this woman had, was made up of men whose daughters were married to colored men, and of women whose husbands and sons are known to be daily doing, in violation of the religion she professes, what she will not allow me to be willing should be done with its sanctions. This intolerant person was an inmate of the same house with myself.

Her character, as it was described to me, (for I never was in the same room with her,) presented a miniature representation of that lamentable condition to which the possession of unlimited power reduces both individuals and communities. She was proud, overbearing, and importunate—impatient of contradiction, greedy of attention, and highly sensitive of fancied neglect. Her mind would have afforded to the psychological anatomist the finest specimen of morbid structure and anomalous functions. She scolded her husband, spoiled her boy, flogged her slaves, boasted of her importance, set up her caprice as the standard of merit and virtue, and disgusted all about her by her vanity and querulousness. Yet she was an orthodox believer, and very zealous for the salvation of her neighbor's soul, while she was risking her own by torturing his body. Her boy (the only child of his mother) was from nine to ten years of age. He was suffered to run about the house without any one to instruct or direct him; teazing the children and servants, and calling out for the unfortunate girl who administered to his wants and his whims,—" Where is my slave?—where is my negro? She is my negro!—she is my slave!" While the " property" he thus claimed was sedulously employed in making or mending the body-linen of the family with no small degree of taste and skill, the little tyrant would spit in her face, and threaten, if she remonstrated with him, to complain of her to his parents. Had he committed any fault, or been thwarted of any indulgence, a lie to his mother brought him a sympathizer with his complaints, and an avenger of his wrongs. A threat that he would not visit her sick room (for she was an invalid) made him the master of her will. With such a disposition he was dreaded by the black girl, and detested by the children for his malice and falsehood. In short, he was an insufferable plague to all who came near him, and bade fair to be a scourge to his parents, and a curse to society.

You might see in his handsome countenance the signs of that fearlessness and self-complacency by which the Southerners are usually characterised. In the selfishness of his smile lay, not yet fully developed, that indifference to the rights of others which is complimented with the title of high-mindedness and generosity; and the fretful frown that succeeded, concealed within the deep foldings of his brow the undaunted recklessness with which he would one day grasp his dirk to avenge an insult, or brandish the cow-hide to enforce a command.

As for the father of this precocious autocrat, he was a mere cipher—too weak to control his wife or correct his child,—a martyr, in his old age, to conjugal and parental dotage,—more degraded than his slaves—for even their enemies admit, that half their manly virtue is still left to *them*.

CHAPTER XXXIII.

Slave of Royal Blood.—Free Blacks Wards to Jews.—Character of Slaves.—Election Riots.—Loss of Life.—Funeral Procession. — " Caucus" System. — Arts of Demagogues. — Last
Day at Philadelphia. — Treatment of English Subjects. —
" Clandestine Marriage," and Conclusion.

AMONG the many persons of color whom I visited at
Philadelphia, was a woman of singular intelligence
and good breeding. A friend was with me. She
received us with the courtesy and easy manners of a
gentlewoman. She appeared to be between thirty
and forty years of age—of pure African descent,
with a handsome expressive countenance and a
graceful person. Her mother, who had been stolen
from her native land at an early age, was the daughter of a king, and is now, in her eighty-fifth year,
the parent stem of no less than 182 living branches.
When taken by the slavers, she had with her a piece
of gold as an ornament, to denote her rank. Of this
she was of course deprived; and a solid bar of the
same metal, which her parent sent over to America
for the purchase of her freedom, shared the same

fate. Christiana Gibbons*, who is thus the grand-daughter of a prince of the Ebo tribe, was bought, when about fifteen years of age, by a woman who was struck by her interesting appearance, and emancipated her. Her benefactress left her, at her death, a legacy of 8,000 dollars. The whole of this money was lost by the failure of a bank, in which her legal trustee (a man of the name of James Morrison, since dead) had placed it in his own name. She had other pro-perty, acquired by her own industry, and affording a rent of 500 dollars a year. Her agent, however, Colonel Myers, though indebted to her for many attentions and marks of kindness during sickness, had neglected to remit her the money from Savannah, in Georgia, where the estate is situated; and, when I saw her, she was living, with her husband and son, on the fruits of her labor.

She had not been long resident in Philadelphia, whither she had come to escape the numerous impositions and annoyances to which she was exposed in Georgia. Her husband was owner of a wharf in Savannah, worth eight or ten thousand dollars. It is much to be feared that the greater part of this property will be lost, or not recovered

* An African prince, (Abou Bekir Sadiki,) born in Timbuc-too, has recently obtained his freedom by obtaining the remis-sion of his apprenticeship, after thirty years' bondage in Jamaica. Specimens of his writing in Arabic, which he acquired in his native land, may be seen at the office of the British and Foreign Society for the Abolition of Slavery, No. 18, Aldermanbury.

without great difficulty. I was induced to call upon her, in consequence of a letter I had received from Mr. Kingsley, of whom I have before spoken. He had long been acquainted with her, and spoke of her to me in the highest terms; wishing that I should see what he considered a " good specimen of the race."

We found her, indeed, a very remarkable woman; though it is probable that there are many among the despised slaves as amiable and accomplished as herself. Such, at least, was the account she gave us of their condition, that we felt convinced of the superiority possessed by many, in moral worth and intellectual acuteness, above their oppressors.

Every free black in Georgia, it seems, is obliged to have a guardian, being considered an infant in the eye of the law, or *in statu pupillari*. I need not add that all are thus at the mercy of their legal protectors. They are highly taxed at Savannah, by the State and the Corporation. The amount of the poll-tax is, to each individual, 9 dollars, 75 cents, exclusive of half a dollar for every child between eight and eighteen. They must take out free papers, or have them renewed every year. They cannot even go to Church, unprovided with a pass; and, if found without one after ten o'clock at night, they are imprisoned, and fined five dollars the next day as gaol-fee to the captain of the guard, who receives for his public services twenty dollars per month, besides the little pickings he may thus make from the violation

of a rule, which he must be more honest than most
men not to turn into a source of emolument to himself. The Jews are generally agents for the colored
people, and are well paid for their services. They
seldom act dishonestly towards their clients, for the
love of gain serves as a check to one another's avarice. They have the whole trade in their hands;
and the wealth it brings secures them respect and a
favorable reception from the whites. The colored
people look upon them as their friends. This is a
curious state of society, and the more remarkable, as
something of the same kind, arising from similar
causes, prevails in Poland. What business belongs
to the Pariahs brings high wages and profits from
the exclusion of rivals from without, and the dis-
esteem in which labor is held within the State.
Part of the harvest is shared between the Jews and
the Government; but enough remains to afford a
comfortable maintenance to the lawful possessors, and
prepare them for that new order of things, which is
in slow but certain progress throughout the Southern
States.

Christiana confirmed every thing I had heard from
others with regard to the character of the slaves.
She never knew one who did not long for freedom,
or who felt contented with his lot. Many have
taught themselves reading and writing; having acquired the requisite knowledge with astonishing
rapidity. All are alive to the injustice done them;

and when irritated, tell their owners openly that
they have no right to the labor they force out of
them.   Some will rather suffer death than be
separated from the objects of their affection.   Their
firmness is so well known, that a resolution to this
effect, when once pronounced, will deter any one, at
a sale, from purchasing them separately.   When
standing on a table to be sold, they often cry out to
any one who is known for his cruelty, "You may
buy me, for power is in your hands:—but I will
never work for you."   One woman exclaimed to a
planter, notorious for his barbarity, "Buy me if you
please ; but I tell you openly, if I become your slave,
I will cut your throat the first opportunity."   The
man trembled with rage and fear:—the latter was
the stronger—and he shrank from the bidding.

Christiana had not forgotten that she had royal
blood in her veins, and she showed herself worthy of
the distinction it implied, by her willingness to engage in any work that did not carry moral degradation with it.   Often had she assisted the whites to
clear away the rubbish from their houses, and arrange
the furniture which their indolence and inattention
to comfort had exposed to damage or decay.   There
was nothing, in which her superiority to the pale-
faced fools among whom she had spent the best
years of her life, shone out more conspicuously, than
her disdain for the paltry prejudice that leads a man
to see in the employment of the bodily powers which

Nature has bestowed upon him, a mark of debasement or a misfortune. She had too much honest pride to blush at being useful, and too much regard for her own dignity to shrink from the exercise of those faculties which are destined to keep the mind in a healthy state, while they contribute to the support of its companion *. Her remarks on this subject arose, without parade or affectation, from the conversation in which we were engaged, and were strictly in accordance with those feelings which observation had led me to attribute to persons in her situation ; feelings that are not the less natural, because they are opposed to those preconceptions, by which we are led to believe that the slave sees nothing in freedom, but the gratification of idleness, and an exemption from the degradation of work. He has no such feeling; and we are as irrational in estimating the results of his position, as we were unjust in fixing it upon him. As for Christiana, if I might judge from the tenor of her conversation, her hand and heart were never at fault, when danger or distress called for the exertion of either. She had a strong sense of

* Even the wisest men of antiquity were not exempt from the weakness which this woman had conquered. Cicero says, that all employments, exercised by slaves, are sordid and degrading. " Illiberales et sordidi quæstus mercenariorum, omniumque quorum operæ, non quorum artes emuntur. Est enim illis ipsa merces auctoramentum servitutis." Cic. de Off. 1. 42.

He makes, however, an exception in favor of agriculture.

religion; and the violation of its injunctions, she had been so long doomed to witness in others, had taught her the necessity and value of practical attention to its duties. Her brother, who had come to Philadelphia, under a promise to return to his owner, had informed her of his intention to obtain his freedom by breaking his engagement. " If he does so," said she, " he shall never enter my house again. Whatever may be his wrongs, his honor ought not to be forfeited." This feeling is so general, and so well understood, that masters often allow their slaves to go into other States, upon their promising not to abscond.

Of all the fallacies and falsehoods, to which the cunning of slave-owners, all over the world, has given such unfortunate currency, there is not one that has a smaller intermixture of truth in it, while it has gained almost universal credit, than the imputation of an irresistible inclination to sloth in all who have become free. Emancipation and indolence are indissolubly connected in the minds of too many, to give those, who are groaning in chains, a fair chance of shewing that they may exist apart elsewhere. Because a man is unwilling to work for the benefit of another, it is taken for granted that he will not work for his own; and labor with profit is supposed to be as distasteful as labor without it; as if the old association would keep out the new, and the remembrance of the whip would have more effect on the imagination than the presence of wages upon the senses. When Homer says, that the day which takes from a man his freedom takes from him half his virtue, he speaks of valor not of honesty. The application of the maxim is even more false than the interpretation of the passage, and has destroyed whole communities, by supporting slavery, where it might have saved them by destroying it; for what is lost to the individual is lost to society; and a foreign foe has no better ally than the privation of which the poet speaks.

A few days before I left Philadelphia, the tranquillity of the city was menaced by party violence, the excess of which had cost one of its inhabitants his life—a young man of excellent character, and inoffensive conduct. From what I could make out from the discordant accounts of the contending sections into which the country was divided, the deceased had fallen by a random blow; the wound, which it inflicted, having been found too slight to alarm the medical attendants for his safety. They had left him, the night before his death, in a favorable state:—an internal hæmorrhage, the existence of which had escaped their observation, carried him off before the morning. From the nature and direction of the wound, which had fallen near the femoral artery, there was good reason to believe that it had been occasioned by some one who was endeavoring to escape, with a drawn dirk in his hand, from an onset of the enemy, and had struck him, while moving his hand, in the hurry and confusion of the moment.

Such, however, was not the opinion of the Jackson party, who claimed him as a martyr in their cause, and availed themselves of the occasion, to convert the sympathy of the people into an instrument of detestation against the supposed perpetrators of the outrage.

It was the Bank, that had hired a bravo to strike the fatal blow ; and the lives of the citizens were menaced by its steel, as its liberties were endangered by its gold ! The most inflammatory language was employed in appeals to the nation ; and thousands attended the funeral, displaying their strength, and their resentment by all the devices, that the dread of a defeat at the ensuing election could suggest. There were eight or ten thousand in the procession, headed by the widow and the chiefs of the faction— the members, past, present, and future, of Congress, and the candidate for the honor about to be bestowed by the spectators of the scene. Nothing could well be more calculated to create or increase excitement, than the ceremonies observed at the preliminary proceedings, a few days before, when the judges were chosen for the coming election. The contending parties were mustered in the open street on opposite sides, that the assessors of the votes by which the judges (or by whatever

name they are known) were to be elected, might be
fixed upon. Partial fights took place on the occasion ; and the fierce looks, that were interchanged,
foretold the storm that was about to burst forth.
Such a spectacle was never perhaps witnessed before
in Philadelphia ; and the pageant, which was got up
by the " tories," as the government party are called,
might well inspire the peaceable citizens with alarm
for the results of an exhibition more suited to the
revolutionary movements of a long oppressed people,
than to a community under the protection, and
assembled for the exercise of liberties, created and
controlled by themselves.

On the following Monday, when the election took
place, the apprehensions, so naturally entertained,
were realized; and another victim (if not more) was offered up to the Moloch of civil strife; while many were
severely wounded, and several houses were destroyed;
the fury of the Jackson men having been sharpened
by the victory which their opponents obtained at
the polls. The same spirit was at work, with
more or less violence, throughout the Union, which
might be said to be divided into two distinct camps,
characterised, in the warfare they kept up, by the
usual marks of political strife. It seemed as if there
were no third party of sufficient weight to check the
exuberance of their tendencies, to give consistency
to their attachments, or to instil courtesy into their
hostilities. In most other countries there is an

independent phalanx, to which the nation may look, in times of great emergency, for a dispassionate support of the public good. No such intermediate or neutral body here, has any vote at elections, or any voice in the halls of legislation. Each side has its committee of management or of nomination, who fix upon the candidates, and arrange the requisite preparations. The great body of the electors are virtually disfranchised by the alternative before them, of voting for the tickets offered to their choice by the " Caucus," or of not voting at all. If they are satisfied with neither batch of candidates, there is no remedy. It would be vain to think of any other ; and the chains they have voluntarily assumed, are an insuperable barrier to freedom of election. The State—the municipal—the county—the town elections, are most of them, if not all, concocted in this fashion, and form a series of concentric movements, the springs and agents of which, are to be found in the attractive focus of the presidential chair. Neither constable, nor governor, can assume the badge of office, unmarked by the livery of masters, who enrich themselves by their subserviency to the leaders, and their dupery of the flock.

In the cities (and it is probably the same in the country districts) the nomination of the candidates for office is entrusted to a committee, composed, for the most part, of tradesmen, who are familiar with the different kinds of argument, that are likely to influence the voters. The expenses are defrayed by a species of assessment, which they graduate by a regular tariff, compounded of the means and the zeal of the combatants. Fifteen dollars from one alderman, or twenty from a common council man, are no great object with men who are ambitious of distinction or patronage. There are always good things, and contracts to be bestowed upon their friends; and that sort of gratitude, which has nothing to do with " the memory of the heart," may safely be relied on. It is thus that charitable institutions, reformatory establishments, and the whole train of useful foundations, are too often marred and frustrated, by the control which each junto successively exercises over their trustees and administrators; and the best contrived schemes are often defeated or delayed, by a revolution at Washington, which displaces the whole machinery, at the very moment perhaps of its most successful operation.

The subjoined printed placard, which was stuck up at this election, affords a fair specimen of the arts by which an oligarchy contrive to govern a democracy.

" NOTICE :—

" IN order that a correct account may be obtained of the legal number of voters polled, favorable tò the cause of James Gowen, notice is hereby given, that, so soon as any voter shall have placed his ticket in the hands of one of the inspectors, at either of the windows allotted for that purpose, at the Commis-. sioner's Hall, on the day of the general election, from the opening of the poll till its last close, (no matter at what hour of the night,) he is requested to call immediately afterwards at the house of

" MICHAEL CAVENAGH,
" Corner of Second and Queen Streets,

and hand in his name to a Committee of five persons of the highest respectability, who will be waiting for that purpose, during the whole time of the election. The request is urgently made upon every independent citizen of Southwark, to use all the exertions in his power to carry into successful effect the above satisfactory arrangement, &c.
" By order of the Committee."

This is inimitable! The committee order it to be stated that they are " respectable!"—Were ever people so duped out of their independence? The party for which this self-complacent " Caucus" are acting, are on the anti-Jackson or Whig side! It is of little consequence, which is in, and which is out; since the weapons of defence and of attack are just the same; and the people are equally slaves whether their " friends" or their " enemies" succeed. If this be, as I suspect, the Democratic Whig Committee of Superintendance, the chairman of this virtuous body, who is an Englishman, is playing the very same game in his adopted country which he condemned at home. He is now the editor of a paper, a political intriguer, and a man of no small consequence. I was introduced to him as a person of thoroughly liberal principles, at a private meeting where unrestricted discussion was said to be encouraged, and the honest advocacy of truth the sole object. On my entrance to the presence of these cosmopolites, I called the attention of the company—they were all Englishmen—to the tyrannical conduct of the Anglo-Americans towards their fellow men, and asked whether it was honest or generous to sanction such brutality by direct participation or acquiescent silence?

This " respectable " man took up the cudgels very warmly, and argued in favor of expediency. The person who had introduced me to these boasting, double-faced, " liberty boys " was as much disgusted as myself; for he had known him equally violent against expediency in England. Still this free citizen of a free country was not inconsistent. He was aiming at popularity, and shewed the sincerity of his ambition by the insincerity of his professions. He had entered his solemn protest, as a free thinking Christian, against an orthodox creed in his native country, and he gave in his adhesion, as a free acting republican, to an orthodox color in his adopted country.

I happened, in the course of conversation, to observe, that a time would come when the Americans would atone for their injustice, as they were not wanting in common sense. — " What ! " he exclaimed in a tone of triumph, " you acknowledge then, that they are superior in common sense to the English ? "—" Quite the contrary," was my reply, " my words implied neither contrast nor comparison. I will, however, say that I am sure your former fellow-subjects would not so easily be led away by designing demagogues as your present fellow-citizens." The national vanity, at which travellers are apt to laugh, is as much owing to the base flattery of fawning foreigners as to any other cause whatever. I may add, that the facility with which strangers obtain the elective franchise has proved highly detrimental to the interests of the country, and is likely, if not remedied, to give rise to the worst excesses of corruption or civil discord.

On the 13th of October, I left Philadelphia for New York. On arriving, in company with two or three friends, at the steam-boat, which was to convey me for ever from this beautiful city, I found several others who had come to take leave of me, and unite with the former in the expression of their wishes for my safe return to England. The affectionate farewell, with which they parted from me, still rings in my ears; and I cannot make a more acceptable return for the hospitality and kind offices I received at their hands, than a fervent prayer, that their countrymen may emulate them in their

pure benevolence and exemption from every de-
basing prejudice.

Before I embarked for Europe, I was made acquainted with one of the worst cases of oppression,
as it involves the violation of existing treaties and
municipal laws. The particulars, as I received
them from the sufferers themselves, were subsequently confirmed by an Englishwoman, whom I
saw at New York, and who had known all the
parties for many years,—both in Jamaica and in
Georgia. In December, 1817, Mary Gordon was
taken from Porto Rio Buono, in Jamaica, with her
three children, in the brig Hope, of London, Captain Potter, to Savannah in Georgia, by a woman
of the name of Cooper; who, under a promise of
giving her her freedom, prevailed upon her to quit
the island. Mrs. Cooper had, at the time, two or
three estates in Jamaica. There were two other
females (Nancy Cooper and Lucinda) who were al-
lured by the same artifices, and shared the same
fate. They were all treated as slaves in Georgia.
The two latter are still there. Mary Gordon, however, about a year before I saw the family, came
to New York with her eldest son, as stewardess and
steward in the vessel; their mistress expecting they
would return by it, as they had returned on former
occasions, the mother from England, whither she
had taken her about eighteen years before, and the
son from Liverpool, voluntarily and on account of

his parent and his brothers. Mary had four children; one born seven months after her departure from Jamaica. Of these, two made their escape, three or four years ago, to Cuba, where they got work and were well treated. From that place they went to Nassau in New Providence, whence they came to New York to join their mother. One of these lads had the appearance of an European. No one, they told me, ever insulted them because of their color, while they were on the island. There seems, indeed, to be little if any distinction of the kind there; the free being treated with nearly equal respect, whatever race they belong to. Both these young men observed that they had been more respected in the South than in New York. They were well acquainted with Georgiana Gibbons, and spoke in high terms of her character. Free papers, they said, were often forged in Georgia, as they are in Virginia.

The eldest son had paid between five and six hundred dollars for his freedom. He shewed me the receipts, signed by M. C. M'Queen, in a neat and clear hand. She was Mrs. Cooper's daughter. There was a large bundle of them. The amount was 244 dollars. Others had been lost. They contained accounts, which, with the former, would make the sum of five or six hundred dollars. He said he believed he had paid, in all, nearly twice that sum for his freedom; having advanced, for three years, during which no written account was kept, about twenty dollars a month. This sort of roguery is very common; complaints are useless where punishment is almost impossible. Mrs. M'Queen, in a paper he put into my hands, calls him " perfectly honest, clever, and useful in many ways; but more particularly as a head-waiter." In this document she agrees to take 350 dollars for him. When she enticed him away from Jamaica, she promised to " make a gentleman of him." She always trusted him, he said,—" but," he added, " I will trust her no more." She often importuned him for money; and he had even stripped his coat from his back to satisfy her. One, that was worth sixteen dollars, he had sold for eight. They were all agreed in their description of slavery. It is a system of inconceivable cruelty.

It is high time that British subjects should be protected from the outrages to which their persons and property are exposed in the United States. Not only are they imprisoned, if they venture into some of the Southern States, but they are liable to be robbed or murdered in New York and Philadelphia. One of them, a quiet man, and a valuable member of society, who has resided many years in the former city, had his house broken into, during the late riots, and goods to the value of five or six hundred dollars stolen or destroyed. He was born in one of our colonies; and, as a residence of nearly forty years in the United States, and the most exemplary conduct can never obtain for him the right of citizenship, he may fairly claim protection from our government in return for the allegiance he still owes it. He keeps a register-office for servants, and is well known in the city as a man of unimpeachable integrity, and most obliging behavior. What offence had he given, and what indemnity has he had? None whatever. He had done no more than those who plundered his house, and those who refuse him redress, make a boast of doing. He wore the skin that the Almighty gave him. Ought not such persons to apply to our ambassador for that security which the law or usage denies them? There is no doubt that British subjects are often imprisoned in the United States, in violation of international law, and with perfect impunity. One case occurred in 1817. It was that of a colored man, born and brought up at Saint Bartholomew's, and a seaman in the service of the American Government. He had been sent with twenty-three others from London to Charleston, in South Carolina. The particulars are detailed in an advertisement addressed by the City Marshal " to the owners of fugitive slaves."

" In the brig Samoset, Captain Stevens, who arrived on the 24th of February last, the undermentioned black and colored persons arrived here. They were sent from the port of London by the

American Consul, as distressed seamen; but, having no papers or documents of any kind to prove their freedom, are held by the City Council, so as to give those who have lost slaves, sufficient time to come forward and claim their property." Then follows a list of the names, with a description of the men. " The above described persons of color, having been detained on suspicion of their being slaves, the gentlemen to whom they referred, as being well known, and who, they say, can prove their freedom, are requested to forward on sufficient evidence, so that they might, if free, be immediately liberated," &c.

This advertisement is dated March 5, and the answers from the evidence and from masters, if any, were to be sent in on or before the first day of the ensuing May; when these unfortunate men were to be disposed of " as the law directs." They would all of them, most probably, have been given up to unprincipled claimants, or sold to defray the costs of their detention, had not a benevolent man (Mr. William Turpin) come forward in their behalf. Having personally examined the poor fellows, he applied directly to the highest functionaries of the federal government, and succeeded in rescuing them from the fangs of the local jurisdiction. All of them were eventually discharged, with the exception of two, who were claimed as slaves, and another who, though well known to be a free citizen of Pennsylvania, had been sold by the son of the man to whom, by the abolition act, he was bound apprentice, and carried into Georgia. In his letter to the Secretary of State, (R. Rush, Esq.,) Mr. Turpin says,—" Only consider, that although Mr. Campbell has vouchers for most of these seamen, that would prove their freedom any where to North or East of Maryland, yet if the City Council or City Marshal had, or even any city constable now should contend, by the strictness of our laws, they must be condemned to slavery, except white persons should come here and identify them to be freemen."

In his letter to the Vice-President, (D. D. Tomkins, Esq.,) his words are—" In this State the laws and policy are that every colored person is a slave, until he can prove his freedom. Any person has a right to take up any negro, that has not proper vouchers of his freedom, put him in the house of correction, where negroes are daily sent to be whipt, and advertise him a certain time. If no one appears, he is sold to pay expenses. The laws punish a man with death for stealing a slave : yet only last month a man was indicted for kidnapping a free black, and selling him in the western country, where he never can be found. The indictment only charged him with an assault and battery, and false imprisonment in some place unknown."

We may observe here, that a man can thus have a
more valuable property in the limbs of another
than he has in his own. The whole of the correspondence that passed on this occasion, was submitted to my perusal by Mr. Turpin, who was then
at the advanced age of eighty, living at New York.
He strongly enjoined me not to publish his name,
as he had an intention to visit Charleston, and was
fearful for his own safety, should it be known there
that he had communicated to me what I have here
stated. He is now no more. He is gone where his
good deeds will not condemn him. Among the
letters he lent me was one from Jonathan Hunn, of
the Society of Friends, dated from Camden, State
of Delaware. I subjoin the postscript.

" There is a person from this place, Henry M.
Godwin, now at Columbia, (South Carolina,) after a
number of free blacks who have been kidnapped in
this part of the country, by inhuman human monsters,
and carried off from all that man holds dear by
Southern soul-drivers. The blacks were stopt and
liberated by Claibourn Clifton of that place. I
received a letter from H. M. Godwin a day or two
back, informing me of his safe arrival at Columbia.
He informed me he had seen most of the blacks,
and understood there were many more around in the
neighborhood of Columbia, not more than twenty
miles distant; and that C. C. wished him to see
them. It is astonishing the number of free blacks

that have been kidnapped not many miles from this place." *

I will add another document that I found among Mr. Turpin's papers—as it will give some faint idea of a country where the charity of a dying man dares not express itself openly and directly. It is a clause in a will written by Moses Bradley, of Charleston, (S. C.,) who died in 1812 :—it is as follows:

" To the Society of Friends, called Quakers, in Philadelphia, I leave my servants named Minda, Andrew, Kitty, Susan, Nancy and child, with their issue for ever. The friends of humanity will not be puzzled to know my meaning. I appoint Daniel

---

* The Manumission Society of New York rescued, between 1810 and 1817, 292 free persons from the horrors of slavery. The kidnapper, however, still carries on his trade; as the slaver laughs at our boast of having snatched from his clutches no less than 26,506 victims from January 1, 1827, to January 1, 1833.

The attempt to put down an illegal traffic, which, in supplying a legal demand, affords a benefit beyond the risk of seizure, necessarily drives it into worse channels. The fault and the crime are in the legislature, which makes an arbitrary distinction between acts that are essentially the same. Damon Jones had as much natural right to the " services" of Mr. Gaston, as Mr. Gaston had to the " services " of Damon Jones ; and the law, whether it punishes the one, or protects the other, for doing the same thing, violates and asserts the same principle at the same time.

Latham and William Turpin, of this place, to take charge of these negroes, and to see that this part of my will is duly executed."

I have mentioned one case of a British subject having been imprisoned unjustly; and another seems to have occurred not long ago. In the "Times" of Aug. 23, 1833, is the report of a trial, in which the plaintiff, (Ferguson,) a colored man, recovered wages for the time during which he had been imprisoned in Charleston; the master of the vessel, who had engaged him for a fixed period, having made the loss of his services during his detention a set-off against his claim for the whole amount. Justice Bolland, before whom the trial took place, declared, that the laws of South Carolina could not set aside a pre-existing contract between parties not amenable to their jurisdiction. The man, it appeared, had gone out in the Oglethorpe, from Liverpool. If he was a British subject, no civil damages to him can compensate the nation to which he belongs for this gross insult.

The French nation has equal ground for complaint. There are some curious facts connected with this subject. At the latter end of April, 1830, the French Minister of the Marine informed the maritime Prefect of Cherbourg, that the legislature of Georgia had recently prohibited all vessels (foreign or not) from entering her ports with colored persons on board, under the penalty of forty days' rigorous

370 TOUR IN THE UNITED STATES. [CHAP. XXXIII.

quarantine, and the payment of all expenses attending the detention; besides giving security for the
due discharge of such claims; the punishment for
refusal being 500 dollars, and imprisonment for a
time not exceeding three months. All captains of
vessels sailing from France to America were to
be notified of the regulations. In a few short
months the minister's master was driven from
his throne; and who were among the most active and the most applauded on that memorable
occasion? Bissette and Fabien—two of those very
men thus given up without a remonstrance to the
jailers of Georgia. The colored subjects of France
have now the same rights and privileges as others
within her dominions; yet one of the former was
imprisoned at Charleston, in South Carolina, and the
captain (Chretin) who had taken him thither in his
vessel, (le Jeune-Ernest,) was compelled to pay all
the expenses. An account of this outrage was communicated by the aggrieved party to the public in
December, 1833; but no redress, it appears, has been
obtained or sought for an injury thus inflicted, contrary to the law of nations—the letter, as well as
the spirit of treaties — and the constitution of the
country where it was perpetrated *.

* To be a slave-holding community is to be exempt from the
ordinary restraints of law and justice. The Antigua House of
Assembly, not long ago, committed with perfect impunity an
outrage, which the British House of Commons would not dare

On the 16th of October I embarked on board the packet Montreal, and arrived, after a favorable passage of three weeks, at Portsmouth.

It seemed as if the demon of cruelty was to accompany me back even to England, and to exhibit its victims on the very ground to tread on which is to be free. On board the ship was a black man who acted as waiter. He had been to New York, with his wife, in search of a white man, who owed him 160 dollars, which the other had borrowed out of his hard-earned savings. He had served in the American navy, in which his debtor was a lieutenant. With great trouble, and after much delay, he had obtained payment of part of the original sum :—less, however, than what the pursuit of it had cost him. Interest was out of the question. I was told the rascal's

to propose. It imprisoned and ruined a British subject (Joseph Phillips) for refusing to give up his private papers. Though both Lord Goderich and Sir George Murray declared officially that the imprisonment appeared to have been " an unwarrantable exercise of power," yet the Solicitor-General, (Tindal,) after stating that there was " nothing in the laws of England which is at all analogous to this course of proceeding, or would give any sanction to it," gave it as his professional opinion, that he could " see no effectual redress, but by an appeal to the good sense and good feeling of the members of the house " of Assembly. Thus has one of the most active and disinterested friends of negro emancipation been robbed of all his property, and left, with a wife and four children, to toil, in his old age, for a mere pittance.

name; but such a man is beyond the reach of shame; and there are too many to keep him in countenance, should he be wanting in that commodity. No one on board knew that the poor fellow was married; though his wife was with him—a very respectable, fair, young Englishwoman. At Portsmouth, where most of the passengers landed, this man waited upon me, during three or four days that I was detained by illness; and it was then that I was informed of his marriage and his adventures. While at New York, he was obliged to visit his wife clandestinely at her brother's house, and observe the utmost circumspection, to avoid the consequences which the detection of this " guilty commerce" would have brought down upon his head. Had the nature of the connexion transpired, his life would not have been safe; and perhaps both husband and wife would have fallen victims to popular fury. What a country to live in, where marriage carries with it the dishonor and punishment of crime; and where natural affection cannot be acknowledged without danger, nor indulged without deception! A more honest, kind-hearted creature I never saw. Every one in the packet spoke well of Trusty; and his wife was equally admired for the mildness and patience she displayed under severe indisposition. When I repaid him for the luggage that had been brought on shore by a boat he had hired for me, he wished some deduction should be made, on account of his own trunks ; and in all the disbursements he made for me, I found him scrupulously exact and fair-dealing. The history he gave me of himself was unaccompanied with any expression of complaint or resentment, and was elicited by questions, that some peculiar circumstances I had remarked in his conduct, induced me to put to him.

THE END.

ERRATUM.

Vol. I. p. 350, line 2, " Ætherias," should be " Æthereas."

APPENDIX.

No. I.

EXTRACTED from the REGISTRY of the PREROGATIVE COURT
of CANTERBURY.

> In the Will of SAMUEL GIST, late of Gower
> Street, in the Parish of St. Giles-in-the-
> Fields, in the county of Middlesex, Esquire,
> deceased, dated the 22d day of June, 1808,
> is as follows.

AND WHEREAS, by an act passed in the assembly at Virginia,
at their session in the month of May, one thousand seven
hundred and eighty-two, intituled " An Act to invest the
Estate of me, the said Samuel Gist, in Mary, then the wife of
William Anderson, (now the wife of Martin Pearkes, hereinafter named,) and her heirs and assigns, and for other purposes " ; after reciting that application had been made to that
general assembly by William Anderson and Mary his wife, for
an act to pass vesting the estate in that commonwealth belonging to me the said Samuel Gist, a British subject, in the said
Mary, (and who was then stated to be my only child,) who was
a native of and resident in that State, and it being judged expedient so to do ; It was enacted by the said general assembly,
that all the estate, both real and personal, in that common-

wealth belonging to me the said Samuel Gist, should be and the same were thereby vested in the said Mary Anderson, now Mary Pearkes, her heirs and assigns : Now I do hereby declare, that the same act was obtained only for the purpose of vesting such my estates in Virginia in the said Mary Anderson, (now Mary Pearkes,) as being a native of and resident of that State, In trust for me and my use, and to be disposed of at any future period in the manner I should direct : And whereas I have hitherto paid the said Mary Pearkes the sum of five hundred pounds per annum, in consideration and on condition that she shall, when required so to do, relinquish and give up all claims whatsoever to my said estates, both real and personal, in Virginia, and which have been settled upon her by that State in manner aforesaid : Now I give and bequeath to my trustees and executors hereinafter named, their executors and administrators, during the life of the said Mary Pearkes, not only the said sum of five hundred pounds per annum, but also the further sum of one thousand five hundred pounds per annum, of lawful money of Great Britain, for her benefit, as hereinafter mentioned, to be paid and payable by equal half-yearly payments, without any deduction or abatement whatsoever ; the first payment thereof respectively to begin and be made within or upon the expiration of three calendar months next after my decease, upon condition, nevertheless, that she shall and do, when thereto required and directed by my trustees and executors hereinafter named, or the survivors or survivor of them, or the heirs, executors, administrators, or assigns of such survivor, relinquish and give up the said estates in Virginia, and convey and assure the same in the most full and ample manner as shall be thought most proper and advisable by them, for the purposes hereinafter in that behalf expressed ; but if she shall refuse or decline so to do upon payment, then I do declare the said yearly sums of five hundred pounds, and one thousand five hundred pounds per annum, shall cease and be void ; and that all and every other sum and sums of money which she the said Mary Pearkes would have been entitled to, and which I may give to her by this my will, shall not be paid to her, and in lieu thereof, I give to her the sum of one shilling only.

The testator then gives direction about the payment of the annuities ; and, having bequeathed other property to his daughter, Mary Pearkes, he provides, in case of her non-compliance with the conditions, that his other daughter, Elizabeth Fowke, as the next in succession, shall be subject to the same obligations, and the same forfeiture upon non-fulfilment. He then proceeds :

And whereas by the laws of Virginia, persons possessed of lands and tenements, and leaving slaves thereon within that State, are authorized and empowered, by their last will and testament, or otherwise, to emancipate such slaves as shall belong to them : Now, in pursuance of such power and authority, I do hereby, by this my will, declare and direct, that all and every my slaves, with their issue and offspring, shall, within one year from and after my decease, be emancipated and made free; and in order to make a provision for my said slaves and their issue, I do hereby give, devise, and bequeath unto John Wickham, of Richmond, in the United States of North America, Esquire, and Matthew Toler, of Virginia aforesaid, gentleman, their heirs, executors, and administrators, according to the nature and quality thereof, all and singular my lands, tenements, and hereditaments whatsoever and wheresoever situate in any part of the United States of North America, together with all the stocks of horses, cattle, sheep, hogs, and every other thing relating to the same estates ; and also all the plantation-tools, and other utensils thereunto respectively belonging or therewith used, upon the several trusts, and to and for the several ends, intents, and purposes hereinafter expressed or declared of or concerning the same, that is to say : Upon trust to take upon themselves the management and cultivation of my said estates, and yearly and every year, after deducting all necessary or proper expenses incurred, and also a reasonable annual allowance for their trouble in managing and cultivating the same, to divide the surplus rents and profits thereof to and amongst all and every my said slaves who shall reside and continue to be resident on any of my plantations and lands in America, including my proportion of the Great Dismal Swamp, when the same shall be divided, and the lands bought by Mr. Toler in the name of Mrs. Pearkes, but paid for by me, in equal shares and proportions, and their respective issue for ever, to and for their own use and benefit: first allowing such annual sum and sums out of the whole of the net rents and profits of my said estates for the maintenance of the children and widows of such of my slaves as shall be living at the time of my decease, and of those my said slaves who shall from age, infirmity, or any other cause be incapable of supporting themselves, as they my trustees or trustee for the time being shall think proper ; and I do declare and direct, that in case any of my said slaves shall happen to die without leaving any issue, then, subject as aforesaid, the share or shares of him, her, or them shall be equally divided amongst the remaining slaves and their respective issue, such issue to take per stirpes : And I do hereby empower and direct my last mentioned trustees for the time being, or any of them, to sell and dispose of the produce of my said last mentioned estates, which shall be made and arise therefrom in the year in which I shall die, and apply the money arising from the sale thereof in building suitable houses for my said resident slaves and their respective families : Provided always, and I do hereby declare my will and mind to be, that in case the devise hereinbefore made to the said John Wickham and Matthew Toler, their heirs, executors and administrators, shall by any means whatsoever be rendered void or incapable of being carried into execution, then I give and devise the same lands, tenements, and hereditaments, unto the said William Fowke, Martin Perkes, Francis Gregg, and George Clark, their heirs, executors, and administrators, upon and for such and the same uses, trusts, and purposes, and under and subject to the same powers, provisoes, declarations, and agreements, as are hereinbefore expressed or declared of and concerning my estates in Great Britain : And I give and bequeath unto the said John Wickham, and Matthew Toler, their executors and administrators, all such sum and sums of money as shall at the time of my decease be due and owing to me from any person or persons whomsoever, residing in any part of the United States of North America ; Upon trust, to collect in and receive the same several sums, and lay out and invest the same, or so much thereof as can be collected or gotten in, in the purchase of American stocks or funds, with power to alter and transpose the same at discretion : And I do hereby declare and direct, that the said John Wickham and Matthew Toler, their executors and administrators, shall stand and be possessed of and interested in the dividends, interest, and annual proceed to arise and be produced from such stocks and funds ; Upon trust thereout to pay any yearly sum, not exceeding fifty pounds Virginia currency, as and for the salary or stipend of each of such four persons they from time to time shall think proper to employ and nominate, for the purpose of instructing the whole of my several slaves and their issue in the Christian religion, according to the Protestant doctrine as taught in England ; And upon trust to apply the residue thereof in establishing schools for the education of the children and issue of the said slaves ; and I do hereby declare and direct, that the said John Wickham and

Matthew Toler, their executors and administrators, shall and may, by and out of the said trust estates and premises, retain to and reimburse themselves, all such costs, charges, and expenses as they or any of them shall be put unto in the execution of the trusts hereby in them reposed, and also all reasonable allowances for their trouble, and that they or any of them respectively shall not be charged, chargeable with, or answerable for the acts, receipts, neglects, or defaults of the others or other of them, &c., &c.

And I do request as a particular favor of my Steward, Matthew Toler, and of all his children after his decease, and of the several brothers and sisters of the said Matthew Toler, and their respective children, that he and they respectively will use his and their utmost endeavors, as long as they shall respectively live, to attend to the comfort and happiness of my slaves and their issue : Provided always, and I do hereby declare my will to be, and direct, that if the general Assembly of Virginia will be pleased to adopt any other plan more beneficial to my slaves and their families and issue, as well as to the State, that the trustees of my American property shall conform thereto in the disposition of that property, any thing before contained to the contrary notwithstanding.

In the FIRST CODICIL to the said Will, (Dated 22d June, 1808,) the said Codicil bearing date the 16th day of December, 1809, is as follows.

And considering that it may be impolitic, and perhaps improper in the legislature of Virginia, to liberate so many as two hundred and seventy-four slaves, which by my last return was the number I possessed,—in that case, I desire they may be kept together for the joint benefit of my two daughters, who are natives of that State, during their lives, and the whole to the survivor, it being my intention to make them as nearly equal as I can in all things, and after their decease to my cousin Josiah Sellick and his heirs for ever.

The FOURTH CODICIL to the said will is as follows.

Considering the great increase of my negroes, there being upwards of one hundred under ten years of age, and as they grow up, the land I at present possess in Virginia may not be sufficient to employ them to advantage, I direct that my executors may be enabled to sell three thousand pounds of the five per cents. of the stock I hold at present in that fund, to enable Matthew Toler, my present steward, or whoever may act for me in that capacity at the time, to be laid out in addition to the land I at present hold, in the most convenient lands adjoining any other lands as it can be bought, subject to the approbation of John Wickham, Esq., where the negroes so growing up may be worked for the benefit of my daughters jointly during their natural lives, and to the survivor during her life, and at both their deaths to Josiah Sellick, my cousin, and at his death to his family in such a manner as he directs, doing justice as nearly as possible to each of them, let the three thousand pounds above mentioned be increased to five thousand pounds, provided it can be laid out with safety. SAMUEL GIST (L.S.).

Proved at London, with four codicils, 10th February, 1815, before the Worshipful Samuel Pearce Parson, Doctor of Laws and Surrogate, by the oaths of Martin Pearkes and Francis Gregg, Esq., two of the executors, to whom administration was granted, being first sworn duly to administer.—Power reserved to William Fowke, the other surviving executor.—William Fowke, the other surviving executor, renounced the probate, 7 April, 1815.

On the 27th of August, 1827, administration (with the will and four codicils annexed) of the goods, chattels, and credits, of Samuel Gist, late of Gower Street, in the Parish of St. Giles-in-the-Fields, in the county of Middlesex, Esq., deceased, left unadministered by Martin Pearkes, and Francis Gregg, two of the surviving executors, and two of the residuary legatees in trust named in the said will, was granted to Josiah Gist (formerly Sellick), Esq., the first named tenant in tail, and as such the residuary legatee named in the said will, having been first sworn (by commission) duly to administer—William Fowke, the other surviving executor and surviving residuary legatee in trust named in the said will, having formerly* renounced the probate and execution of the same, and four codicils as the letters of administration with the said will and codicils annexed, of the goods of the said deceased—James Gist, a devisee for life, named in the said will, died in the life-time of the said testator, without issue.

CHARLES DYNELEY.
JOHN IGGULDEN. } Deputy Registers.
W. F. GOSTLING.

No. II.

SOME Advertisements from the Southern Newspapers are here inserted. They will give some faint idea of the atrocities practised under the system which prevails there.

CASH FOR ONE HUNDRED AND FIFTY NEGROES.

WE will pay the highest prices in cash, for one hundred and fifty likely young Negroes, of both sexes, families included. Persons wishing to sell will do well to give us a call, as we are permanently settled in this market. All communications will meet attention. We can at all times be found at Mr. W. Robey's, on 7th street, south of the Centre Market House, Washington City, D. C.

June 4.   JOSEPH W. NEAL & CO.

---

* *Sic* in the extract.

Fifty Dollars Reward.

Ran away from the subscriber, on Tuesday night, the 8th inst., negroes Hal and Davy. Hal is a dark mulatto, five feet eleven inches or six feet high, and about forty-five years of age. He was formerly the foreman on the Hill's Ferry Plantation, in Hertford Co., N. C., where he is very well known; he has a wife at Mr. Timothy Ridley's in Hertford Co., in which neighborhood it is more than probable he will conceal himself. Davy is about five feet five or six inches high, of dark complexion, and twenty-four or five years old; he was raised in Hertford Co., N. C.; and his father, who calls himself Doctor Dave, lives in or near Murfreesboro'.

I will give the above reward for their apprehension and confinement in jail, so that I get them again; or Twenty-five Dollars for the apprehension and confinement of either of them, so that I get him again.

Smithfield, April 11.   Jno. H. Purdie.

Notice.

Will be sold, at the prison of Washington County, District of Columbia, on Saturday the 12th day of April next, for her prison fees and other expenses, a Negro Girl, who calls herself Sarah Ann Robinson, committed as a runaway slave. She is of light complexion, and about five feet high. She has no particular scars except a hair lip.

Sale to take place at 11 o'clock, A. M.

James Williams,
Keeper of the Prison of Washington County, District of Columbia, for

Alexander Hunter,

March 15, 1834.   Marshal D. C.

Cash for Negroes.—I shall be absent two or three months from Richmond. During my absence, Mr. Wm. H. Goodwin will attend to my jail and the purchase of slaves for me. Liberal prices will be paid.   LEWIS A. COLLIER.

———

I WISH to exchange the following tracts of Land, lying in Montgomery county, Maryland, being within nine or ten miles of Washington city, for Negro Slaves, for my own use, in the State of Missouri, or will sell them very low for cash. The tract of land I now reside on contains 593 acres, on which I have lately erected a frame Dwelling-house, which will contain twelve rooms, passage, piazza, and kitchen, with an overseer's house, houses for people, barn, and blacksmith's shop, and is one of the best watered farms in the county. This land lies between the farms of William and Robert Brents, Esqs., and is supposed to be as handsome a situation as any in the neighborhood, there being in view from the dwelling-house, three churches, two turnpike roads, with an extensive view of the surrounding neighborhood—neither of the churches exceeding two miles; the Catholic church, half a mile; Presbyterian and Methodist church, one mile; Episcopal church, two miles; City turnpike, half a mile; Georgetown pike, two miles; and is about nine miles from Washington City. Also, one other tract, containing 200 acres, adjoining the lands of Mr. Thomas Cramphin, lately deceased, which is equal to any land in the neighborhood. Also, one other tract, adjoining the former, containing 103 acres. Also, one other tract of 148 acres, and another tract of eighty-five acres, together with all my farming utensils, consisting of three wagons, 1 horse cart, two ox carts, six of Davis's ploughs, ten horses, cattle, hogs, and all necessary utensils for farming. Those wishing to buy a great bargain will do well to give me a call, as I have determined to move to the West, and will sell very low. Inquire of JOHN C. RIVES, at the Globe Office, or of the proprietor on the premises.   ROBERT BROWN.

———

Twenty-Five Dollars Reward.—Ran away from the Subscriber, about the 25th of Nov. last, a Negro woman, named Matilda. She is a little above the common size of women, of a brown complexion, and about twenty-five years old. It is thought that she may be some where up James River, or lurking above the Basin, as she was claimed as a wife by some boatman in Goochland. The above reward will be paid on her delivery at Captain Prentis's jail, either by him, or by the Subscriber.

May 2. Joshua Alvis.

———

Notice.—For hire, a Wet Nurse, of good character. Enquire at the Whig Office.

May 3.

———

200 Dollars Reward.

Ran away from me, on the 6th of June, 1833, Edward, aged eighteen years, dark complexion, inclined to be round shouldered, when spoken to has a down cast of the eyes, of common height and size.—He has always lived in Richmond, and was sold to me a few weeks ago, by Mr. David Barclay, of Richmond, who has owned him for several years. His father is named Solomon, who belongs to Mr. William Rowlett, of Richmond, and there is no doubt but Solomon has been the cause of his elopement; and as Mr. R. has employed his father, as a drayman in Richmond for several years, he has acquired considerable acquaintance with the crew of vessels sailing to this port, and from that acquaintance, I have no doubt he will endeavor to get him off to the North on some vessel. It is thought that he may have got away on one of the following schooners that sailed on that day from Richmond, the Effort, or George Wheaton, for New York; and in case he should get away on any vessel, and not be returned to me by the owner, master, or some person who may act as agent for the vessel, I will pay the above reward, 200 dollars, to any person whose evidence may be the means of obtaining a verdict for damages against the master or owner of the vessel who may be found guilty: but if he should get off without the knowledge of the master of the vessel, then, for his return to me, by him, or any person acting under his instruction, the law as to plead for damages, will be relinquished by me. For the apprehension of Edward, within the limits of this State, and his delivery to me, at Richmond, or security in some jail, so that I get him, I will pay fifty dollars reward. If he should get out of the limits of this State, I will pay 200 dollars reward to any person who will inform me where he is, provided I get him. I am determined to be at any trouble or expense that may be necessary in obtaining him, provided he should be taken out of the limits of the State; therefore any person knowing where he is, will please forward me the information, by mail, to Richmond. Gentlemen living in the Northern States, who are willing to support the rights of the constitution of the slave holding States, are respectfully requested to notice this advertisement.

Richmond, June 19. LEWIS A. COLLIER.

———

NOTICE.—Whereas I, Littleberry Clark, of the county of Prince Edward, Va., having bought of Thomas E. Scott, of said county, four negroes, and given my bond for ten hundred and fifty dollars, Beverly Cox being witness, and now finding the right to said property not to be sufficiently satisfactory, do hereby forewarn and prohibit any person or persons from trading for said bond, bearing date, April 12th, 1834, as I do not intend to pay it until satisfied.

April 25th, 1834. LITTLEBERRY CLARK.

———

Cash.

I WISH to purchase a number of likely SERVANTS, (slaves,) of both sexes, from about twelve to twenty-five years of age, of good habits. They are for two gentlemen, (citizens of this State,) for their own individual use, and not for speculation—I can give the most unquestionable satisfaction, as to that, from one of the best houses in this city. Persons wishing to part with their slaves, will do well to call or communicate with me, as I will give at all times the highest prices in cash.

JOHN BUSK.

Office, opposite the Exchange, South Gay Street, Baltimore.
Jan. 4.

A Card.

A. WOOLFOLK wishes to inform the owners of Negroes in Maryland, Virginia, and N. Carolina, that he is not dead, as has been artfully represented by his opponents, but that he still lives, to give them CASH and the highest prices for their NEGROES. Persons having negroes to dispose of, will please give him a chance, by addressing him at Baltimore, where immediate attention will be paid to their wishes.

Oct. 6.

By Fernandez and Whiting.

ON SATURDAY, the 19th inst. will be sold at Hewlett's Exchange Coffee House, at twelve o'clock, Slave Noele, aged about forty-five years, good French cook, &c., and is now rented permanently at twenty-five dollars per month; fully guaranteed against the vices and diseases as prescribed by law.

Terms, four months credit for an approved endorsed note and mortgage until final payment, acts of sale to be passed before Louis T. Caire, Notary Public, at the expense of the purchaser.

NOTICE.

THE undersigned are desirous of purchasing from forty to fifty negroes, for the use of their plantation in Louisiana. They would be preferred in families, and as many from the same plantation as possible. Persons having servants to dispose of, will receive fair cash prices, and satisfactory evidence that they are intended for our own use, and that they will not be separated, by applying to us through the Post Office at Easton.

FELIX HUSTON,
WALTER BYRNES.

August 24th, 1833.

ONE HUNDRED DOLLARS REWARD

FOR the apprehension and delivery of Negro Girl Louisa, aged about seventeen, if taken out of the District of Columbia, Maryland, or the State of Virginia, and all reasonable expenses in addition for bringing her home, or to the subscriber, residing in Georgetown, D. C.

FIFTY DOLLARS REWARD

If taken in the District of Columbia, and if in the State of Maryland or Virginia, the expense of her delivery will be added. She is low in stature, well made, and inclined to be fat; and neat in her appearance; smooth brown skin, round face, with features peculiar to the negro, but quite likely—wears her hair neatly combed, tied up with a black ribbon, and parted on her forehead. She wore away a linsey frock, black and red striped, cross barred collar ruff, and straw bonnet trimmed with broad red ribbon. She took with her, calico frocks, worked ruffs, ribbons, &c., besides a small sum of money. She has relations at Arlington, the residence of Geo. W. P. Curtis, Esq., and at Alexandria. Although I have no doubt but it is her object to make her escape to Pennsylvania, I have reason to believe she is yet in the District of Columbia, and is now harbored by her relations, or the free people of color who are numerous on our borders.   Reference to

JOHN GRAY, Agent and Police Officer, Georgetown, D. C.
March 28.

STOP THE RUNAWAY!!—Twenty-five Dollars Reward.—Ran away from the Eagle Tavern in this place, on Sunday evening last, a negro fellow named NAT—he is a carpenter by trade, is of low stature, and stoutly made, has an intelligent countenance, and is about thirty-five years of age; had on a white bell-crowned hat, with wide brim, and grey kersey coat and pantaloons. He is a shrewd, sensible negro, and is no doubt attempting to follow his wife, who was lately sold to a speculator named "Redmond," who was lately in this city. The above reward will be paid by Mrs. Lucy M. Downman, of Sussex county, Va., as soon as it is ascertained that the said negro is safely lodged in any jail in this State.

N.B.   The above described negro was brought to this place on Sunday morning last for sale, at his own request, and gave the young gentleman under whose care he was, the slip the same evening.

March 14.

WANTED.—A female WAITER in a small family, one that can be well recommended as to capacity and character—a slave would be preferred, by the year.   Apply at the Patriot office.

May 3.

HOUSE SERVANTS FOR SALE.—A family of valuable servants, consisting of a woman twenty-four years old, a good American cook, her daughter eight or nine years of age, a smart house servant, and her son a boy of four years old; all good cha-racters, and fully guarantied.   Apply to Jas. Armor.

———

Good Servants Wanted.

The Subscriber wishes to purchase or hire, (the former would be preferred,) four first rate servants, two for waiters, and two female servants, capable of waiting on ladies, and taking charge of chambers.   None need apply but those that can bring good recommendations as to industry, honesty, &c., &c.

Feb. 27.   John Gadsby, National Hotel.

———

Sale of Negroes.—Will be sold at Terrell's tavern, in the county of Hanover, to the highest bidder for cash, several likely young negroes belonging to the estate of Burnley Duke, dec'd., on the 28th day of the present month (April), to satisfy the claims against the estate of the said decedent, at which time and place, those having claims are requested to present them.

April 11.   By the Executor.

———

A Great Bargain in Main Street Property, for cash or on time, or it would be exchanged for Young Negroes, by contract or at valuation, or for Tobacco or Iron.—Enquire of

May 15.   Howel Davies.

———

Cash for 200 Negroes.

We will pay higher prices in cash, for two hundred negroes, of both sexes, from twelve to twenty-five years of age, than any purchaser who is now or may hereafter come into this market.

All communications promptly attended to. We can at all times be found at our residence, west end of Duke Street, Alexandria, D. C.

Oct. 3.   FRANKLIN AND ARMFIELD.

A NURSE WANTED.—Wanted immediately, a middle aged woman, without incumbrance, as a nurse. For one that is capable, and can come well recommended, I will give a liberal hire.

ED. W. TOMPKINS.

No. III.

THE following CONFESSION was published Nov. 5, 1831, by T. R. GRAY, of Jerusalem, Southampton, Virginia, with an address to the public and an attestation from the judicial court, in whose presence it was read to NAT TURNER, and acknowledged by him to be correct.

CONFESSION.

AGREEABLE to his own appointment, on the evening he was committed to prison, with permission of the jailer, I visited NAT on Tuesday the 1st November, when, without being questioned at all, he commenced his narrative in the following words :—

SIR,—You have asked me to give a history of the motives which induced me to undertake the late insurrection, as you call it. To do so I must go back to the days of my infancy, and even before I was born.　I was thirty-one years of age the 2d of October last, and born the property of Benj. Turner, of this county.　In my childhood, a circumstance occurred which made an indelible impression on my mind, and laid the ground work of that enthusiasm, which has terminated so fatally to many, both white and black, and for which I am about to atone at the gallows.　It is here necessary to relate this circumstance —trifling as it may seem, it was the commencement of that belief which has grown with time, and even now, sir, in this dungeon, helpless and forsaken as I am, I cannot divest myself of.　Being at play with other children, when three or four years old, I was telling them something, which my mother overhearing, said it had happened before I was born.　I stuck to my story, however, and related some things which went, in her opinion, to confirm it; others being called on were greatly astonished, knowing that these things had happened, and caused them to say in my hearing, I surely would be a prophet, as the Lord had shewn me things that had happened before my birth.　And my father and mother strengthened me in this my first impression, saying, in my presence, I was intended for some great purpose, which they had always thought from certain marks on my head and breast—(a parcel of excrescences which I believe are not at all uncommon, particularly among negroes, as I have seen several with the same.　In this case he has either cut them off or they have nearly disappeared).— My grandmother, who was very religious, and to whom I was much attached—my master, who belonged to the church, and other religious persons who visited the house, and whom I often saw at prayers, noticing the singularity of my manners, I suppose, and my uncommon intelligence for a child, remarked I had too much sense to be raised, and if I was, I would never be of any service to any one as a slave.　To a mind like mine, restless, inquisitive, and observant of every thing that was passing, it is easy to suppose that religion was the subject to which it would be directed, and although this subject principally occupied my thoughts, there was nothing that I saw or heard of to which my attention was not directed. The manner in which I learned to read and write, not only had great influence on my own mind, as I acquired it with the most perfect ease, so much so, that I have no recollection whatever of learning the alphabet; but to the astonishment of the family, one day, when a book was shewn me to keep me from crying, I began spelling the names of different objects. This was a source of wonder to all in the neighbourhood, particularly the blacks; and this learning was constantly improved at all opportunities. When I got large enough to go to work, while employed, I was reflecting on many things that would present themselves to my imagination, and whenever an opportunity occurred of looking at a book, when the school children were getting their lessons, I would find many things that the fertility of my own imagination had depicted to me before; all my time, not devoted to my master's service, was spent either in prayer, or in making experiments in casting different things in moulds made of earth, in attempting to make paper, gunpowder, and many other experiments, that although I could not perfect, yet convinced me of its practicability if I had the means *. I was not addicted to stealing in my youth, nor have ever been. Yet such was the confidence of the negroes in the neighborhood, even at this early period of my life, in my superior judgment, that they would often carry me with them when they were going on any roguery, to plan for them. Growing up among them, with this confidence in my superior judgment, and when this, in their opinions, was perfected by Divine inspiration, from the circumstances already alluded to in my

* When questioned as to the manner of manufacturing those different articles, he was found well informed on the subject.

infancy, and which belief was ever afterwards zealously in-culcated by the austerity of my life and manners, which became the subject of remark by white and black.—Having soon discovered to be great, I must appear so, and there-fore studiously avoided mixing in society, and wrapped my-self in mystery, devoting my time to fasting and prayer.— By this time, having arrived to man's estate, and hearing the scriptures commented on at meetings, I was struck with that particular passage which says: " Seek ye the kingdom of Heaven, and all things shall be added unto you." I reflected much on this passage, and prayed daily for light on this sub-ject.—As I was praying one day at my plough, the spirit spoke to me, saying, " Seek ye the kingdom of Heaven, and all things shall be added unto you."

QUESTION.—What do you mean by the Spirit?

ANSWER.—The Spirit that spoke to the prophets in former days;—and I was greatly astonished, and for two years prayed continually, whenever my duty would permit—and then again I had the same revelation, which fully confirmed me in the impression that I was ordained for some great purpose in the hands of the Almighty. Several years rolled round, in which many events occurred to strengthen me in this my belief. At this time I reverted in my mind to the remarks made of me in my childhood, and the things that had been shewn me—and as it had been said of me in my childhood by those by whom I had been taught to pray, both white and black, and in whom I had the greatest confidence, that I had too much sense to be raised, and if I was, I would never be of any use to any one as a slave. Now finding I had arrived to man's estate, and was a slave, and these revelations being made known to me, I began to direct my attention to this great object, to fulfil the purpose for which, by this time, I felt assured I was intended. Knowing the influence I had obtained over the minds of my fellow servants, (not by the means of conjuring and such like tricks—for to them I always spoke of such things with contempt,) but by the communion of the Spirit, whose revelations I often communicated to them; and they believed, and said my wisdom came from God. I now began to prepare them for my purpose, by telling them something was about to happen that would terminate in fulfilling the great promise that had been made to me. About this time I was placed under an overseer, from whom I ran away; and after remaining in the woods thirty days, I returned, to the astonishment of the negroes on the plantation, who thought I had made my escape to some other part of the country, as my father had done before. But the reason of my return was, that the Spirit appeared to me, and said I had my wishes directed to the things of this world, and not to the kingdom of Heaven, and that I should return to the service of my earthly master:— "For he who knoweth his Master's will, and doeth it not, shall be beaten with many stripes, and thus have I chastened you." And the negroes found fault, and murmured against me, saying, that if they had my sense they would not serve any master in the world. And about this time I had a vision—and I saw white spirits and black spirits engaged in battle, and the sun was darkened—the thunder rolled in the heavens, and blood flowed in streams—and I heard a voice saying, "Such is your luck, such you are called to see, and let it come rough or smooth, you must surely bear it." I now withdrew myself as much as my situation would permit, from the intercourse of my fellow servants, for the avowed purpose of serving the Spirit more fully;—and it appeared to me, and reminded me of the things it had already shown me, and that it would then reveal to me the knowledge of the elements, the revolution of the planets, the operation of tides, and changes of the seasons. After this revelation in the year 1825, and the knowledge of the elements being made known to me, I sought more than ever to obtain true holiness before the great day of judgement should appear, and then I began to receive the true knowledge of faith. And from the first steps of righteousness until the last, was I made perfect; and the Holy Ghost was with me, and said,— "Behold me as I stand in the Heavens!"—and I looked and saw the forms of men in different attitudes—and there were lights in the sky to which the children of darkness gave other names than what they really were—for they were the lights of the Saviour's hands, stretched forth from east to west, even as they were extended on the cross on Calvary for the redemption of sinners. And I wondered greatly at these miracles, and prayed to be informed of a certainty of the meaning thereof—and shortly afterwards, while laboring in the field, I discovered drops of blood on the corn as though it were dew from heaven—and I communicated it to many, both white and black, in the neighborhood—and I then found on the leaves in the woods hieroglyphic characters, and numbers, with the forms of men in different attitudes, portrayed in blood, and representing the figures I had seen before in the heavens. And now the Holy Ghost had revealed itself to me, and made plain the miracles it had shown me. For as the blood of Christ had been shed on this earth, and had ascended to Heaven for the salvation of sinners, and was now returning to earth again in the form of dew,—and as the leaves on the trees bore the impression of the figures I had seen in the heavens, it was plain to me that the Saviour was about to lay down the yoke he had borne for the sins of men, and the great day of judgement was at hand. About this time I told these things to a white man, (Etheldred T. Brantley,) on whom it had a wonderful effect; and he ceased from his wickedness, and was attacked immediately with a cutaneous eruption, and blood oozed from the pores of his skin, and after praying and fasting nine days he was healed; and the Spirit appeared to me again, and said, as the Saviour had been baptised, so should we be also; —and when the white people would not let us be baptized by the church, we went down into the water together, in the sight of many who reviled us, and were baptised by the Spirit. After this I rejoiced greatly, and gave thanks to God: and on the 12th of May, 1828, I heard a loud noise in the heavens, and the Spirit instantly appeared to me and said the serpent was loosened, and Christ had laid down the yoke he had borne for the sins of men, and that I should take it on and fight against the serpent; for the time was fast approaching when the first should be last and the last should be first.

QUESTION.—Do you not find yourself mistaken now?

ANSWER.—Was not Christ crucified? And by signs in the heavens that it would make known to me when I should commence the great work, and until the first sign appeared, I should conceal it from the knowledge of men. And on the appearance of the sign, (the eclipse of the sun last February,) I should arise and prepare myself, and slay my enemies with their own weapons. And immediately on the sign appearing in the heavens, the seal was removed from my lips, and I communicated the great work laid out for me to do, to four in whom I had the greatest confidence, (Henry, Hark, Nelson, and Sam). It was intended by us to have begun the work of death on the 4th July last. Many were the plans formed and rejected by us; and it affected my mind to such a degree, that I fell sick, and the time passed without our coming to any determination how to commence: still forming new schemes and rejecting them, when the sign appeared again, which determined me not to wait longer.

Since the commencement of 1830, I had been living with Mr. Joseph Travis, who was to me a kind master, and placed the greatest confidence in me; in fact, I had no cause to complain of his treatment to me. On Saturday evening, the 20th of August, it was agreed between Henry, Hark, and myself, to prepare a dinner the next day for the men we expected, and then to concert a plan, as we had not yet determined on any. Hark, on the following morning, brought a pig, and Henry brandy; and being joined by Sam, Nelson, Will, and Jack, they prepared in the woods a dinner; where, about three o'clock, I joined them.

QUESTION.—Why were you so backward in joining them?

ANSWER.—The same reason that had caused me not to mix with them for years before.

I saluted them on coming up, and asked Will how came he there; he answered, his life was worth no more than others, and his liberty as dear to him. I asked him if he thought to obtain it? He said he would, or lose his life. This was enough to put him in full confidence. Jack, I knew, was only a tool in the hands of Hark; it was quickly agreed we should commence at home (Mr. J. Travis's) on that night; and until we had armed and equipped ourselves, and gathered sufficient force, neither age nor sex was to be spared (which was invariably adhered to). We remained at the feast, until about two hours in the night, when we went to the house and found Austin; they all went to the cider press and drank, except myself. On returning to the house, Hark went to the door with an axe, for the purpose of breaking it open, as we knew we were strong enough to murder the family if they were awaked by the noise; but reflecting that it might create an alarm in the neighborhood, we determined to enter the house secretly, and murder them whilst sleeping. Hark got a ladder and set it against the chimney, on which I ascended, and hoisting a window, entered and came down stairs, unbarred the door, and removed the guns from their places. It was then observed that I must spill the first blood. On which, armed with a hatchet, and accompanied by Will, I entered my master's chamber: it being dark, I could not give a death blow, the hatchet glanced from his head; he sprang from the bed, and called his wife—it was his last word; Will laid him dead with a blow of his axe, and Mrs. Travis shared the same fate as she lay in bed.

The murder of this family, five in number, was the work of a moment,—not one of them awoke; there was a little infant sleeping in a cradle, that was forgotten until we had left the house, and gone some distance, when Henry and Will returned and killed it. We got here four guns that would 'shoot, and several old muskets, with a pound or two of powder. We remained some time at the barn, where we paraded; I formed them in a line as soldiers, and after carrying them through all the manœuvres I was master of, marched them off to Mr. Salathul Francis's, about six hundred yards distant. Sam and Will went to the door and knocked. Mr. Francis asked who was there; Sam replied it was him, and he had a letter for him, on which he got up and came to the door; they immediately seized him, and dragging him out a little from the door, he was dispatched by repeated blows on the head; there was no other white person in the family. We started from there for Mrs. Reese's, maintaining the most perfect silence on our march; where, finding the door unlocked, we entered, and murdered Mrs. Reese in her bed, while sleeping; her son awoke, but it was only to sleep the sleep of death: he had only time to say, who is that? and he was no more. From Mrs. Reese's we went to Mrs. Turner's, a mile distant, which we reached about sunrise on Monday morning. Henry, Austin, and Sam, went to the still; where, finding Mr. Peebles, Austin shot him, and the rest of us went to the house; as we approached the family discovered us, and shut the door. Vain hope! Will, with one stroke of his axe, opened it, and we entered and found Mrs. Turner and Mrs. Newsome in the middle of a room, almost frightened to death. Will immediately killed Mrs. Turner with one blow of his axe. I took Mrs. Newsome by the hand, and with the sword I had when I was apprehended, I struck her several blows over the head, but not being able to kill her, as the sword was dull. Will turning around and discovering it, despatched her also. A general destruction of property, and search for money and ammunition, always succeeded the murders. By this time my company amounted to fifteen, and nine men mounted, who started for Mrs. Whitehead's, (the other six were to go through a bye-way to Mr. Bryant's, and rejoin us at Mrs. Whitehead's.) As we approached the house we discovered Mr. Richard White- head standing in the cotton patch, near the lane fence; we called him over into the lane, and Will, the executioner, was near at hand, with his fatal axe, to send him to an untimely grave.

As we pushed on to the house, I discovered some one run round the garden, and thinking it was some of the white family, I pursued them; but finding it was a servant girl belonging to the house, I returned to commence the work of death, but they whom I left had not been idle; all the family were already murdered, but Mrs. Whitehead and her daughter Margaret. As I came round to the door I saw Will pulling Mrs. Whitehead out of the house, and at the step he nearly severed her head from her body with his broad axe. Miss Margaret, when I discovered her, had concealed herself in the corner, formed by the projection of the cellar cap from the house; on my approach she fled, but was soon overtaken; and after repeated blows with a sword, I killed her by a blow on the head with a fence rail. By this time, the six who had gone by Mr. Bryant's, rejoined us, and informed me they had done the work of death assigned them. We again divided, part going to Mr. Richard Porter's, and from thence to Nathaniel Francis's, the others to Mr. Howell Harris's, and Mr. T. Doyle's. On my reaching Mr. Porter's, he had escaped with his family. I understood there that the alarm had already spread, and I immediately returned to bring up those sent to Mr. Doyle's and Mr. Howell Harris's; the party I left going on to Mr. Francis's having told them I would join them in that neighborhood. I met these sent to Mr. Doyle's and Mr. Harris's returning, having met Mr. Doyle on the road, and killed him; and learning from some who joined them, that Mr. Harris was from home, I immediately pursued the course taken by the party gone on before; but knowing they would complete the work of death and pillage at Mr. Francis's before I could get there, I went to Mr. Peter Edwards's, expecting to find them there, but they had been here also. I then went to Mr. John T. Barrow's; they had been here, and murdered him. I pursued on their track to Capt. Newit Harris's, where I found the greater part mounted, and ready to start; the men, now amounting to about forty, shouted and hurraed as I rode up; some were in the yard loading their guns, others drinking. They said Captain Harris and his family had escaped, the property in the house they destroyed, robbing him of money and other valuables. I ordered them to mount and march instantly, this was about nine or ten o'clock, Monday morning. I proceeded to Mr. Levi Waller's, two or three miles distant. I took my station in the rear, and as it was my object to carry terror and devastation wherever we went, I placed fifteen or twenty of the best armed and most to be relied on, in front, who generally approached the houses as fast as their horses could run; this was for two purposes— to prevent their escape, and strike terror to the inhabitants,— on this account I never got to the houses, after leaving Mrs. Whitehead's, until the murders were committed, except in one case. I sometimes got in sight in time to see the work of death completed, viewed the mangled bodies as they lay, in silent satisfaction, and immediately started in quest of other victims. Having murdered Mrs. Waller and ten children, we started for Mr. William Williams's, having killed him and two little boys that were there; while engaged in this, Mrs. Williams fled and got some distance from the house, but she was pursued, overtaken, and compelled to get up behind one of the company, who brought her back, and after showing her the mangled body of her lifeless husband, she was told to get down and lay by his side, where she was shot dead. I then started for Mr. Jacob Williams, where the family were murdered. Here we found a young man named Drury, who had come on business with Mr. Williams; he was pursued, overtaken, and shot. Mrs. Vaughan was the next place we visited, and after murdering the family here, I determined on starting for Jerusalem. Our number amounted now to fifty or sixty, all mounted and armed with guns, axes, swords, and clubs. On reaching Mr. James W. Parker's gate, immediately on the road leading to Jerusalem, and about three miles distant, it was proposed to me to call there, but I objected, as I knew he was gone to Jerusalem, and my object was to reach there as soon as possible; but some of the men having relations at Mr. Parker's, it was agreed that they might call and get his people. I remained at the gate on the road, with seven or eight; the others going across the field to the house, about half-a-mile off. After waiting some time for them, I became impatient, and started to the house for them, and on our return we were met by a party of white men, who had pursued our blood-stained track, and who had fired on those at the gate, and dispersed them,—which I knew nothing of, not having been at that time rejoined by any of them,—immediately on discovering the whites, I ordered my men to halt and form, as they appeared to be alarmed. The white men, eighteen in number, approached us in about one hundred yards, when one of them fired, (this was against the positive orders of Captain Alexander P. Peete, who commanded, and who had directed the men to reserve their fire until within thirty paces,) and I discovered about half of them retreating, I then ordered my men to fire and rush on them; the few remaining stood their ground until we approached within fifty yards, when they fired and retreated. We pursued and overtook some of them who we thought we left dead; (they were not killed;) after pursuing them about two hundred yards, and rising a little hill, I discovered they were met by another party, and had halted, and were re-loading their guns; (this was a small party from Jerusalem who knew the negroes were in the field, and had just tied their horses to await their return to the road, knowing that Mr. Parker and family were in Jerusalem, but knew nothing of the party that had gone in with Captain Peete; on hearing the firing they immediately rushed to the spot, and arrived just in time to arrest the progress of these barbarous villains, and save the lives of their friends and fellow-citizens;) thinking that those who retreated first, and the party who fired on us at fifty or sixty yards distant, had all only fallen back to meet others with ammunition. As I saw them reloading their guns, and more coming up than I saw at first, and several of my bravest men being wounded, the others became panic-struck and squandered over the field; the white men pursued and fired on us several times. Hark had his horse shot under him, and I caught another for him as it was running by me; five or six of my men were wounded, but none left on the field; finding myself defeated here, I instantly determined to go through a private way, and cross the Nottoway river at the Cypress bridge, three miles below Jerusalem, and attack that place in the rear, as I expected they would look for me on the other road, and I had a great desire to get there to procure arms and ammunition. After going a short distance in this private way, accompanied by about twenty men, I overtook two or three who told me the others were dispersed in every direction. After trying in vain to collect a sufficient force to proceed to Jerusalem, I determined to return, as I was sure they would make back to their old neighborhood, where they would rejoin me, make new recruits, and come down again. On my way back, I called at Mrs. Thomas's, Mrs. Spencer's, and several other places : the white families having fled, we found no more victims to gratify our thirst for blood, we stopped at Major Ridley's quarter for the night, and being joined by four of his men, with the recruits made since my defeat, we mustered now about forty strong. After placing out sentinels, I laid down to sleep, but was quickly roused by a great racket ; starting up, I found some mounted, and others in great confusion, one of the sentinels having given the alarm that we were about to be attacked ; I ordered some to ride round and reconnoitre, and on their return the others being more alarmed, not knowing who they were, fled in different ways, so that I was reduced to about twenty again ; with this I determined to attempt to recruit, and proceed on to rally in the neighborhood I had left. Dr. Blunt's was the nearest house, which we reached just before day ; on riding up the yard, Hark fired a gun. We expected Dr. Blunt and his family were at Major Ridley's, as I knew there was a company of men there ; the gun was fired to ascertain if any of the family were at home ; we were immediately fired upon and retreated, leaving several of my men. I do not know what became of them, as I never saw them afterwards. Pursuing our course back and coming in sight of Captain Harris's, where we had been the day before, we discovered a party of white men at the house, on which all deserted me but two; (Jacob and Nat;) we concealed ourselves in the woods until near night, when I sent them in search of Henry, Sam, Nelson, and Hark, and directed them to rally all they could, at the place we had had our dinner the Sunday before, where they would find me, and I accordingly returned there as soon as it was dark and remained until Wednesday evening, when discovering white men riding around the place as though they were looking for some one, and none of my men joining me, I concluded Jacob and Nat had been taken, and compelled to betray me. On this I gave up all hope for the present; and on Thursday night, after having supplied myself with provisions from Mr. Travis's, I scratched a hole under a pile of fence rails in a field, where I concealed myself for six weeks, never leaving my hiding place but for a few minutes in the dead of night to get water which was very near; thinking by this time I could venture out, I began to go about in the night and eaves-drop the houses in the neighborhood; pursuing this course for about a fortnight and gathering little or no intelligence, afraid of speaking to any human being, and returning every morning to my cave before the dawn of day. I know not how long I might have led this life, if accident had not betrayed me, a dog in the neighborhood passing by my hiding place one night while I was out, was attracted by some meat I had in my cave, and crawled in and stole it, and was coming out just as I returned. A few nights after, two negroes having started to go hunting with the same dog, and passed that way, the dog came again to the place, and having just gone out to walk about, discovered me and barked, on which thinking myself discovered, I spoke to them to beg concealment. On making myself known they fled from me. Knowing then they would betray me, I immediately left my hiding place, and was pursued almost incessantly until I was taken a fortnight afterwards by Mr. Benjamin Phipps, in a little hole I had dug out with my sword, for the purpose of concealment, under the top of a fallen tree. On Mr. Phipps discovering the place of my concealment, he cocked his gun and aimed at me. I requested him not to shoot and I would give up, upon which he demanded my sword. I delivered it to him, and he brought me to prison. During the time I was pursued, I had many hair-breadth escapes, which your time will not permit me to relate. I am here loaded with chains, and willing to suffer the fate that awaits me.

I here proceeded to make some enquiries of him, after assuring him of the certain death that awaited him, and that concealment would only bring destruction on the innocent as well as guilty, of his own color, if he knew of any extensive or concerted plan. His answer was, I do not. When I questioned him as to the insurrection in North Carolina happening about the same time, he denied any knowledge of it; and when I looked him in the face as though I would search his inmost thoughts, he replied, " I see, sir, you doubt my word; but can you not think the same ideas, and strange appearances about this time in the heavens might prompt others, as well as myself, to this undertaking." I now had much conversation with and asked him many questions, having forborne to do so previously, except in the cases noted in parentheses; but during his statement, I had, unnoticed by him, taken notes as to some particular circumstances, and having the advantage of his statement before me in writing, on the evening of the third day that I had been with him, I began a cross examination, and found his statement corroborated by every circumstance coming within my own knowledge or the confessions of others whom had been either killed or executed, and whom he had not seen nor had any knowledge since 22nd of August last, he expressed himself fully satisfied as to the impracticability of his attempt. It has been said he was ignorant and cowardly, and that his object was to murder and rob for the purpose of obtaining money to make his escape. It is notorious, that he was never known to have a dollar in his life; to swear an oath, or drink a drop of spirits. As to his ignorance, he certainly never had the advantages of education, but he can read and write, (it was taught him by his parents,) and for natural intelligence and quickness of apprehension, is surpassed by few men I have ever seen. As to his being a coward, his reason as given for not resisting Mr. Phipps, shews the decision of his character. —When he saw Mr. Phipps present his gun, he said he knew it was impossible for him to escape as the woods were full of men; he therefore thought it was better to surrender, and trust to fortune for his escape. He is a complete fanatic, or plays his part most admirably. On other subjects he possesses an uncommon share of intelligence, with a mind capable of attaining any thing; but warped and perverted by the influence of early impressions. He is below the ordinary stature, though strong and active, having the true negro face, every feature of which is strongly marked. I shall not attempt to describe the effect of his narrative, as told and commented on by himself, in the condemned hole of the prison. The calm deliberate composure with which he spoke of his late deeds and intentions, the expression of his fiend-like face when excited by enthusiasm, still bearing the stains of the blood of helpless innocence about him; clothed with rags and covered with chains; yet daring to raise his manacled hands to heaven, with a spirit soaring above the attributes of man; I looked on him and my blood curdled in my veins.

I will not shock the feelings of humanity, nor wound afresh the bosoms of the disconsolate sufferers in this unparalleled and inhuman massacre, by detailing the deeds of their fiend-like barbarity. There were two or three who were in the power of these wretches, had they known it, and who escaped in the most providential manner. There were two whom they thought they left dead on the field at Mr. Parker's, but who were only stunned by the blows of their guns, as they did not take time to re-load when they charged on them. The escape of a little girl who went to school at Mr. Waller's, and where the children were collecting for that purpose, excited general sympathy. As their teacher had not arrived, they were at play in the yard, and seeing the negroes approach, she ran up on a dirt chimney, (such as are common to log houses,) and remained there unnoticed during the massacre of the eleven that were killed at this place. She remained on her hiding place till just before the arrival of a party, who were in pursuit of the murderers, when she came down and fled to a swamp, where, a mere child as she was, with the horrors of the late scene before her, she lay concealed until the next day, when seeing a party go up to the house, she came up, and on being asked how she escaped, replied with the utmost simplicity, "The Lord helped her." She was taken up behind a gentleman of the party, and returned to the arms of her weeping mother. Miss Whitehead concealed herself between the bed and the mat that supported it, while they murdered her sister in the same room, without discovering her. She was afterwards carried off, and concealed for protection by a slave of the family, who gave evidence against several of them on their trial. Mrs. Nathaniel Francis, while concealed in a closet heard their blows, and the shrieks of the victims of these ruthless savages; they then entered the closet where she was concealed, and went out without discovering her. While in this hiding place, she heard two of her women in a quarrel about the division of her clothes. Mr. John T. Baron, discovering them approaching his house, told his wife to make her escape, and scorning to fly, fell fighting on his own threshold. After firing his rifle, he discharged his gun at them, and then broke it over the villain who first approached him, but he was overpowered, and slain. His bravery, however, saved from the hands of these monsters, his lovely and amiable wife, who will long lament a husband so deserving of her love. As directed by him, she attempted to escape through the garden, when she was caught and held by one of her servant girls, but another coming to her rescue, she fled to the woods, and concealed herself. Few, indeed, were those who escaped their work of death. But fortunate for society, the hand of retributive justice has overtaken them: and not one that was known to be concerned has escaped.

G. Woodfall, Printer, Angel Court, Skinner Street, London.